D0200174

1510

Crest given to the Grivas family in 1510 by the British.

A Greek Odyssey
in the American West

Helen Papanikolas

University of Nebraska Press
Lincoln and London

In memory of my parents
Emily and George Zeese

Αἰωνία ἡ μνήμη σας
(*Eons be thy memory*)

© 1987 by Helen Papanikolas
All rights reserved
Manufactured in the United States of America

☉ The paper in this book meets the minimum requirements of American National Standard for Information Sciences—Permanence of Paper for Printed Library Materials, ANSI Z39.48-1984.

First Bison Books printing: 1997

Library of Congress Cataloging-in-Publication Data
Papanikolas, Helen Zeese.
[Aimilia-Geōrgios. English]
A Greek odyssey in the American West / Helen Papanikolas.
p.   cm.
"Originally published in 1987 as Emily-George by the University of Utah Press, Salt Lake City, in the Utah centennial series"-T.p. verso.
Includes bibliographical references.
ISBN 0-8032-8747-X (pa: alk. paper)
1. Greek Americans—Biography.   2. Zeese, Giōrges, 1886–   .   3. Zeese, Emily.
4. Papanikolas, Helen Zeese—Family.   I. Title.
E184.G7P3713   1997
973'.0489'00922—dc21
[B]
97-19099   CIP

The names of several people mentioned in this book have been changed to protect the privacy of their descendants.
Originally published in 1987 as *Emily-George* by the University of Utah Press, Salt Lake City, in the Utah Centennial Series.

Contents

Acknowledgments

In bringing my parents' story into print, I would like to thank the following: my daughter Thalia Smart whose love for her grandparents impelled me to continue the long search for their beginnings; my son Zeese for his continual encouragement, suggestions, and editorial help over a period of several years; my husband Nick who overcame my reluctance at publication; Miriam Murphy, editor of the manuscript, whose insistence that readers beyond the family have access to the biography, led to its publication; my aunts, Maria Alexopoulou, Vasiliki Papagheorghiou, Angeliki Zisimopoulou of Athens, and Sophia Papachristos of Chicago for their vivid oral accounts of family history; my cousin Ioanna and her husband Panos Giovas of Athens who supplied me with information and many important publications; my Chicago cousins Thalia and Katherine Papachristos who made numerous telephone calls within the country and to Greece, searched for and supplied documents and photographs, and substantiated aspects of family lore.

Others who assisted me are: my cousin Helen Anderson, my nephews Marcus and George Theodore, Ginna Allison, and Professors Charles S. Peterson, Utah State University, and S. Victor Papacosma, Kent State University, who read the manuscript with care and whose suggestions I greatly appreciated. I acknowledge also that immigrant heritage that has enriched my life and inspired my writings.

Αἰμιλία — Γεώργιος
Emily — George

I

What will I have to remember if I reach their age, my father in his late nineties, my mother a few years younger? What have I to remember like my father's memory of himself, a boy of fifteen sent by the village midwife to bury a panful of his mother's bloody afterbirth and uncovering five valuable Turkish coins? What memory have I like my mother's, a child walking with her grand mother the far distance across a Macedonian plain to the Turkish festival of Ramadan where the segregated, veiled women huddled, stricken at the sight of a spying Turk?

Will I remember a night, perhaps many nights now become one in my memory, when in the living room of our three-room half of a house my father, his cousin Lambros, my godfather, and other *patriotes* were feasting and singing the old songs of their guerrilla ancestors waiting to ambush the Turkish conquerors?

"*Kyria*," my father called. He never called her by name as Americans and some Greeks called their wives, but *Kyria*—Madame. "Bring more food!" With platters and bowls of lamb, *pilafi*, and other fragrant delicacies, my mother hurried from the kitchen, through the bedroom where my sisters and I were supposedly asleep in the golden suffusion of the icon light, and into the *sala*.

Tselingas—Master Shepherd—and Tall One the men called my father. When my mother opened the door that separated us from that distant world of men, I caught a glimpse of them sitting around the table under floating layers of blue tobacco smoke: my

3

father, narrow head on a bull neck; his cousin Lambros, long grieving face like the martyrs on the icon screen in church; and my godfather wearing a high white collar, a diamond stickpin in his tie, eyes mellow brown, hair carefully parted and smelling, I knew, of lilac scent. Heads held high, they sang one song after another, their deep voices rising slowly, heavy with fatalism, descending mournfully, of men "who never ate warm bread, the battle was their dowry; the yataghan their talisman, and off they sped like a bullet."

On the dresser the vigil light illuminating the icon of the All-Holy and Her Infant Christ swayed and sent graceful shadows across the ceiling, and the dark clothes hanging on the door pegs were what they were, the family's wardrobe, not the night shapes that could suddenly change into dangerous phantoms.

Water ran steadily from the kitchen tap; dishes clicked and cupboard doors opened and closed. The singing faded; after a silence the men spoke in low tones. At the rock mountain gates a freight train whistled its heavy warning call. Someone passed the house playing a harmonica and far off a piano tinkled. The town's ten o'clock whistle began to tumble from the fire station, slow, heavy, like a fat man laughing ever deeper until he could go on no more.

Through the crack of the door to the kitchen, I watched my mother embroidering a white altar cloth under the dangling electric light globe with its delicate red filament. My eyes closed as she put the embroidery aside and opened a green book. A passenger train called from the canyon, a lingering, regretful cry.

I awoke at dawn, my possession, for I alone was awake. My three sisters breathed evenly, unaware. The scents of freshly unearthed coal, acrid sagebrush, stale tobacco smoke, and leftover incense from Saturday's ritual cleaning for Sunday were in the coolness. I knew my father was gone, to the canyon beyond the rock mountains where he was bringing a water line through the chasm and into town, called Helper after the engines sent to help pull trains over the summit. Leon went with him. Leon had suddenly become a big mongrel, worthy of the name Lion, a different dog from the blackish brown puppy that Lambros, or Louis as he was called in English, had held down on newspapers in the *sala* and using a pocketknife had cut off its tail. Leon slept in the tent at the foot of my father's cot and growled whenever a laborer on the Mexican gang came near. Next Sunday my father and Leon would return. My father would sit in the kitchen at the oilcloth-covered table, a cigar in his mouth, and write in a gray ledger. He wrote in English, in fluid, rounded letters, the e's old-fashioned. On the table were a red Greek-English grammar book and a small black Greek-English dictionary with gilt-edged pages. From time to time he looked into the books. The index finger of his left hand was missing.

I waited in the stillness, my eyes on my parents' wood-slatted immigrant trunks on either side of the dresser. The room was dim; the vigil wick had used up the layer of olive oil in the glass of water and burned out. I examined the water stains down the blue calcimined walls; the designs changed each time my mother stood on a kitchen chair and poured hot water out of a kettle to kill cockroaches. I waited, wondering how the sky would be.

Slowly the gray gathered color and transformed itself into golden-rimmed clouds of red, magenta, purple. While I gazed, the colors changed slowly, subtly, to violets, mauves, and blue grays. A familiar, nameless bird called from far off, sweetly sad.

The sky turned a pale blue. The Italian family on the other side of our walls stirred; coal rattled into stoves; privy doors slammed. From the nearby rail yards came clangings, groanings, chuggings. A train whistled to signal its leaving. Acrid engine smoke seeped into the room while the house rumbled, shook, and was left shuddering as freight cars went by. The town whistle rolled out; mine whistles in the hidden canyons faintly shrilled and screeched. It was all over and we were eating Cream of Wheat in the dark, crowded kitchen, the morning coolness dispelled by the warmth from the coal stove.

Will I forget that first white frame house, one of a row owned by the Bonaccis who, at the end of the street, had an entire house to themselves? The rest of us polyglots, Irish railroaders, Greeks, Italians, Americans, lived in double houses divided down the center into three rooms for each family.

In and out neighboring women came to have my mother read from the worn dream book she kept on top of the green wooden cupboard. Because she had been raised in the holy city of Constantinople and knew several languages, she read in Greek and then translated the interpretations. Pandemonium! Italian women screamed and tore their hair when their dreams of black birds alighting on a person's head and other ominous images foretold disaster and death.

In the communal backyard, the dirt shiny and smooth from the soap and lye of wash water thrown over it, boys with grimy fingers played marbles; girls made dolls out of clothespins and scraps of gingham. "Andy-I-Over," the older boys called and threw balls over the roofs of houses to each other. The mothers hung up their wash on clotheslines stretched between privies—my father's long underwear had a rust spot in the middle from the gun he kept behind his belt. The mothers spoke in a special language: "Go-a-Gringholga, tell-a im rossa warra an-a glickerina"—Go to Greenhalgh and ask him for rose water and glycerine. Ashamed and defiant, I grimaced at passing Mormon and other American children who laughed at the mothers, and with wonderful fear I watched the boys of our row and the flaxen-haired Mormons throw rocks at each other.

"Dirty foreigners, go back where you come from!"

"Take one step on our property! We dare you! Mormon hicks!"

"Yah! Yah! Wear your religion round your necks!"

"Yah! Yah! Wear your religion round your ass!"

I kept the cross my godfather had given me at baptism under my collar and hoped some day to see the Mormon undergarments with their mysterious symbols hanging on a clothesline.

How many years did we live in that first house with my mother serving visitors, cleaning, cooking, giving birth? Perhaps until my second year in school. People moved into the row of houses and out again. The plump, pretty Italian woman on the other side of our walls was visited, the boys in the backyard said, by an Irish railroader when her bowlegged husband was on the graveyard shift at the mine. The American wife of a dour Greek barber, who dyed his hair black, disappeared one day. "She stole things," women from Greek Town said, sitting on the leather sofa and chairs of the *sala* sipping and eating, "even when she had no use for them. He warned

6

her once, twice, and the third time he beat her and threw her out. That's what Greek men get for marrying Amerikanidhes!"

On the other side of the barber lived a Greek family without *filotimo*, without honor. The portly father was home at all hours, a cigar clenched between his teeth, gold-covered to show his affluence. Before the children were born he had taken his wife to western mine, mill, and smelter towns to dance in coffeehouses; then he became a labor agent and lived by cheating newly arrived immigrants.

The woman's father and stepmother lived with them. One morning I saw my mother surreptitiously give the old man a silver dollar as he walked by on his daily excursion to the coffeehouse. When his fragile old wife came to drink Turkish coffee, my mother became sprightly and spoke soothingly to her while she rocked in a straight-back chair lamenting, "When my man dies, what will *she* do with me?"

The most frequent visitor in our kitchen was an Irish neighbor, Sarah "Kilarney" Reynolds. From her my mother learned American cooking: lemon meringue pies, Parker House rolls, fruitcake, oatmeal raisin cookies. For our after-school treats she made these American delicacies we thought far superior to Greek honey and nut sweets. When yeast and cinnamon scents filled the house, I watched entranced as she beat, mixed, and baked. Her hands were strong, magical.

But when she made Greek cheese pastries, it was a bright occasion, my father's name day or my godfather's visit. Using a bleached broomstick, she deftly rolled out paper-thin circles of dough on the floured table. She draped each circle over the broomstick and spread it on the sheet-covered furniture in the other two rooms where that day we were forbidden to enter. Back and forth the floured hands rolled the slender broomstick, the tips of the little fingers turned gracefully inward.

Kilarney Reynolds told our mother to send us to the YMCA Sunday School, although she attended the small frame Catholic church near Nigger Town east of the rail yards. Greeks would sit in the Catholic church only for funerals. The Mormon ward, as the

Helen Papanikolas, back row, right, and her sisters, Josephine, center, Demetra on the left, and Sophie seated.

Latter-day Saints called their church, was beyond understanding—those Mormons who had been, and some still were, polygamous as were the hated Turks. Real church was the Greek church, seven miles away in Price, the county seat, where we went on the important days of the year: Christmas, Holy Week and Easter, and August 15, the day of the *Kimisis*, the Falling Asleep of the All-Holy.

Seldom smiling, even when she played Irish tunes on an accordion, Kilarney Reynolds told my mother about visiting days at the grade school, about American customs, about cures for childhood illnesses. Obediently, my mother pushed an index finger dabbed with Vicks down our throats. Mrs. Reynolds gave my older sister, Josephine, her American name. Jo's godfather had had her christened with the name Panaghiota after Panaghia—All-Holy, one of the titles for the Virgin. Mrs. Reynolds advised an American name. Trying to explain who the Panaghia was, my mother said, "She was the wife of Joseph." Kilarney slapped one palm over the other. "Then call her Josephine," she said. And so the odd, un-Greek name was given Panaghiota instead of Mary, the name of the Virgin.

Perhaps Kilarney Reynolds also explained mysterious happenings to my mother. We stood at the living room window, my mother and I, and watched a long procession of cars following a hearse. On the radiator caps of each car were two blue and white Greek flags tied in opposite directions. The people in the open touring cars were like us, Greeks; they were dressed in black and each held a small Greek flag. The next day or so we were again at the window. Soldiers marched down the dusty road, dressed like my godfather in his World War I picture. Unshaven miners looked on, and boys with mock-serious faces walked stiffly at the side of the column holding stick guns on their shoulders. Kilarney might have explained the strike to my mother. To us, our mother said nothing.

Greek women came often to the three-room house, holding babies, their older children pulling on their skirts. Unselfconsciously they nursed the babies, little noses pushed into blue-veined, swollen breasts. Sipping liqueurs and Turkish coffee and eating the indispensable honey and nut sweets, they talked in high-pitched visiting voices, each in her dialect, about *patridha*, the fatherland, oddly exhorting and pining at the same time for their "good, honest fathers," their "poor, overworked mothers," for "sweet *patridha*" where grapes were sweeter, lemons larger, water colder.

The women brought dandelion greens, cleaned, washed, and tied in a dishtowel, a loaf of bread, still warm from their outdoor earth ovens, or goat cheese pastries. They exclaimed over the square gray washing machine in a corner of the dim kitchen and pretended to spit at it to counteract the envy that could give it the evil eye and break it. We sisters sat with the visiting children on the floor, nibbled on cookies, and eyed each other. When the visitors left my mother talked to herself. "Tsk, tsk. Hm. And now what? Tsk, tsk." Then she relapsed into her usual silence.

Will I remember that narrow dry valley bounded by towering dun-colored rock mountains, boulders and acrid-smelling junipers on their sagebrush slopes? Across from our row of houses green tumbleweeds gave off a disagreeable smell and sunflowers wilted in the heat and dust of summer. In winter, snow and wind swept over the mountains leaving frosted designs on our bedroom window. Then the black coal stove burned with spit and sizzle and melted the fairyland frost on the kitchen windows into opaque moisture that shut us off from the outside world.

Has the town dimmed for me? Not yet. I still see the gardens and white and dark green frame houses of Wop Town and Bohunk Town on a plateau on the other side of the river, the Nigger Town shacks near the Catholic church east of the Denver and Rio Grande Western rail yards, the Cretan enclave north where two mountain slopes almost converged, Greek Town by the grade school, the yellow and brown frame D&RGW railroad houses on either side of the tracks, Main Street with its American and immigrant stores, and the rolling clouds of heavy black engine smoke spreading and settling over the narrow, dessicated valley.

On Main Street, Greek coffeehouses, both mainlander and Cretan, basil plants growing in rusty cans in the windows, resounded with table poundings and chair smashings over church and old-country politics; in markets young mustached Greek fathers

The main street of Helper, Utah, center of the eastern Utah coal camps, at the foot of Steamboat Mountain. The early twenties. *Courtesy of the Utah State Historical Society.*

hacked at carcasses; others, clean shaven, well dressed, presided over fragrant candy stores and overstocked clothing stores. The short, bald manager of the Grill Cafe wore a dinner jacket and black bow tie, like restaurant men in Salt Lake City, and leaning over a window tank of green water, scooped up flapping trout. In the basement banquet room of the Grill, visiting Greek lodge officers, Greek-language newspaper reporters, and Orthodox bishops and sometimes the archbishop—tall black *kalimafkia* on their heads, flowing black robes, swinging pectoral crosses—fervently admonished our parents and us children to keep up the Greek language and customs.

The Italian stores were of less interest: the Helper State Bank, the Ricci Meat Market; yet in the windows of the Quilico Furniture Store stood the new electric stoves and refrigerators that were replacing coal ranges and wooden iceboxes.

The nauseous-smelling Japanese Fish Market—the mother energetically cleaning the glass case—had to be quickly passed, then the mysterious noodle house next door where no one ever went in or out; but the import store was for long lingerings: wondrous creamy-skinned, black-haired kimonoed dolls, pretty spread-out fans, dragon-embossed dishes.

Fascinating, too, were the placards on the outside walls of the Strand Theater, actresses with cupid-bow lips and cowboys in ten-gallon Stetsons and high-heeled boots riding noble horses, Tom Mix's black stallion, Tony, decorated with silver-tooled bridle and saddle.

The bare-looking Chinese–American Cafe had two signs in the window: WHITES ONLY and WHITE HELP ONLY. Sometimes, wiry, stunted men stood outside it, their faces weather-browned, hand-rolled cigarettes in their bleached mouths, their stockmen's hats—not the Stetsons of prosperous Greek, French, and Mormon sheepmen—discolored above the band from years of sweat. Their women with toothpicks in their mouths were scrawny, their skin netted with wrinkles, their blue eyes squinting, even on gray days, from the wind and sun of their open terrain. In fall they shivered in striped suit coats worn over J. C. Penney dresses. Their children, little girls in too-long cotton dresses and boys, whose straw-colored hair was whacked close to their heads, stared big-eyed at passersby. A long time passed before I realized that those stunted, wiry men from the sagebrush land and Tom Mix were supposed to be the same people—cowboys.

Set between the Greenhalgh and Rexall drugstores, the newspaper plant, doctors' and dentists' offices above, were several South Slav stores and Stein's Mercantile. "The Jews are like us," my mother said of the only Jewish family in town. Rouged and mascaraed women gazed down from walk-up hotels. "Don't look up!" our mother hissed.

Our excursions through Main Street were a prelude to visiting Greek Town. At the Rexall Drugstore we turned right and came to the Liberty Hall where the American Legion and Kiwanis held meetings and the Greeks wedding and baptismal celebrations. We were there when two white doves suspended above the bride's and groom's wedding crowns were released and flew and swooped over the crowd.

We turned left, down a dirt road through a neighborhood where several feuding Cretan matriarchs reigned, all in black, lace-trimmed caps of mourning covering their hair. On name day visits they denounced each other, blue veins swelling in their throats while my mother made noncommittal *achs*.

At the end of the street stood the squat, two-story, yellow brick schoolhouse in a dirt yard. A wide cement walk led to double wooden doors. Two months after my fifth birthday, I had trooped after my older sister, Jo, into the building, which smelled of urine and must, and into the room she pointed out. Inside, children squealed and laughed until two teachers, their hair fashionably short and marcelled, hit rulers on a desk and divided us into the High and the Low. I was put into the Low with miners' children, American girls in faded ginghams too long or too short, immigrant girls in homemade dresses cut like nightgowns, and boys in old bib overalls. I burst into sobs and could not stop. The teacher put me into a closet and closed the door. When I was let out, I would not look up from the scarred desk top. "I'll change your name to Bill," the teacher told Vasileos Psaroudakis. "Your last name's bad enough." At the end of the day she rapped the ruler sharply on her desk. "And tell your mothers I won't stand for you eating garlic. Tell them it don't cure colds."

My mother quirked her lips when Jo told her I was in the Low. Four years of studying the times tables and spelling lists before school, at recess, at lunch time, after school, and in bed and I was at last in the fifth grade High.

During recess boys fought with bare knuckles, and if tears ran down their dirty faces, the children chanted, "Cry baby! Cry baby, go suck your mother's titty!" The boys caught dogs and sicced them on each other. Cretan children played by themselves, ran, chased, shouted in their dialect, angering me that they spoke Greek on the school grounds. At coffeehouse doors, on the street, anywhere, they kissed their godfathers' hands, and they spoke English as if it were Greek: "I have to comb my hairs," the girls said.

The school's cement walk was no-man's-land. My godfather had fought in no-man's-land in France, that strip of shelled craters between the Allies and the Germans. I had seen it in a movie at the Strand. The American soldiers crawled out of their trenches and the Germans out of theirs, both carrying guns with fixed bayonets. While Irene Holmes pounded fast on the piano below the stage and bombs flashed on the screen, the smudged, handsome Americans clashed heroically with the mean-faced Germans in spiked helmets.

At times the American and Mormon children stood on one side of no-man's-land and the "foreigners," as they called us, crowded opposite them. "Dirty Greeks! Dirty Wops! Dumb Bohunks! Go back where you come from! Sappy Japs!" Yet the Japanese never took part but stood near the door on the periphery of no-man's-land. The blacks, too, were onlookers, sitting on the rusty pipe rungs of the fence.

The leader of the immigrant children, who lived in a cave in Wop Town, shouted back, "This ain't your land! It belongs to the Indians! Mormon shit-asses! We wuz born here same as you! We got just as much right! Stick that up your ass!"

All the time eyes glanced at the door, expecting the looming figure of blue-eyed, bald Mr. Horsley, the principal, to appear at any moment. Mr. Horsley's office was at the top of the wide central stairs. On his rolltop desk was a length of black rubber hose. A boy and girl had been sent to him by the second grade teacher for three strokes of the rubber hose: when she had asked the students to stand up and name their flag, the two had said "Greek." Another teacher had sent up an Italian girl. The girl's mother had rampaged into the school, yanked the teacher outside by the hair and beaten her. Then she had shouted for Mr. Horsley to come out for his beating, but he remained inside.

Into the screeching of recess they swarmed, Mormons and other Americans with names like Eliza, Wanda, Charlotte, Mildred, Dwayne, Weldon, and Elroy; immigrant children, the Serbian and Slovenian Millies who had been christened Milka, the Greek Anastasias, Demetras, Yoannas, Penelopes, called by their diminutives Soula, Lula, Noula, Popy; the boys called Sam whose given names had been Soterios, Spyros, Salvatore, Savas, Shiguru; the Mikes who had been baptized Mihaêl, Manoli, Emmanuel, Manos, Michael; the Iosifs, Josips, Giuseppis, now all Joes; the Yiannises, Johans, Giovannis, Jacques—Johns; and those others whose American names made no sense at all, like Alcibiades Diamant's Walker and Alexandra Pappas's Olive.

My stomach constricted on school mornings, and I would not drink even a glass of milk despite my mother's angry exhortations. Often I could not eat the lunch Jo doled out to us sisters from a large black lunch bucket. By the time I reached home my head ached and I felt withered inside as I sat down to eat the after-school treats my mother had waiting for us on the kitchen table: a bowl of cinnamon-sprinkled *rhizoghallo*—rice pudding, pies, and cookies. When she was sick—although we had no inkling of it because she neither complained nor went to bed—she prepared a plate of bread heavy with butter, sugar, and cinnamon or boiled rice with honey, spices, and cream. "Eat, eat!" she demanded of me. "You're skin and bones."

At the end of my first school year, I was left with a Cretan family homesteading on the Ute reservation—we were related by godfatherhood—because the mothers knew the clear air would miraculously give me an appetite.

As soon as my father's new Hudson drove off in a cloud of reddish dust, I was overwhelmed with loss and despair, and struck with homesickness, nearly starved the following weeks until my father and a friend drove on roads turned to rivers of mud by summer storms. I sat in the back seat while they talked, told anecdotes, and sang old *kleft*, guerrilla, songs. My father maneuvered the car expertly, but I thought we would never reach our white frame house. My heart almost burst at the sight of it. My mother was in the kitchen with Jo helping her. I barely ate. Later I wandered from one room to the other, away from the table strewn with soiled dishes and the leavings of chicken bones and Kalamata olive pits, their purple juice staining *pilafi* and *feta* bits. I was unworthy. I had pined and grieved with "that homesickness that has no cure," as the Greek proverb said, and they had gone on, laughing, eating their fill, not giving me a thought.

West of the school another dirt road led to Greek Town. On its boundaries poor Americans lived in dilapidated houses. Cardboard replaced broken windows, rags plugged smaller holes. Chickens pecked in dirt yards cluttered with discarded bedsprings, assorted broken chairs, hand wringers for washtubs, and old automobile tires, although no car or truck was ever in sight. When the women of Greek Town sneered at *Amerikanidhes*, they usually meant these gaunt or obese women with lank hair and missing teeth who "washed clothes on Sunday and hung them out shamelessly." A thin woman with bad teeth always had a cigarette hanging from her lips. "In broad daylight! Like a man! Smoking!" And Americans "threw their daughters to the dogs! They don't care enough about them to protect them from men," the mothers said, fuming over the American custom of dating.

At the end of the road on barren dirt stood a small frame building that had once been a meat market for supplying lamb to Greek boardinghouses. There our Greek school was held. It was suffocatingly hot when the sun's heat filtered through the cobwebbed rafters and freezing cold in winter when only the teacher next to the furiously burning potbellied stove got any warmth from it.

Previously we had stayed after American school while the other students went home snickering at us for having to learn Greek; then for a short time we were taught in the black wooden railroad chapel. That ended when the older boys locked in the dapper little teacher. Almost every session he had ordered one or two boys and sometimes all of them to come forward, line up, and put out their hands, palms down. Then going from one to the other he whacked them with a force that lifted him up by the heels.

One late, cold afternoon, the wind picking up the cinders at the side of the tracks and flinging them against the windows and walls, the teacher kept us in, screaming that we were no different from American children who had no respect for their elders, that we Greek-American children were depraved and children in Greece were dutiful, respectful, well-mannered. "No! They have not been spoiled by easy living like you in Ameriki! They know that life is more than"—with poisonous sarcasm he exploded the English words—"the *good time*! That's all the Amerikani think about—the *good time*!"

Once outside in the howling wind, older boys picked up rocks and pieces of coal and ran around the chapel breaking windows. The screams inside were barely heard in the whistle of the wind. The next day he left, just as most teachers and priests left, raging that they would leave us peasants and return to civilization, and my father was again at the wall telephone talking with editors of Greek newspapers in the East and to the Archdiocese in New York about a replacement.

Greek school was moved to the former meat market. We sat at nine or ten rows of slanted, unpainted planks with attached benches that served as desks. Their hair home cut, the boys had seats on the right side of the room, the girls, almost all of them with long thick braids down their backs, on the left. About two feet of decorous space separated the boys and girls.

We recited from books written in the *katharevousa*, the language of the academy and the courts, the purist language we never heard spoken and never would hear. Pompous fathers came to pontificate in village dialects about the catastrophe that would befall us if the Greek language died out in America. A succession of teachers

17

taught us; some came and left so quickly they were as quickly forgotten. One of the earliest was the "Cretan Hothead" who tried to burn an American flag during a strike and was run out of town by the Greeks themselves. Another cried for Greece constantly: "The land that gave birth to Demosthenes, Alexander the Great"—a long list of names followed; then with eyes closed dramatically and finger pointing to the warped floor, "lying there, slave to the tyrant Turk, prostrate for over four hundred years!" And the tears flowed.

Demetrios Kyriopoulos, James Gray in English, was one of the few teachers holding a diploma. His hair was thick and glossy black, his sagging cheeks gray, and his horn-rimmed glasses magnified sad, black eyes. He had left his family in Chicago, overridden with Greek teachers, to languish in the Savoy Hotel and in bouts of frenzy—his loneliness no doubt—to direct us in a series of plays and programs.

Twice when teachers had caught the first D&RGW for the East we were taught by two women who converted their living rooms into classrooms. One was a pretty blonde, blue-eyed Cretan woman, the wife of a handsome miner, whose small children roamed in and out wanting water or their sticky hands washed. The other was Mrs. Frickson, a strict, childless woman, whose husband had butchered meat on the far outskirts of Black Hawk, a coal town set among sagebrush and junipers. When immigration restriction laws cut off the constant spillage of young Greek men and boys into the coal fields, the boardinghouses and then the meat market closed. The Fricksons were nearly destitute. The slender, gray husband and his short, stout wife with thick eyebrows and large moles sprouting stiff black hairs raised pigeons for eating. Their poverty was probably the reason they were often at our Sunday dinner table. To our mother a person could be sick or grief stricken, but to be hungry was the worst evil to befall him. So they ate, the docile husband absorbed in eating; his wife, cheeks bulging, denounced political events in Greece. My father glowered at a woman's discussing politics.

In one way or another almost every teacher left the Greeks in an uproar, but none to the extent of Kyria Eleni—Madame Helen.

Kyria Eleni's black-dyed hair was cut short; Egyptian eyes glared under her black eyebrows, white powder generously covered her incipiently sagging face, and rouge was bright on her eyelids, cheeks, chin, and the cleavage of her pendulous breasts.

Nothing daunted her, except for the day that Psaroudakis came in leading his red-eyed son, Bill, by a rope around his neck and proclaiming, "He'll learn Greek or I'll beat him until the priest looks like a donkey to him!" Kyria Eleni collapsed into her chair and a horrified stillness filled the room.

A few days later, with Kyria Eleni ensconced next to him, the oldest student, Chris Jouflas, drove several of us to the Greek church in Price to practice for a March 25 program to celebrate the anniversary of the Greek revolt against the Turks. As we approached the church, Kyria Eleni told Chris to drive her on to the priest's house and then return to church to wait for her. Driving off, we glimpsed the priest in long underwear, his black hair parted in the middle and wetly plastered to his head, put on metal-rimmed eye-glasses and unlatch the door. Their liaison was exposed. For several years Kyria Eleni pressed a breach-of-promise suit against the priest, then, half-paralyzed by a stroke spent the rest of her life in the Salt Lake County Infirmary.

Greek Town surrounded the frame school, its cluster of houses like small oases set in dessicated earth. Rows of vegetables grew at the side of grass patches shaded by young fruit trees. Planks or brick paths led to porches covered with cascades of silver-lace and morning -glory vines.

Crammed in backyards of dirt, shiny and smooth as clay from splashed soapy water, were washhouses, coal and wood sheds, rabbit hutches, wire-fenced areas for pecking chickens, pigeon coops, and domed earth ovens supported on wooden platforms. How joyous when the warm yeasty scent of baking bread filled the air.

In and out of each other's houses the Greek Town children ran while mothers scolded, threatened, and, snapping dish towels, drove swarms of flies through open screen doors. The children ran down narrow dirt alleys lined with battered washtubs and boxes filled with ashes and clinkers and jumped over rivulets of gray wash water that trickled into mud puddles. Boys, and sometimes girls, fought and threw rocks at each other. They were beaten by their mothers: the girls for reading worn *True Story* and movie magazines they kept hidden under mattresses and in washhouse niches when they should have been washing dishes or ironing, the boys for roaming too far or for having been seen smoking by the river or for not going to Greek school.

With dish towels tied about their heads, the mothers irrigated their gardens with America's plentiful water. They pushed mounds of white dough on wooden paddles into earth ovens and took out golden brown loaves of bread. The mothers were quick to cut us large pieces and slather them with butter. This admonition we heard daily from the mothers: "Don't drop the bread! Bread is holy. If you drop it, make the sign of the cross and kiss it before eating. If it can't be eaten, bring it to me to burn. Never throw bread in garbage. Bread is holy!"

During autumn's ritual making of tomato paste, the mothers carried out bucketsful of tomato skins, which were immediately pounced upon by a mass of droning, iridescent blue-green flies. All the while the mothers called to each other over wire fences, mostly about their children. Folk cures for fevers, for the dread *pounta*—pneumonia—and croup, judicious advice on who was best for dispelling the evil eye—Barba Yiannis, Uncle John Diamanti, the favorite—and "putting meat on children's bones" were the hysterical concerns of mothers whose wedding pictures showed them thin, even scrawny, but who had become heavy in America where a person could eat meat every day. Aunts, godmothers, village friends, and neighbors cajoled children, brought delicacies, recalled old-country stories of lethargic children suddenly eating voraciously after some seemingly insignificant remedy or occurrence. Every school recess Nicky Pappas ran across the road to Eleni Koulouris, his mother's village friend, for a soft-boiled egg to "give him strength."

Nearly every Greek Town house had extra men living in it: brothers, cousins, or fellow villagers of parents. A bevy of adults disciplined the children. In memory I see the stealthy, excited face of a boy as he climbs into a coop, brings out a chicken, pushes a splintered stick under its tail feathers, and screams as it runs around the yard, wings flapping, squawking, the bloody stick trailing after it. Then I see his mother chasing him, brandishing a broom handle.

Chris Jouflas was the leader of the boys. At the end of the school year, he lined them up in his backyard, shaved and then dunked their heads into a tub of water. With their shaved heads—said to make hair grow in stronger and prevent future baldness—and bare feet, the boys were ready for summer. In the fall when immigrants ordered carloads of grapes for wine-making, Chris filled galvanized tubs with them and he, his brothers, and many cousins wearing hip-length boots stamped out the juice.

Often in Greek Town a sheepman butchered a lamb, first making the sign of the cross three times to help him do the job quickly and cleanly to minimize the animal's suffering. As the sheepman pulled back the lamb's throat, its blue-veiled eyes gazed out from white bristled lids. Dark red blood spurted. More slashes, a meticulous working of bloody fingers, and the gray, thick pelt was thrown over a wire fence to dry, the gray innards were spilled into a washtub, and the small naked carcass was hung head down against a shed by a wire through its shanks. Finished, blood up to his elbows, the sheepman again made the sign of the cross three times.

Although visiting Greek Town was usually satisfying, I did not want to live there in the houses with their lean-tos, sheds, washhouses, and where mothers baked wonderful bread in backyards but also wrung the necks of chickens and pulled off their wet, smelly feathers, chopped off the heads of rabbits and skinned them in a flash. I was always eager to return to my silent house.

2

*I*t was always so, wanting to be somewhere and not wanting to be there. When we left our compact, dusty valley for the greenness of Mud Springs, I could hardly bear the long, slow uphill climb. I wanted to be in the greenness at that very moment.

A long line of sedans chugged up the narrow dirt road; far below the railroad tracks shone like two blue satin ribbons. Halfway up, the fathers turned off their engines, got out, and with handkerchiefs wrapped around hot radiator caps, quicky turned them and jumped back as steam shot up in slender streams.

Then we were there. Blue, white, yellow, and pink flowers spread over a high meadow surrounded by pines, and the cool breeze mingled the scents of piquant evergreens and roasting lambs.

Men squatted on the ground and turned poles on which the roasting lambs were impaled. At their heels glasses of red wine caught the rays of the sun, and drops of fat sizzled on ash-covered coals while the men hummed *kleft* songs, cigarettes quirked in their mouths, their eyes half-closed from the blue smoke and the heat of the fire. Sheepherders and town gamblers worked in relays turning the poles while mothers spread their delicacies on tablecloths smoothed over the meadow grass. Children ran and darted, wondrously happy.

Then it palled: I wanted to be there, yet I wanted to be home reading one of the books my mother indiscriminately bought from every salesman at the door or in her garden where she grew vegetables and flowers in mingled confusion.

A picnic in the mountains. "The cool breeze mingled the scents of piquant evergreens and roasting lamb."

After the banquet, musicians brought out a *laouto*, *clarino*, and Cretan *lyra*, and mothers retrieved hidden gunnysacks and filled them with the soft, black dirt fathers complained turned their cars into gypsy wagons. The men sang "songs of the table," of exile in America and other foreign places, of their guerrilla heroes. A favorite was old General Grivas whom the Turks had hunted all his life and who later brought down Othon, the Bavarian prince the Great Powers had placed on the throne of Greece:

> *Grivas, the king wants you.*
> *And what does the Bavarian want, lads?*
> *Does he want me for good, to make me a general?*
> *Or does he want me for ill, to lock me up?*
> *If for ill, I'll change my clothes,*
> *I'll adorn myself.*

Grivas would adorn himself with his slaughtering knife and silver-chased pistols. My father sat in the center of the group, head back, eyes closed, singing of Grivas's manliness, his *leventia*. I watched him unwaveringly. Still I wanted to be in a corner of the garden breathing in the scent of flowers, alone.

On the way down the steep canyon one Sunday, we sisters with our feet on the dirt-filled gunnysacks destined for our mother's garden, I leaned forward. "Papa, who was General Grivas?"

"The patriarch of my clan."

Will I remember our second Bonacci house, a four-room one all to ourselves? On a dirt road at a right angle to the tracks not twenty feet away, the house faced the rail yards, the black water tipple and roundhouse, the frame chapel painted black so that engine smoke would go unnoticed, the yellow and brown wooden Denver and Rio Grande Western depot and houses, and beyond, the YMCA where railroad men stayed between runs and where my father went for his weekly shower with a bundle of clean clothes under his arm.

When tramps came to the back door in the evening and night, eyes darting, on the lookout for railroad detectives, begging, even shouting, "Hurry the train's comin'!" my mother deftly wrapped sandwiches in newspaper together with an apple and a Greek cookie, opened the screen door latch, and handed out the packages with no fear at all. At night when our father was still at work and something or someone rustled in the backyard, she took the *blasti*, the broom handle for rolling out sheets of dough, walked heavily across the kitchen and porch, and disappeared into the blackness, and I, quaking, knew I was a coward. I would never have courage like hers.

Across the dirt road from our house was a ravine or wash. Rainstorms had dislodged great sand-colored boulders from the mountain slopes and flat slabs from the cliff faces and sent them cascading into the yellow silt of the wash. The flash floods came suddenly, roared, and were gone. Then the mourning dove called most clearly.

Red, orange, and yellow sunsets touched the wash with a golden haze that rose shimmeringly and filled us children with an ethereal buoyancy that sent us from boulder to boulder, with no certain focus of play, in a slow-motion leaping and a joyful calling in the miniature golden valley.

All day freight trains passed by that second house, each gondola filled with a certain size of shiny coal, some as large as boulders,

Yoryis's great grandfather Theodhoros Grivas, a leader in the revolt against the Turks, 1821–29.

others as small as pebbles. Acrid clouds of smoke billowed from the engine stacks. So close did the trains go by that I could see the color of the engineers' eyes. With red bandanas tied around their necks and in striped gray and white railroad caps and coveralls, the honorable vestments of their work, they lifted their hands to grasp the whistle cords. Every engine call had its own tone—piercing, mellow, or low—and signal of long and short notes. Decades later I would learn that each engineer had his own whistle to alert his wife to get his food on the table. Happily, I did not know this then and could believe in their mystique. A whistle was like the voice of a person, distinctive, and all were pleasing to hear. At intervals the whistles sounded farther away, fainter as the trains entered the canyon.

The freights carried other cargo besides coal: sheep, cattle, pigs that left a stench; grapes, peaches, pears that scented the air briefly with a delicate sweetness. Bumping their couplings the cars went by. The boxcars were painted a special color and bore a symbol and name—the white mountain goat of the Great Northern forever climbing a mountain slope—and always the favorite of all, our own Denver and Rio Grande Western, a little zephyr trailing its logo. It had been built over the roughest terrain in the country, through the Rocky Mountains.

I gazed at the long Denver and Rio Grande Western passenger trains when they stopped at the depot to discharge mail, pick up travelers, and funnel on water from the tipple. People sat on green velour seats or in the dining car at tables covered with white cloths, flowers in glass vases, their orders taken by black men in white jackets. Sitting on the front yard grass in warm weather or at the dining room window in winter, I contemplated these people so different from me who lived in a house of silence. My parents were unlike other parents.

I had stayed at the Jouflas house one night when my parents had gone to Salt Lake City, for what reason I did not know—perhaps, I believe now, to see a doctor for my mother. Mae Jouflas and I lay next to her parents' bedroom, listening to their talking long into the blackness about news Koumbaro—for we were related by godfatherhood—had heard in the coffeehouse earlier. He snorted when Koumbara told about Mrs. Psaroudakis's visit that afternoon. Obese, blue-eyed Mrs. Psaroudakis had asked how to stop having children. Koumbaro growled, "Why didn't you tell her to take a knife and cut it off." The sound of leisurely talk did not come from my parents' room.

Melancholy, I watched the unusual, privileged people on the green seats and at the dining room tables begin moving slowly by. Faster the wheels turned, clicking rhythmically; the whistle sounded, the observation platform flew by, and from far off the whistle came again, muted, almost lost. At night an insolence was in the whistle as it heralded the taking of people away, away, away.

From our house we walked on the cinders at the side of the tracks to the yellow brick YMCA, the town landmark. The two-story front faced the rail yard; the three-story back had an entrance that led directly to the hall used for Sunday school. According to age we sat on circles of chairs and listened to middle-aged teachers read Bible stories from a children's book.

On the first floor was a long, carpeted room; three walls were entirely of windows, the fourth lined with book shelves from which Jo and I eagerly began to take home new-found treasures: Gene Stratton Porter's *Boy of the Limberlost, Girl of the Limberlost, The White Flag, Freckles*.

We Greek children, a Japanese girl, and "Americans" posed for a photographer one day along with several women teachers, and Julius Shepherd, the director. Mr. Shepherd may have been a minister, but he dressed in business suits just as the lay Mormon church leaders called bishops did. We were used to Catholic priests who wore clerical collars and vests; Greek priests but recently in dusty black robes, tall *kalimafkia* on their heads, and flashing pectoral crosses had been successfully harangued by church boards to dress like them on streets.

Mr. Shepherd was old, slender, and clean shaven, his hair white and thin. When he talked about his Jesus, that blond, wavy-haired, blue-eyed man who knelt with hands clasped against a rock in the Garden, his voice quavered. With Mr. Shepherd gathering us together, telling us about Jesus, we were safe. No one used the word *foreigners* in the Y.

Our Greek priest, Papa Yiannis—Father John—was a real man of religion, bearded, long haired, sonorously chanting the Divine Liturgy, dispelling the evil eye by reading passages from the Scriptures. He was not a real priest, however, but a chanter ordained on the spot during the Balkan Wars so that he could carry messages hidden in his robes through enemy lines. After Papa Yiannis left town in humiliation when the newspaper scoffed at him for not knowing English, mothers took their whining babies, suffering from colic no doubt, to the new priest who "had his papers" for a rereading of the baptismal ceremony: Papa Yiannis could have left out a word and the "holy oil of baptism not taken."

If I had known all this at the time, would it have made a difference? No. Papa Yiannis was of the church with his faded robes, tall priest hat, and beard; and Mr. Shepherd ascetic and lean, speaking of Jesus lovingly, without even a clerical collar, was the man who ran the YMCA.

But whenever we sang in the YMCA basement, a poignancy held me, sentimental as the words were about the kind, all-loving Jesus who forgave and understood and would lead us to Heaven. Not the words but the sad sweetness of the music brought me close to tears for something I could not comprehend.

> *I come to the Garden alone,*
> *While the dew is still on the roses,*
> *And He walks with me and He talks with me,*
> *And He tells me I am His own.*

Often we sang that martial song:

> *Mine eyes have seen the glory*
> *of the coming of the Lord.*
> *He is trampling out the vintage*
> *where the grapes of wrath are stored.*
> *He hath loosed the fateful lightning*
> *of His terrible swift sword.*
> *His Truth is marching on.*

Glory, glory, Hallelujah!
His Truth is marching on.

The music stirred me, but Jesus and God had nothing to do with it. Like harmonica music, it left me pleasantly sad. In the hot dusty summer afternoons, on the Jouflas porch swing with morning glory vines screening us from the night, or on our own front porch in the twilight, harmonica music wafted gently beyond. I was becoming aware of grossness, bathos, and false emotion, but I listened, again with a sweet sadness, to songs about convicts who wished they had the wings of an angel to "fly over these prison walls," about dread letters of death edged in black, about love:

> *Oh, I'll take you home again, Kathleen,*
> *Across the ocean, wild and wide.*
> *Oh, I will take you back again,*
> *To where your heart will feel no pain.*
> *And when the fields are fresh and green,*
> *I'll take you to your home again.*

And there were all those songs from World War I a few years back that were played on Victrolas in candy stores in town and in houses on Main Street, but they were more poignant by far when unseen boys or men blew the tunes on their harmonicas at night:

> *It's a long, long way to Tipperary.*
> *It's a long way to go.*

And after a movie showing Colleen Moore as a French farm girl in love with Gary Cooper, the American soldier who had to leave her at lilac time for the front lines, the Victrolas tinkled out "Lilac Time" constantly.

Who knows why I sat in sad bliss at the music of the harmonica. But I know that the YMCA, the books on its shelves, Mr. Shepherd and the American Jesus, the songs we sang in the basement Sunday school, the harmonica and Victrola music were all lumped together for me: they were what being American was.

Greek school, the robed priests, incense and candles, long-faced saints on icons, screeching mothers in the *sala*, men singing of their ancestors waiting to ambush the Turks: they were what Greekness was.

May I never forget that in this second house I learned Easter was the most important day of the year, that every day led inexorably to it and then Christ's journey to the cross began all over again. The forty days of Lent signaled an exhaustive housecleaning. Soap, ammonia, and fresh calcimine chilled the house; then, in arms floured up to her elbows, my mother rolled out sheet after sheet of pastry, and the scents of baking honey and nut sweets dispersed the harsh smells of overcleanliness.

Fasting began in earnest for us two weeks before Easter. Neither fish, poultry, nor meat could be eaten because of the blood in them, in memory of Christ's shedding His blood. Nor was anything that came or was made from blooded animals allowed: milk, eggs, cheese, yogurt. Many households lived on beans, lentils, and greens, and some mothers would not use olive oil for taste because it was holy. Our food was bread, pickled peppers, squid with rice, spinach with rice, beans with rice, and, for something sweet, halvah. Between meals we munched on salted, dried chick-peas. Bloodless shrimp, crab, and lobster were sold in the Japanese Fish Market, but we had little of them. Lent was not the time for delicacies, our mother said. All penny candy, too, was forbidden because she did not know what ingredients were in it.

Holy Week came and there was no playing at all, no listening to the new, arch-shaped table radio or the hand-cranked Victrola. Daily and nightly services were conducted in the dimmed church, reliving Christ's life. On Great Thursday and Great Friday, the most terrible days of the year, our mother admonished us severely not to play at recess, not to laugh. We returned to a mute house, a grieving throughout. Outside, Mormon children played and called to one another. Never was the chasm so wide and deep between us and them as at Eastertime. Mothers shook their heads over the Mormons. "What does Christ hanging on the cross mean to them? It's only Joseph Smith they care about. They even marry on Great Fri-

A rash of marriages followed the arrival of Father Markos Petrakis, the first Greek Orthodox priest in Carbon County, Utah. 1916. *Courtesy of the Utah State Historical Society.*

day! All the world is singing dirges at His bier and they marry on Great Friday!"

Peeking under the green blinds one Holy Week, I saw Mormon children coming from an Easter party at the railroad chapel. They were holding baskets woven out of colored crepe paper and eating

The Greek Orthodox Church in Price. Looking toward the *ikonostasion*, "the Bible of the unlettered." *Courtesy of the Utah State Historical Society.*

candy Easter eggs. I looked at them with the utmost disgust, with that sneer of Greeks when they called a worthless person without self-respect a "gypsy."

I remember especially one Easter week. On Great Thursday the mothers in black sobbed as they kneeled on the oil-spotted wooden floor while a black wooden cross was carried slowly about the church. The following day one of the fathers drove us girls to the church to transform a dome-shaped, wood and chicken wire frame with carnations, daffodils, and blue irises into the flower-studded Tomb of Christ. In the evening, walking behind as it was carried outside and around the church, we sang the Lamentations.

> O, Life, how can You die? How can You dwell in the Tomb? You broke down the Kingdom of Death, and raised up those who were dead in Hades.

We sang His Mother's lament:

> O, My sweet Springtime, my most loved Child,
> Where has Your beauty gone?

On Great Saturday morning the air was alive, expectant. We talked in low voices, but as the day wore on, excitement grew in the house. Our mother prepared the traditional *mayeritsa*, the chopped brain, intestines, and liver of the paschal lamb, and baked the sesame-sprinkled sweet Easter bread, decorated with ropes of dough forming a cross and with a red egg, for His Blood and symbol of rebirth, at each end of the cross and in the center.

At midnight all lights were turned off in the church. Babies shrieked and were silenced. Then a small light moved forward from the altar, and the priest called us to come and receive light from the unwaning Light. In a few moments the church was ablaze with hundreds of swaying candle flames. The priest raised his candle high and the song of Resurrection came from him tentatively:

> Christ has risen from the dead
> By death trampling Death, has bestowed
> life upon those in the tomb.

The congregation joined in singing, over and over again, each time more sure, louder and louder until the windows and walls of the church quivered and the floor trembled. Still singing the people pushed outside, cupping their hands about their candles in an attempt to light the vigil tapers of their family icons and insure good health for the coming year. In the church yard people embraced saying, "Christ is risen!" and were answered, "Truly risen!" Women and men cried happily and several enemies asked each other's forgiveness.

We were home and eating anything we wanted. At the dining room table eating the *mayeritsa* were Louis and Nick Zeese, my father's second cousins; my godfather; our youngest sister Sophie's godfather, Raekos, called behind his back Liar; and Stylian Staes, the Greek vice-consul. Joy shimmered in the house.

The next day, Easter, real Easter, was celebrated in the three o'clock Agape service. Because the Orthodox church used the ancient Julian calendar, only once in four years did we celebrate Easter with Protestants and Catholics. The other three years we had two Easters. (In the YMCA basement Easter lilies were set on top of the upright piano, and Mr. Shepherd talked about Jesus dying on the cross for our sins. This "dying on the cross for our sins" was one of the strange things about American religion. Americans talked more about it than about Christ's dying to give us eternal life, but what did it matter.)

In the din of the church basement the feasting and dancing began. Children pushed through the packed crowd and ran wildly into the yard and back again, screaming in ecstasy, hurrying to mothers, godmothers, and aunts for honey and nut sweets that were indulgently given out. The mothers covered planks set on sawhorses with white tableclothes and spread their delicacies on them. The freshness of newly washed hair came from the mothers' heads, the smell of vinegar from their armpits, and the scent of cloves from their mouths.

Men, called "sports," ostentatiously carried in roasting lambs on poles and at one end of the hall hacked them into pieces. Their silk shirt sleeves rolled up, dishtowels tied around their waists, they rushed big platters of lamb, oozing pink and red juices, to people clustered at the tables. The sports often brought American women with them. We girls from Greek school knew exactly what these women would say after eating and burst out laughing to the warning glances of our mothers. Probing their teeth with lipstick-covered toothpicks, they said it: "You Greeks sure can cook."

The mothers gave the women evasive looks and glanced with annoyance at the men whom they had known in their villages. "Foolish boys," they said under their breaths, as if they were talking about their sons.

Girls pointed out people and told us about them. Otherwise we would not have known anything about the life of the immigrants. We did not dare repeat what we had heard to our mother. "Never gossip! Never criticize! Be modest, modest!" The word for modest, *semni*, came so often from her mouth it was hateful. As for our father, he never talked with us, except to ask us in English for the newspaper or to bring him a glass of water. I was awed by what the other girls knew.

One successful businessman was ashamed that his wife could not speak English—he fancied he could—and would not allow her to shop: "He even buys her corsets!" The girls giggled about Tsikouris who had been shown a plump, pretty woman for his approval, but when she lifted her veil at the conclusion of the wedding ceremony, her dark, oily skinned sister had been substituted instead. And there was Monoyios who gaped when his ugly picture bride stepped off the D&RGW, then ran to one sheep camp after the other, chased by her brother who caught him and begged him not to destroy his family's *filotimo*, its self-respect, by refusing his sister who would then be left forever unmarried. Mrs. Papakostis, distracted, had stepped off the train and realized that the thin, hook-nosed man approaching her was not the man whose picture she held in her hand. Papakostis had sent his handsome brother's picture instead of his own. The bride turned to get back on the train, but she had nowhere to go.

Because Easter had come late that year, lambing was over and Nikos Linardos, a sheepherder, was in town for his annual leave from camp. Tall, immensely dignified, he resembled the hawk-nosed British colonels stationed in India we saw in movies. He had been named after the church of Saint Nicholas where his mother, fleeing with fellow villagers from Turks out to avenge the killing of one of their officials, gave birth to him. The villagers would not allow her to take the baby with her: his cry would give them away to the Turks swarming over the mountain slopes. His mother wrapped him in her petticoat and placed him under the altar of the church. Three days later the villagers filtered back and his mother found him alive. Sitting near Nikos was red-faced, effusive Sampalis devouring lamb with gold-covered teeth. He had had to have the diamond embedded in a front tooth removed to pay a gambling debt or be murdered.

A roar exploded as the first dancers took to the floor. All evening the gaiety resounded against the basement windows. Late at night we walked to our cars. "Christ is risen! Truly risen!" The calls came fainter and fainter into the blackness.

The house was quiet, the silence taut. Angry talk from the front bedroom. "To men like Sampalis a nod is enough! A handshake is not given lightly!" My mother stridently: "People saw!" My father: "Let them fuck themselves!"

I lagged going home from school, my eyes on the sidewalk— "Step on a crack, break your mother's back." Then nothing could be done but enter the silent house where my mother sat at the dining room table and practiced writing English words or read from an orange red book, a Greek translation of *Les Misérables*, or the old green one.

No memories are so stark for me as those associated with this second Bonacci house. It had space for proper entertaining in a dining room. The wooden floor was covered with brown linoleum patterned with yellow roses, the round oak table with a beige linen cloth from which crocheted grape clusters hung. A corner glass cabinet displayed my mother's new dishes and glassware. A sewing machine was placed under the window where we sisters read from our Greek books while our mother sewed and tried to counter our unspoken belligerence by intoning what she had probably read in a Greek-language newspaper—that all words come from the Greek: nephrology, pathology, biology, and on and on.

Women continued to come for afternoon visits. In the evening my father brought home men passing through town with whom he had "eaten bread and salt" on labor gangs in his first years in America. Priests came on Epiphany in black robes and *kalimafkia* to cleanse the house of sin, bless it with a bunch of basil dipped in holy water, and stay for dinner. My father's cousins, Louis and Nick Zeese, sat at the table often, Louis arriving from the McGill, Nevada, copper mine, Nick from making the rounds of mining towns on paydays, gambling with money staked him by Nick the Greek. My father gnashed his teeth at Nick who dressed in the immaculately pressed suit of a gambler, rippling silk shirt, gray fedora set rakishly on his sleek hair—a Greek Rudolph Valentino. With a pleased smile, Nick appeared one day looking like a twin of the champion golfer Bobby Jones in tweed cap, knickers, and argyle socks. "Where's your golf stick?" my father said sarcastically. Soon he was storming at Nick, "Cardplayer! White slaver! Smudge on our clan's name!" Nick looked down at his plate with a pretense at shame. Louis joined in chastising him. His old black suit was shiny; a deep line on either side of his mouth pulled down his thin cheeks. When we read our Greek lessons to Louis, we smelled the whiskey on his breath.

My godfather died soon after we moved into the house. He had come home from war in France with a mastoid infection. I heard when I was grown that people marveled at my grief, barely eating, sobbing at the mention of his name, but I remember only my father, sisters, and I waiting in the car for our mother and the drive to the funeral. The engine was running and our father's muttering kept us silent. Our mother hurried out in that heavy way of hers, with much moving of arms yet covering little ground. She was dressed all in black. My father slammed the gearshift, cursing her saints and All-Holy for dressing like a *vlahissa*, a peasant. The black stockings, especially, drove him to horrendous oaths. From that day on, when masses of small cumulus clouds spread across the blue sky, I thought that one of them was my godfather.

It was in this house that I saw boys running down the dusty road and across the tracks whooping, "A Nigger's gittin' hanged!" Later, I saw the black man's picture as I idly turned the pages of a staple in Greek homes, the photograph album. The mothers screaked on in the room dimmed by rubber and basil plants at the windows. I scrutinized the pictures of weddings, baptisms—naked

George Anton, Yoryis's closest friend and godfather of his daughter Helen.

boy babies propped against pillows, their penises like ridged buttons, girl babies in demure embroidered baptismal dresses—picnics with squatting men turning lambs on spits and dancing in rounds against the mountain pines, and on the last page a black man dangling from a tree and under him men, women, and children, arms crossed, smiling for the photographer.

In this house my mother and we four sisters stood at the kitchen window and looked in silence at a Ku Klux Klan cross burning on the blackness of a mountain slope and across the valley the immigrants' circle of fire flaming in answer.

Outside this house I stood on the new sidewalk one clear blue March day and the ground moved under my feet, then once again. People hurried out of their houses. Our obese neighbor came puffing and calling, "I just called Central! The Castle Gate Mine Number Two has exploded!"

Orphaned Greek girls returned to American and Greek schools with their long braids tied with black ribbons and wearing black dresses that smelled of acrid dye. The boys wore black shirts with the same pungent odor and sweaters and jackets with black arm bands sewed on the sleeves. When fights broke out at recess, children chanted at them, "Orphan! Orphan!"

I have a memory that comes to me at intervals. May it never fade. I had come home from school to a still house. I was alone. Afternoon sunlight in golden motes fell across the worn kitchen linoleum. I walked quietly toward the dining room to put my books on the sewing machine and stopped. On the table covered with the beige linen cloth with crocheted grape clusters was a low bowl of tall green shoots topped with delicate white flowers. A sweet scent came from them. I gazed. I breathed in the scent. After a while, I tiptoed to the table and looked at the brown bulbs pushed into white and pink bits of pebbles. I leaned forward to smell the flowers, looked into their yellow centers at fragile filaments on which yellow tabs sprouted. The peace, the beauty in the room was profound.

3

We moved north, still at the side of the tracks, at the foot of Steamboat Mountain, a strange name for the massive rock upthrust thousands of miles from water. Now prosperous, my father had built us a spacious red brick house that had a tiled bathroom; a large, airy kitchen with electric stove and refrigerator and a long drainboard of small white sexagonal tiles; a living room of blue and gray Karastan rugs, plush furniture, the latest combination radio and phonograph, an upright piano, and carved tables; a dining room with blue brocaded draperies embroidered with white chrysanthemums and a massive oak table that could be extended into the adjoining living room. On this table our mother regularly set platters and bowls of steaming food for church dignitaries, for traveling Greek newspaper reporters and editors from New York, Chicago, and San Francisco, and for brides from Constantinople, the holy City, and other parts of Asia Minor, women whose families had lost their ancient properties in the aftermath of Greece's futile invasion to regain its former land. Dowryless they had come to America to marry, most often men with little or no education.

Vivacious and *moderna* compared with the village women of the town, they were led by a black-eyed woman with short hair and flat curls—"spit curls" they were called—in front of her ears. In the afternoons she pulled a small child just learning to walk and carried a baby to visit systematically one Greek house after the other. Taking advantage of the old hospitality edict, she knew when her husband came to take her home, they would be asked to stay for dinner. She regaled those around the dinner table with stories about the *hodjas*, teachers and sometime religious leaders of the Turks. While the baby pulled on a swollen brown nipple, she gave us sisters advice: for perfect spit curls we were to use egg white or lemon juice; to make powder stick we were to pat it on immediately after we washed our faces. She was oblivious to our not yet wearing makeup.

Nick Zeese, who had a nickname for everyone, called her Theda Bara after the sultry silent film star. Theda told my mother which phonograph records and sheet music to order from the New York Atlas catalogue. No *kleft* songs for her, but sentimental love songs. "Romanza, romanza!" she exclaimed, she who was married to a stone-faced attorney Nick Zeese called Calvin Coolidge. Her eyes transfixed, she clamped her palms at the sides of her breasts and pushed inward, breathing deeply over Rudolph Valentino, Antonio Moreno, and other sleek-haired movie stars playing the roles of gauchos and Arab sheiks.

My mother's eyes opened wide as she and Theda talked animatedly about the *Polis*—the City—Constantinople. Theda spoke lovingly about her parents, brothers, and sister; about the servants they once had, the leisurely life; comic anecdotes.

One day as my mother was rolling out sheets of dough in the new kitchen, I said, "Mama, don't you have any brothers and sisters?" A gasp. A terrible cry, the broom handle still, and her sobbing, sobbing. In horror I walked out of the room.

Another day: she was sharpening a butcher knife. It slipped and gashed her from the wrist to the elbow. Fat seeped from the cut skin where drops of blood formed. Wrapping her cut arm with a dish towel, she hurried to her bedroom and returned with one of my father's leather belts. Her injured arm against her waist, she scraped the inside of the belt until she had a small pile of shavings. After pushing the fat back in place, she tamped the shavings along the cut and wrapped the towel tightly about her arm, then picked up the knife to continue sharpening it. All the while I stood, unable to move.

My mother joined the Ladies Guild with the wives of railroad men; Kilarney Reynolds, her mentor; and Mrs. Gease whose husband manufactured cigars called Flor de Helper in his basement. Several of the women had cut their hair, and my mother followed; now she looked almost American. She served the women American dishes: salmon loaf with peas in cream sauce, chicken croquettes with potatoes au gratin, chicken a la king, Waldorf salads, pies of all kinds, strawberry shortcake, and caramel custard, exquisitely shimmering on the plate with a Nabisco biscuit. "You just serve too much food," a salesman's wife said after she had eaten heartily, and my mother rubbed her hands together and looked liked a chastened child.

The Ladies Guild members were the "good" women of the town, tidily dressed, easily distinguishable from the immigrant women, the poor Americans, and the wives of doctors, dentists, and the newspaper editor who had nothing to do with the other three groups. Across the narrow dirt road, our doctor's wife often entertained her bridge club. Their laughing and high spirited talking came clearly to me sitting on the cement steps of the front porch. The women clipped their words; their voices were raspy, and cigarette coughing interrupted their conversations. Only one had a child. "I'll be damned if I'll raise cannon fodder!" a voice snorted. Bootleggers drove up late at night to deliver packages or sent their sons in the daytime with newspaper-wrapped bottles. Their Saturday night parties lasted into early morning.

Between the festive dinners and luncheons in our new house came the long silences, the strain of eating at the table when no one spoke after outbursts from my mother and cursings from my father that awoke me at night. A gray pall hung over the town. Child kidnappings, murders, appalling abuse of people filled the newspapers. Late at night a drunken man passed the house singing. "Shell shocked," the women across the street had said about him.

Almost every Sunday we sat in lodge meetings and heard the old harangue about preserving "our heritage, our language, our Orthodox faith for which our ancestors watered with blood the valleys and mountains of Greece." We girls sat dressed in club uniforms of blue and white, the colors of the Greek flag. Speakers told

43

us we were the future mothers of the race and on us lay this responsibility. The boys of Greek school managed to be somewhere beyond the banquet room of the Grill Cafe. Sitting next to girls whom I avoided in American school, whose armpits smelled, who believed in the evil eye and all village superstitions, who had been embroidering dish towels for their trousseaus since they were six, I fantasized about the passenger train that I would someday board to be carried through the rock mountain gates into the canyon beyond and away, away.

On an October morning in 1929, I stared in perplexity at the stark headlines of the *Salt Lake Tribune*: STOCK MARKET CRASHES! Months later the mines began to work half shift. Unshaven miners leaned against the buildings of Main Street even on windy days. Freights rumbled down from the canyon mines less often, and the whistles at the mountain gates were further and further apart.

With President Roosevelt's campaign promise to allow collective bargaining, two unions vied for the miners' membership. One, at first unknown to them, was a Communist front. The members went on strike, and the heavy, dull smell of old rubber tires they burned to keep warm saturated the town.

Then company houses were boarded up, and miners, both American and immigrant, piled children and belongings into old cars and drove west to California, the Cretan Greeks hoping to find work in the vineyards of countrymen. Now the freights that slowed down to take on water at the tipple were filled with unsmiling young men, ignored by railroad detectives, sitting in the doorways of box cars, their feet hanging over, also on their way to California. As months passed, older, unshaven men appeared in the boxcars, a bundle or scruffed suitcase at their sides. Then came old men, boys as young as ten, old women, and at last young families, men and women holding children and babies, and they were all going to California and all gazed out unsmiling.

There could be no God. One morning as I picked up the *Salt Lake Tribune* on the front porch, the mourning dove called. I waited, and as I listened, it changed from a bird to a slinky, furry animal standing on its hind legs, its mouth pursed into a small o.

4

Our mother told us to pack: we were moving to Salt Lake City. Our parents chose the first house that they looked at because it was near three schools. It was old, of a purplish, rough brick, and smaller than our new one in Helper. There was a small bay off the living room where we put our piano and an even smaller one off the kitchen, supposedly a breakfast nook, where not even a miniature table would fit. Each of the three bedrooms could barely contain a bed and dresser, and their flowered wallpaper was tinged with a lifeless brown. "We'll get a bigger house later," our father said at our silence. I lay awake at night, unable to sleep in the quiet. I thought of rumbling trains and calling whistles that had once lulled me to sleep.

Depression though it was, our father with his partner opened a series of grocery stores, eleven in all. He became the president of the church and president of his lodge and later its district governor. Again we sisters were the nucleus around which a girls' club was formed; at meetings we wore blue skirts and white tunics bordered with a blue Greek key design. I wrote skits for the club to perform on Mothers' Day. I harangued the members on etiquette, glowered at them when Jo drove us to the A&W drive-in after meetings and they giggled with abandon, attracting the attention of others sitting in cars and looking on with mild interest.

Again we had to listen to pompous men tell us to keep up the Greek customs and ideals and to our mothers' exhortations to be *semni,* "modest." Hysteria lay just beneath our skin, waiting. During one meeting Kolokithas—"Squash"—short, red-faced, went to the bathroom at the back of the hall. The long rush of urine hitting the toilet bowl came back as clearly as if he were in the middle of the room. Strangled giggles from us girls, our hands clamped over our mouths, shuffling about in our chairs in a futile attempt to hide brought hundreds of parental eyes to glare at us and moments later at returning Squash. With a serious look on his round face, he pulled down his vest in a businesslike manner, took his seat, and folded his arms across his chest, his head cocked, to resume hearing the importance of keeping up the customs and culture of the fatherland.

At the next meeting I said I could not go: I had lessons and an important examination. My mother not only made no attempt to force me but had food simmering on the stove. I was a serious student with almost all A's on my report card and fervently believed I would become a doctor. I used the same excuse to absolve me from the ceremonial name day visiting. My last such visit came the day my mother and I had gone to Auerbach's department store to buy me a coat on sale. I had annoyed her by insisting on a navy blue, too near black, the color of mourning. In the streetcar on the way home, she pulled the cord and announced we would stop at a house to pay our name day respects to the father. An improbable thought overcame my churlishness: perhaps the daughter, Tina, and I could go across the street to Liberty Park to watch the ducks swim in the lake.

Tina opened the screen door for us and with a tilt of pride to her chin invited us into that world of immigrants who had moved from the Greek Town of church and rail yards to the east side of the city, into the milieu of massive, ornate furniture, thick carpets, cut glass, and hand-painted china. Two women who visited my mother regularly were there. One was Mrs. Vassiliou, the childless wife of the man who made the communion wine because he was "pure of thought and action." The proof was, Nick Zeese said, they had no children. Mrs. Vassiliou followed a strict routine; one Monday when an earthquake shook the city, she resolutely continued hanging up her wash. The other visitor, "the College Grad," as our youngest sister, Sophie, called a small sharp-faced woman, one of the Asia Minor refugees married to a laborer, was expounding on something she had read in the *Readers' Digest*. Mrs. Vassiliou, barely literate in Greek, immediately contradicted her.

The women began discussing a story in the *Kambana* [The Bell] about a woman who had "fooled" a hard-working Greek immigrant and after spending all his money left him destitute. The women clucked over these stories prevalent in Greek newspapers and fiction. They were so ready to believe the worst of women.

Tina served the visitors in the ceremony of the tray, linen, glasses, dishes, and pastries elegantly placed about a small nosegay of sweet william. She answered the women's toasts, "to your wedding crowns," in the purist Greek, overpolitely, bowing slightly and smiling sweetly in the manner my mother praised as being well bred and modest.

When she and I sat at the dining room table to drink a Coke and eat a honey and nut sweet, Tina curling her little finger, I tried to think of something to say and remembered visitors in my mother's house mentioned her beautifully embroidered and crocheted trousseau linens.

"Well, yes," Tina said, "I guess I wouldn't be boasting to say I do have a few nice things. I'll show them to you someday. I have everything put away just so. I've got this book on storing linens. Like tablecloths. I don't fold them. I roll them on big cardboard tubes."

The sound of a toilet flushing came from the back of the house. Tina stood up, smiling indulgently. "That's my little brother Petey. I've told him according to Emily Post he should lower the seat afterwards, but you know how boys are. Excuse me."

At about this time, 1935, my father went back to Greece to see his family. He took a compartment in a Denver and Rio Grande Western passenger train. Only one other traveler occupied a compartment, Jack Dempsey, the boxer. Together they rode to New York, smoking cigars and talking about the fights and fighters.

I did not know until he was near death that my father, no doubt with my mother's goading, had gone to Greece with the intention of moving us there. "But why didn't you ask us if we wanted to go?" I inquired. "What if we had told you we didn't want to go?" He pulled down his lips at this unexpected, belated argument. "You spoke Greek, you went to Greek schools, Greek church, Greek clubs," he said. "I didn't think it would be very different. But I didn't like it. Everywhere you went men were bunched together talking about which girls had the biggest dowries. Let them go to hell!"

I went on to the university, but I did not become a doctor. My resolve dissipated after dissecting preserved worms in parasitology class. In the pathology specimen room, where diseased organs were kept in formaldehyde, a reinforced shelf supported a mammoth glass jar holding the huge uterus of Mrs. Psaroudakis. For no more than a second I stood before the repulsive gray monstrosity and a distant pity evoked her image, waddling down a dirt road, her swollen hands holding up her great abdomen. She had begged to be told how not to have more children.

Her son Bill, whose father had led him by a rope around his neck through Main Street and into Greek school, strode across the campus in gray flannel pants and highly polished shoes. During high school he had worked for the town undertaker and had prepared his mother's body for burial. He, too, was going to be a doctor, paying his way by selling Real Silk Stockings to well-to-do, middle-aged women who thought his blue eyes and sleek black hair handsome. Before the year was out, he married one of the women, moved to Las Vegas, and hanged himself a few years later.

Other reminders of the mining town years came often. As a medical technologist in the county hospital laboratory, I always stopped in the Infirmary to see paralyzed Kyria Eleni, my old Greek school teacher, because my *filotimo* demanded it. Lifting her pudgy, good hand, she fumed and cursed her keepers, especially the stout, gray matron, refered to as the "madam" because she had once run a house of prostitution. She and Kyria Eleni often screamed and pulled each other's hair. "That she-ass!" Kyria Eleni sputtered through her fat rouged lips, her eyes glittering.

My sisters and I married men with ancestral roots in the Peloponnese. Our marriages began a year before Pearl Harbor, and our ten children were born during the Second World War. When the first child was born our mother stopped dyeing her hair and our father stopped cursing—openly; however, our mother used, without success, a salve to bleach out age spots. "When I was a child," she said sadly, "I didn't want my grandmother to touch me because of the brown spots on her hands."

We sisters tended each other's children and arranged that one of us would always be present to help our mother with her dinners. She gathered soldiers stationed at nearby army bases who were drawn to church by loneliness and had my father drive them home where she plied them with food. Laden with butter and other foods in short supply, which she managed to get from my father's stores, she took streetcars to visit mothers mourning the loss of sons in the service.

After the war came spurious prosperity and a harried release into parties and enormous name day celebrations. Letters again arrived from Greece, and the relatives I had never heard my parents speak of became people. During the German occupation of Greece, my father's brother Pericles had starved to death far from his village while searching for clan members who might help his family. When he could hold on no longer, he had sold his mother's family icon of the All–Holy and Child in a gold-leaf frame of carved roses. His wife and three daughters had left the village for the valley and worked in the fields of strangers for a pittance of grain. His son Spyros had joined the Communists because they pledged abolition of the dowry system. He was caught and imprisoned for alleged involvement in a political murder. His letters asked for a radio and money to buy food from his jailers. My father sent money, I the radio. "They'll never give it to him," my father said. My mother and I collected used clothing from the family and supplemented it with thrift store articles to avoid the relatives' having to pay exorbitant import taxes on new clothing with money they did not have.

My father's life revolved increasingly around the church. On election day, just as on the opening of local and national polls, he telephoned to instruct us how to vote. His *komma*, party, had to win or some unspoken disaster would follow. During these Sunday elections, while the entire family was seated at our mother's table, babies asleep in bedrooms or whining on our laps and older children wandering about with a drumstick in hand, the telephone rang constantly. Springing up, my father listened eagerly to the latest tabulations. He began a drive to erect a memorial hall next to the church for the American-born Greek servicemen killed in the war. As I read their names on the plaque, a haze came over them—not too long ago young, smiling, getting out of Greek school, alive, now dead.

Our mother's preoccupation next to food was sending our children to Greek school and Sunday school. Daily we were reminded that *all* her friends' grandchildren were attending Greek school, all but hers. She still cooked bountiful dinners for a procession of visiting church dignitaries. The dinners stopped suddenly in the late 1950s. An officious little bishop brought his mother, unannounced, to stay with my parents. Before the dinner—he had ordered the menu earlier—he asked that the *nykokyra*, the lady of the house, be brought to him. While my mother stood before him, he explained how he wanted the food served—everything on separate dishes, the soup hot not lukewarm, all plates removed completely after each course. Pastries would be served at the table but the demitasse of coffee in the living room. After the guests had gone, my father cursed the bishop; my mother said firmly, "I will never cook another dinner for bishops and archbishops."

New immigrants and their children who had come at the close of the war took up most of the church pews. They, the aging, and a sprinkling of second-generation women were the regular churchgoers. On church celebrations the new immigrants filled the memorial hall and danced joyously to the *laouto, clarino,* and *lyra*. At church assembly meetings they shouted against paying dues; it wasn't done in Greece. They were as quick to take offense at the new American-born priests as were the immigrants of my childhood against those from the old country.

Each time a new priest arrived and stood in the middle door of the altar screen, I thought of the priests I had known who had once appeared at the Holy Gate. Before the American-born priest, angrily looking out, had been "Goatbeard" who had answered every question with a "That's how it's done"; earlier the round, flat-faced priest, the first to lead the dancers, who said himself he should never have taken vows because he loved pleasure too much; before him, young, saintly Father Artemios from the Holy Land, sent away because his voice creaked while chanting; farther back stood Kyria Eleni's seducer, then Father Yiannis who "did not have his papers," and farther and farther back to giant Father Petrakis, black robed, *kalimafki* on his head, long hair, bearded.

The American-born priests instilled order, forbade visiting during liturgy, gave Sunday school teachers literature from the archdiocese and lectured them not to deviate with their own explanations. Boys were brought together and properly trained as altar boys. The liturgy was translated, biblical Greek on one side of the page, English on the other. The long calls, the haunting supplications were no longer in obscure Greek; they were there in black and white:

> *Thee, the ever-blessed and most pure Virgin and Mother of our God. Thee, that art more honorable than the Cherubim and incomparably more glorious than the Seraphim, that, without spot of sin, didst bear God, the Word: and Thee, verily the Mother of God, we magnify.*

Each new priest looked younger than his predecessor. The mothers, now grandmothers and great-grandmothers, kissed their hands while receiving the *andithoro*, the piece of consecrated bread, from them and said, my mother among them, "Father, why are you growing a beard? You must shave it off." Remembering, no doubt, unclean, old-country monks and perhaps even priests, the mothers had a great aversion to the beards the new priests were growing.

As the priests grew younger, the altar boys grew older. They had begun as seven- and eight-year-olds, tittering when they stumbled over their stoles, yawning, probably from late-night television, freezing under the black looks of priests. Suddenly they were gawky, arms and legs too long for their cassocks, head acolytes bearing the glinting cross and standards, and then suddenly they were no longer there. Younger boys had replaced them and they were married, fathers.

Funerals were becoming as common as weddings and baptisms. As bachelors died off, coffeehouses dwindled. Mothers and fathers of children I had sat with in Greek school were dying. Men who had sung "songs of the table" in our two Bonacci houses were all dead. Louis Zeese had died of alcoholism; Nick Zeese from cancer and the insidious life with a woman he had not realized when he became respectable and married was mentally ill. Once part owner of four brothels in the Intermountain West, he knew nothing about women.

My father still held himself tall and looked far younger than his age, witness to his name which meant "son of the long-lived." My mother, though, had become extremely wrinkled and often spoke and acted peculiarly. Whenever we left her house, she asked us, her middle-aged daughters if we had gone to the bathroom—to preclude being inconvenienced on our way. Far too generous to her children and grandchildren, she darned her stockings and mended her underclothing as if they had to last out her lifetime. At a dinner for her widowed friends, she picked up a whole chicken and tore it into serving pieces. She was still cooking constantly and forcing her food on us. At times it was excellent as in her younger days; most often it was ruined, the *dolmadhes* too full of rice, an infinitesimal amount of ground meat, and boiled until the grape leaves fell apart.

I often stopped to clean her dining room and kitchen. She and her friends ate, left the table with a hill of soiled dishes, and sat in front of the television set to watch soap operas. Each had a different version of what was happening on the screen: "See, she's getting what's coming to her," one said about a victimized, pregnant woman. "She lost her virginity, so now she 'can dance to the tune she paid the musicians for.'" "And look at that beast, cavorting around like a young boy!" another said of a cuckolded husband who had gone to his mother with the bad news. "Instead of staying home where he belongs, he finds this older woman for a lover!"

Avidly they watched the screen, four aged women, children and grandchildren grown, three of them in black mourning, one soon to die of cancer, the other of heart disease, my husband's mother to be relegated to a wheelchair, and my mother to more and more strokes.

Twice I drove my father to funerals in the mining towns; alert and hardy he was rapidly losing his eyesight. Old women contemporaries of his had taken to wearing black kerchiefs about their heads as if they were back in their villages.

My children were grown, parents themselves, living away. I often looked at my parents, sad and frustrated that I knew so little about them. After buying their groceries, bringing them back from doctors and dentists, I prepared lunch. While drinking coffee in the small familiar kitchen—for they had never moved although they could well have afforded it—I asked them questions. They answered readily, surprised at my interest. And I was surprised at their inner life, at how deeply my mother had been stirred by colors, hues, scents, the tone of voices; at how sharp the rage still was in my father at the poverty of his village and what it had done to people's lives and characters.

I filled several notebooks and wrote down incidents that Nick Zeese and my father had told my husband, stories they would never tell a woman. My husband and I traveled throughout the West looking for the places where my father had worked. I listened to events I had researched for my work, but hearing from their mouths, seeing through their eyes, they became indelibly theirs. They spoke in the oral tradition of their people, remembering with amazing recall. I traveled to Greece and found my parents' people. Beyond Athens and the provincial towns, I was lulled by the barren land receding past. Gray green thyme very like sagebrush dotted the arid earth. In the distance rocky hills were patched with scrub oak and on the horizon hazy blue mountains rose. The pink of an occasional oleander bush was the same hue as the wild rose found at the side of a Utah irrigation stream, and the far-off lone cypress on the plain of thyme and those growing about graveyards were but a darker green than young Mormon poplars. It was all familiar, the dessicated earth that hoarded its meager rainfall to nurture small-leafed plants. At times I forgot that I was traveling in my parents' land until a Venetian battlement, stark white against dark green foliage and rock on a mountainside, reminded me where I was. It was all familiar, the land, the people, the churches.

I visited the provincial towns where my father had lived while his father had served as secretary of courts and his mountain village where winter came early. An old guidebook said of it: "Winter was a horror. . . . The mountaineers fear neither snows nor rain, only the powerful, wild, bitter, frigid, burning north wind." I went to my mother's birthplace in western Thrace and to the cobbled streets and alleys of Constantinople, the City, where she had grown to womanhood.

I met the remnants of their families: my father's blue-eyed sisters and first, second, and third cousins; my mother's nieces and nephews. As I walked up the road of her village, a woman came toward me, as tall as I but thinner, wearing a faded brown kerchief with which village women still covered their heads. With a little leap in my heart I looked into eyes identical with my own. She was my mother's sister's daughter. Her name, like mine, was Eleni and we were the same age.

After my fourth visit, I was ready to write my parents' story.

5

Yoryis was born into the Zisimopoulos clan in 1886, or perhaps 1888. The name Zisimos—long-lived—and poulos—son of—had come to them from an ancestor who had lived to a great age. Down through the generations his progeny carried his traits of "going to their graves with clear mind and hair and teeth intact."

Yoryis had been born in Klepá, Roumeli, in central Greece, his father's ancestral village, but he spent most of his young years in Mitikas, a town on the Ionian seacoast. Where his family lived depended on the ruling political party which appointed judges and their assistants.

Yoryis's father, Yiannis, noted for his remarkable brown eyes that "saw into one's soul," but with compassion, had taught himself law. As a young man he had walked to the provincial towns of Nafpaktos, Lamia, Karpenisi, and Agrinion and bartered for old law books. He worked in the fields from dawn to evening, then read by the fading light until he could no longer see.

When Yiannis decided he was ready, he walked down the mountains to Messolonghi to take the bar examination. He did not know that a month previously the Greek Parliament had enacted a measure making university attendance mandatory for acquiring a law degree. Although Yiannis passed the examination, he was allowed only the title "Secretary to the Court." He prepared cases, prosecuted them, often served as judge, was called "Judge" all his life, but was paid a secretary's wages and his employment depended on whether Harilaos Trikoupis was in office as premier.

After passing the bar examination, Yiannis rode the family mule to Athens and presented Premier Trikoupis with a letter of introduction from the powerful Sismani clan who ruled the wild mountains of Yiannis's province. Trikoupis was called "The Englishman" because of his un-Greek reserve. Yiannis himself had this same reserve. Trikoupis believed in the Great Idea, the regaining of Greek lands conquered by the Turks centuries earlier, and like all Greeks that it was their destiny to retake Constantinople, the City, and its great cathedral Ayia Sophia—Holy Wisdom. First, though, Trikoupis exhorted the Greeks to rebuild the country that had deteriorated under four centuries of Turkish rule.

In 1881, Trikoupis sent Yiannis to Mitikas on the Ionian coast to hear cases. It looked on the map like its name, Great Nose. One of his first assignments was on the island of Corfu. Crossing the turbulent water in a caique during a storm, he became drenched, developed pneumonia, and suffered from asthma the rest of his life.

In Mitikas Yiannis met Demetrios Grivas, son of the old general Theodhoros Grivas. Demetrios had been left with four orphaned nieces to dower. To provide the dowries he sold a portion of land given his father by the Greek government for his services during the Revolution of 1821. The land was north of Mitikas, opposite the island of Lefkas. It was guarded by a round rock battlement known as the Castle of Grivas. Because of Greece's poverty, Demetrios sold three thousand *stremmata*, a *stremma* being about one-fourth of an acre, for the equivalent of twenty-five cents each. Demetrios was educated, unlike his almost illiterate father; his mother was a daughter of the famed widowed Bouboulina who had taken over her sea captain husband's command and routed the Turks in more than one battle. Demetrios offered Yiannis his niece Zaferia, her eyes the color of sapphires for which she was named. She was six-feet tall, prized as women of height had been for centuries to produce tall sons to fight and panic the short-statured Turks.

As a notable, Demetrios was called by the diminutive Demetrakis, just as his father was called Theodhorakis in legend and in song. Demetrakis had lost his right arm following a foray into northern Greece, still held by the Turks. After drinking a glass of ouzo and while he smoked a cigarette, the gangrenous arm was cut off. Demetrakis learned to use his left hand expertly and became renowned for his swordsmanship.

In 1882 Demetrakis exchanged the wedding crowns for his niece Zaferia and Yiannis; a year later Zaferia gave birth to a son, Pericles. Demetrakis, "the absolute ruler of Akarnania," western central Greece, inexplicably lost the next election. Inexplicably, because all he had had to do before previous elections was send a servant to lead his great gray stallion through the towns and villages of his province to remind them of him. He summoned Yiannis from Mitikas to Patras where he was to board a ship for Paris. "When I return," he told Yiannis, "we'll work out something so you won't be dependent on politics for your bread."

Two years later, Demetrakis was dead. According to family legend, his fame with the sword had preceded him and France's foremost duelist sent him a challenge. Demetrios vanquished the Frenchman and was summarily poisoned for humiliating French honor. That was family legend. History records that after a brilliant career, he "resigned completely from politics and lived a quiet life, mostly in Paris. In April of 1889 returning from Nice to Paris, he became ill with pneumonia and died in Massalia [Marseilles]."

Without work and help from Demetrakis forever lost, Yiannis led his loaded mule, his pregnant wife, and children to his desolate, barren mountain village, Klepá, too high for growing olive trees to give its people oil for food and for the vigil lights of their icons, too rocky on the mountain face to grow wheat which they tasted only when someone died. To prepare memorial wheat for the dead, they traveled to valleys where it could be grown. Gheorghios—Yoryis was born there soon after they arrived.

In Klepá Yiannis was more often called Tanga than Yiannis or Judge. In his boyhood he had pulled the church bell; *tanga-tanga* it had tolled. Two married sisters and two tall, gaunt brothers lived in Klepá, Christos, as a priest called Papa—Christos, and unmarried Konstandinos. The family moved into the ancestral two-story gray

Beneath the granite-topped mountain Xerovouni lay Yoryis's ancestral village of Klepa in the province of Nafpaktias. 1927.

rock house with Konstandinos in Lower Klepá, separated from Upper Klepá by the Great Torrent.

On the first floor, no more than a square cave, the mule was stabled; in summer two goats and their kids were also penned there. In winter the goats and kids were kept above at one end of the one large room of the house. At the other end was the blackened hearth. Battered metal jugs of water were set on shelves together with tin plates, bowls, and a few knives, forks, and spoons. There Zaferia placed her dowry china. On a corner shelf were two family icons, the All–Holy and Christ and Saints Demetrios and George. The fourth wall had a central door leading to a small balcony and a window like a giant eye looking over the steep slopes to the river below. The floor was made from planks of various sizes and covered with several layers of hand-loomed rugs that generations of brides had brought with them. In the attic was the universal food of the poor, a mound of squash and homespun bags of dried beans and corn.

The family slept on the floor with sheep pelts for mattresses and goat-hair blankets for covers. In the morning the bedding was folded and stacked against a wall. In the center of the room was a rough table and four chairs and in a corner a pail of dirt that Konstandinos used to make mud mortar. During the long winters, wind, rain, and snow battered the rock walls, ate away the mortar, and threatened to bring down the house. With frostbitten hands Konstandinos mixed dirt with water, removed one rock at a time, and troweled in new mud. Only the churches and school had a sturdy mortar made by burning limestone at the riverside on the valley floor until it became powder.

Far below the house on widely separated patches, Yiannis worked with Konstandinos to raise more squash, beans, and corn to see the family through winter. After coming home in the evening, he sat at the window reading until the room darkened and he could no longer make out the words on the page. Only then did he light a candle that he had cut into notches. When the flame burned down to the next notch, he blew out the candle to save it for other nights of reading.

To the mud-mortared house Zaferia was brought, to the slopes of Xerovouni—Dry Mountain—where trees had long ago disappeared for fuel, where the soil had lost its nutrients a hundred years ago and more. She came wearing a hat that only the middle class and those above wore. The women esteemed her, they who tied kerchiefs about their heads in the ancient sign of modesty to hide their hair, woman's glory. Not only was Zaferia of the Grivas family but the only woman they had ever seen wearing a hat.

Zaferia had never worked in the fields; she knew how to cook delicacies and to embroider with silk thread, but soon she was doing woman's work: supplying fuel and water for the family. Almost daily she climbed to the wooded area above the village for twigs and branches to store for the onslaught of winter. She joined the procession of women to a spring a quarter of a mile upward, next to the chapel of Saint John, to fill jugs with water. There alongside the

Zaferia, Yoryis's mother, who came to Klepá wearing a hat but soon donned the traditional head scarf of village women and became one with them.

kerchiefed women she did the family's wash and carried it back to hang on bushes to dry. She sometimes climbed higher to Kokkinia, the red peak, where she could see Mount Boumstos of her childhood, and gazed in silence.

Zaferia cooked, cleaned house, and milked the family goats to be ready for the traveling cheesemaker, but all her thoughts were on her first-born, Pericles. He had had typhoid in Mitikas and nearly died from the fever. He was thin, slow thinking. If he coughed, she hurried to Papa–Christos for a Scripture reading. If he sneezed, she lighted candles to the All–Holy. If his face was hot, she sent her husband or Konstandinos for the midwife in Upper Klepá to come with her herbs and magic. Like all Greeks, educated or not, she was superstitious.

Three years after Yoryis was born, Zaferia gave birth to Olga, christened after King George's queen. The baby screamed day and night, and then Zaferia had two of her three children to consume her thoughts and strength. She had no time, no inclination to talk about the illustrious—or notorious—Grivas clan.

To help his distraught sister-in-law, Konstandinos of the thick dark hair and mustache pulled sideways into points often took Yoryis with him to the fields and set him on the dirt to amuse himself with rocks and twigs. As Yoryis grew older, he played with his cousins, the older Papa–Christos boys and the sons of his aunts of the Zisimopoulos clan. They played *tslika*, hitting at stones with sticks to see who sent his the farthest. Sometimes Pericles watched them, sitting far enough away to avoid being hit by a rock, but usually Zaferia kept him at her side. When the boys heard the music of the gypsies' clarinets, *gaïda*, bagpipe, and *daouli*, drum, they stealthily made their way to neighboring Arahova and hid on the slopes above, between boulders and scrub oak, to watch the baptismal or wedding festivities below.

One day a distant wailing summoned them. They hurried through the bushes and rocks to see a funeral procession they would learn was that of an unmarried pregnant girl killed by her brothers under the ancient code of death to women who bring dishonor to the family. The black-dressed procession left the church, and while the coffin was carried to the grave on the shoulders of the girl's brothers, her womenfolk keened and wailed.

Yoryis's closest friend beyond the family was Kostas Mástoras. On May 1 Yoryis and Kostas took off their European-style pants, made from cheap cloth manufactured in Piraeus, and put on white, pleated kilts they wore on name days and festivals. From door to door they went singing the first of May song in return for honey and nut confections; at home their sisters waited to divide the sweets.

From the time Yoryis was six years old he was sent with letters containing legal advice from his father to villages throughout the mountains. With Pericles looking on, his mother screeched as he started out: "Yoryis, close your ears to the shepherds' pipes! Yoryis, jump over a crosspath! Yoryis, say the Lord's Prayer if you see a black animal! It's a kalikanzari! It'll harm you! Yoryis!" He went on, heart beating at every crackle of a twig, running at the mountain's whispers. At times he was too far from home and had to remain overnight in a stranger's house. On his return he waited for an opportunity to kick Pericles.

When leaving the village with his father, though, he gave Pericles the traditional goodbye: *Yiassou!*—Life to you. From time to time, to earn a few drachmas, Yiannis traveled to the port of Nafpaktos to fill orders from villagers on the way. He, Yoryis, and the mule descended the zigzag path to the ancient Evinos River the villagers called "Snake," crossed over a rock bridge, and climbed to the villages clustered at intervals on the opposite mountain face. Often Yiannis made his own path through boulders and bush with Yoryis following and leading the mule. At the outskirts of each village Yiannis began calling, "A newspaper! A newspaper! Does anyone have a newspaper?" "—paper! —paper! —have a newspaper?" the echo bounded back from the mountains.

A villager or coffeehouse owner would sometimes rush out waving a months'-old newspaper and invite the judge to sit down to read it. Whenever the judge was given the paper to keep, he smiled, his eyes bright, and with his son and mule went on his way. They were often late in reaching Nafpaktos because someone invariably needed legal advice. If night caught them, they stopped in a travelers' hut where a small charcoal fire burned in the center of a dirt floor. Dank-smelling travelers lay in a circle, their feet toward the fire.

Often Papa–Christos called Yoryis to swing the smoking censer. When the priest's youngest son was sent from the village to apprentice as a carpenter, Yoryis took his place at the altar. Sunday after Sunday in the small, dim church, miserably cold in winter, the deep rumbling voice of his uncle chanting the Scriptures reverberated. On many Sundays the two of them were its only occupants.

Although Papa–Christos was as tall as his brothers, he was emaciated from his many fastings. His skin stretched tightly, thinly over his bony face and his full, gray beard caved in at his sunken cheeks. From under his dusty priest's hat his hair hung to his shoulders. Beneath the wide band that crossed over his faded, oil-stained robe of cheap satin the original rose color shone.

Each Sunday Yoryis stood expectantly at the right of the altar holding in one quivering hand the smoking censer by its long chains and in the other a cup of warm water. His priest-uncle intoned: "But one of the soldiers pierced His side and forthwith came there out blood and water." Papa—Christos added the water to the wine and crumbs of bread in the chalice in enactment of Christ's Passion on the cross. In the stillness, in the incense-heavy enclosure, the moment when the wine and bread would be changed to the Gifts neared. Slowly the priest lifted the chalice and looking upward, his voice tremulous, asked that the wine and bread become the Body and Blood of Christ. From his beseeching eyes tears flowed copiously into his beard. The priest and Yoryis knelt at that most holy of all moments in the liturgy, and there with them was Christ, not merely his spirit but himself, there.

After this thousandth upon thousandth reliving of the Passion, they hurried out, the priest's once-black robe faded and ringed with green. Against his scarecrow legs the skirt flapped, and he pressed a long yellow palm on his hollow stomach. When they neared Yoryis's stone house, Papa—Christos called out in a voice as deep and resonant on the mountainside as in the small church, "Bride! Put on the brik!"

And Yoryis's mother, who would be called "Bride" until she died and beyond that in reminiscences, sprinkled roasted barley and a few grains of coffee on water simmering in a long-handled brass pan set among burning twigs. She also cut a piece of corn bread and, because it was Sunday, dribbled a spoonful of olive oil on it. Papa—Christos sat at the rough-planked table, crossed himself, peered at the cup of coffee and corn bread and ate noisily. His own house was too poor even for barley coffee.

Papa—Christos was so holy that when he cut into a loaf of bread brought by a village woman to be consecrated and given out at the end of the liturgy, he would begin to itch violently if the bread were unclean. He would cut into another parishioner's loaf. If he still itched, he ordered his wife to take a bath and bake the bread. The *papadhia* put on clean petticoats and dress, always at hand for such a crisis, and to be sure she was spotless left off her only pair of garters.

Papa—Christos had that Zisimopoulos impatience. He saw what

had to be done and "like a streak of lightning" did it. Periodically, locusts would whir down the slopes and devour the crops. At the first sound of their loathsome crunching the priest dispatched a villager to the monastery in Kozitsas for the arm and hand bones of Saint Polycarpos.

The monastery had been established in 1456 while the Turks were sweeping through Greece after conquering the City. In the monastery was the icon of the Theotokos, the Virgin, a work said to be by the Evangelist Luke. The icon had been thown into the Pineus River by the invaders on their march of destruction.

The bones of Polycarpos, bishop of Smyrna, ordered martyred by Marcus Aurelius in A.D. 167, arrived in the monastery after a long journey from Asia Minor. The fingers were awesomely held, middle finger and thumb touching in the ancient manner of blessing.

Racing against the gluttony of the locusts, runners carried the box holding Polycarpos's bones to the village. Papa—Christos celebrated the liturgy. Then, chanting and holding high the saint's relics, he led a procession through the village with Yoryis swinging the incense burner and other boys and young men bearing the standards of the church. Immediately the locusts swarmed down to the river and drowned.

When August rainstorms threatened to wash away the small fields, Papa—Christos took his umbrella in one hand and the altar cross in the other to the chapel of Saint Paraskevi, one of ten *exokleissies*, out-churches, surrounding the village, chanted prayers to the holy ones, and the rains stopped. During droughts, he called for help again and rain fell.

In all the surrounding mountain villages Papa—Christos was revered. Forty days before Christmas he began fasting and conducting daily liturgies. He, as did his sisters, lived on water and one dried fig or small glass of liqueur a day and with each liturgy grew weaker. In his way he was even revered by his brilliant young relative Zisimos—Bellos whose constant cheating and practical joking drove the priest to pray for his soul to the Trinity, to the All—Holy, to the numerous saints and martyrs. "I don't know what it is,"

The narrow valley below Klepá under the old bridge spanning the ancient Evinos River, now called the Fidheris, the Snake. Center, the practical joker, a cousin of Yoryis, Zisimos Bellos; second from the right, George Papachristos, who would come to America and return to marry Yoryis's sister, Sophia.

Zisimos—Bellos told Papa—Christos whenever he was caught, "but evil is in me, I can't help it."

All of Papa—Christos and Yiannis's efforts to "turn Zisimos from the bad road he had taken" failed. An immigrant to Rumania had sent money to the priest to be divided among destitute families in the region. Papa—Christos instructed Zisimos to make a list of such people. It was some time before the horrified Papa—Christos and Yiannis learned that Zisimos had added a number of dead to the list and kept the money for himself. (He would try it again in his old age, after the Second World War, with American relief.) "It's the evil in me, Pater," he said. "I can't help it."

At two o'clock one morning the village was awakened by the ominous ringing of the church bell of Saint George. The people rushed out to find what calamity had befallen the village. Pulling the church bell was a white monster. Paralyzed, the villagers listened to the monotonous, apocalyptic knell. Zisimos had dusted a donkey with lime, tied him by the neck to the bell rope on which, a foot or so beyond the animal's reach, he had bound a sheaf of barley.

And could the villagers ever forget when Zisimos–Bellos fashioned a dummy with *foustanella* and an ancient Greek helmet—as Saint George was represented on icons—propping it in the bishop's throne, and hiding to await fast-weakened Papa–Christos's entrance into the dim church? With what glee he saw Papa-Christos run out of the church calling, "Come quickly! Saint George is sitting in the church! Quickly!"

Yoryis wondered why Zisimos–Bellos didn't play his tricks on only mean and spiteful villagers, but no one was exempt, not even his uncle Konstandinos whom everyone called O Kalos—The Good. Konstandinos often took Yoryis with him when he went to neighboring villages or to the large ones, Karpenisi and Platanos, to barter. Jabbing the rocky goat trail with a gnarled shepherd's crook, Konstandinos instructed Yoryis on the events that had taken place in the villages, ridges, cliffs, and ravines of the mountains. They had swallowed invaders, villagers, and bandits over the centuries.

In a ravine called the Bishop's Hand, a palm print was deeply etched into a sheer rock wall. It reminded generations of villagers that a bishop had once demanded forty groschen to perform a liturgy. He was refused and in rage strode off toward the next village, slipped, and fell into the ravine, his desperate gesture leaving his palm print forever on the rock face.

On Mount Oxa the nomad Vlachs summered their goats and sheep. They were rustic people who took to the mountains, it was said, when the City fell to the Turks. For centuries they had driven their flocks to the mountains in summer and to isolated valleys in winter. They carried only the rudiments to meet life's demands: a few pots, blankets, and their burial clothes. The dead were buried at the wayside, far from church and priest.

Konstandinos and Yoryis came upon a group of Vlach women on one of their journeys. Women went ahead to find a campsite and build shelters of branches for the night. The old women in faded black skirts, the young also in black, their skirts bordered with bands of colored triangular designs, all, young and old, with burnished, leathered faces, looked down as Yoryis and Konstandinos passed. The tinkling of goat bells grew louder as Yoryis and his uncle walked. Suddenly, on rounding a jut of mountain, they stopped before a throng of goats, Vlachs, and dogs. "Sit down," Konstandinos said. As the dogs rushed snarling toward them, Yoryis sat next to his uncle, his heart beating fast even though Konstandinos had told him more than once to expect such a confrontation. Konstandinos laid down his gnarled staff. At that, the dogs stopped in their tracks and became quiet as they had been trained. The *tselingas*, the master shepherd of the Vlachs, a slender, bearded man, the peaked hood of his long, black, goat hair cape on his head, smiled and hailed the travelers. In a thick dialect, he said they were coming down from The Forty. After an exchange of talk on weather and fodder, the Vlachs went on.

The Forty was a mountain pass above the village of Arahova. From the village a bridegroom with thirty-nine kin had gone to a distant village to fetch his bride. Of the family only the groom's mother remained behind: it was bad luck if she accompanied the party, and custom decreed she should be standing in the doorway of her house to welcome the bride. On the mountain trail the party was caught in a late snowstorm and all forty froze to death.

One of Konstandinos and Yoryis's journeys took them to Kefalovrisson—Head Waters, the mule carrying a winter's supply of squash, dried beans, and corn to Yiannis who was presiding over the district court there. Yoryis was nine years old and excited over seeing Kefalovrisson for the first time. A cousin, Konstandinos said, was a doctor and would lend them his horse and carriage to drive wherever they wished. Konstandinos sometimes sang as they trudged of Roumeliot heroes—Grivas and his horse Black, Athanasios Diakos roasted over a fire by the Turks, Karaïskakis, son of a *kleft* and a nun, and Markos Botsaris, the greatest of the *klefts* from Souli in the Agrapha mountains northward. Markos had at last been killed as the despot Ali Pasha vowed. Konstandinos sang of the Romaioi's, the Greeks', grief, funereal, his deep throb echoing through the mountains:

> And when the Romaioi heard the news,
> And when they heard the tidings,

67

They dressed themselves in clothes of black
They clad themselves in mourning
They're taking Markos to the church
They're taking Markos to the grave
Twenty bishops go before
And sixty priests behind.

Deep into the mountain passes and far from the nearest village, snowflakes began to float down. The two trudged more quickly over the trail. The snow came thicker, faster. Konstandinos lifted Yoryis on his powerful shoulders. (And how could it be that mountain men existing on beans, goat cheese, and greens, could be so long of leg, so wide of shoulder?) Yoryis, riding high in the cold, snowy air, was jostled from side to side and pitched forward several times when his uncle fell to his knees. Yet Konstandinos's strong grip securely clutched his ankles and he felt no fear.

One of the last journeys Yoryis and Konstandinos made was to the village of Dhomnista, three hours by donkey, two by foot, as distance was measured. Konstandinos's eyes had been failing, and he read the family's Bible and a few books with difficulty. Not having money for eyeglasses sold in Platanos, he and Yoryis set off to visit a *koumbaghianitis*—false doctor—in Dhomnista. Villagers touted his cures. Konstandinos and Yoryis left as soon as "God brightened." The *koumbaghianitis* threaded a large needle with a red ribbon, pinched the base of Konstandinos's neck, and pushed the needle through the flesh. He left the ribbon hanging on either side of the piercing. "Each morning," he intoned, like Papa–Christos reading from the Holy Book, "take hold of both ends of the ribbon and slide it back and forth."

On the way to and from Dhomnista, they had to pass through neighboring Arahova. The village was the stronghold of the powerful Sismani clan who had produced mayors and senators and were feared for their cunning.

The first Sismani to come to Arahova were Bulgarians who had fled the Turks a century or two earlier. Their name had been Sismanoff. In the early 1800s Ali Pasha ordered the Sismani to send one of their daughters to his harem in Yiannina. The Sismani tried to save her by making excuses. Ali Pasha then sent his army to Arahova to destroy them. Only an infant boy was saved by villagers who spirited him to Macedonia. When the boy was ten years old, villagers brought him back. He became the ruthless head of the new Sismani clan, known throughout the mountains for their crime toward a *kleft* family.

In Konstandinos's youth the mountains had been filled with *klefts* who had fought for the Revolution. When the Great Powers put the seventeen-year-old Othon on the throne of Greece, he brought with him six thousand Bavarian soldiers to protect him. The devastated country had to support them while *klefts* were starving. The *klefts* took to the mountains, to their *kleftolimeria* that had been their province all the years they had harassed and fought the Turks. There, they turned to brigandage, pouncing on travelers making their way through the mountains. The government put a price of one hundred fifty drachmas on the head of each *kleft*, the equivalent then of five hundred dollars. Demetrios Grivas had been sent to rid the mountains of them.

The Sismani held godfatherhood with *kleft* families, the holy bond deeper than blood relationship because it was sanctified by God when the *koumbaros*, the godfather, laved the infant's body with consecrated oil. The Sismani forgot the sacred vows at the government's announcement of the bounty and invited a *kleft* family to dinner. Some of the Sismani remained outside on a pretext, ready to thrust their gunbarrels through holes they had bored into the walls of the house. The leader of the *klefts* had a foreboding and looked at his men in warning. Suddenly the matriarch of the family, Koumbara Yoryina, stood up, shouted the sign "Salad!" and fled. Bullets zinged into the room. One *kleft* threw his cape out the window, drawing a fusilade of bullets, jumped out another window, and escaped to tell of the treachery.

Konstandinos sang the old song of Sismani dishonor:

> *You, Koumbara Yoryina,*
> *Koumbara, friend!*
> *The oil we put on your children,*
> *May it ignite and burn them!*

69

The Sismani continued to rule the mountains around Arahova. The timber was theirs. Yoryis was thrilled with the potential of danger whenever he and his uncle Konstandinos walked through the Sismani stronghold. The Sismani also had beds to sleep on.

But Konstandinos's eyes did not improve. The ribbon rotted away; the flesh swelled and stank where it had been punctured. The village midwife made poultices of boiled onions and mountain herbs to draw out the putrefaction.

6

In 1894 Yiannis was sent to Karea on the island of Lefkas in the Ionian Sea; the following year he was posted in the capital, Lefkada. With elections almost two years away, Yiannis wrote his family to come to the island. No snow fell on Lefkada in winter, only rain. Yoryis's fingers were never stiff and blue while sitting in the schoolhouse. In summer, lemon-scented breezes swept through their spacious white-stuccoed house, and pink oleander reached to the roof. Yoryis's father rented an Italian bicycle for him and he pedaled it around the island. On the topmost hill he sat and gazed at the Ionian Sea where the old general Grivas had sailed with a flag given him by the British government for safe passage flying from the mast. He looked on the shore where men put fifty-gallon wine and oil barrels at the water's edge to be rocked by the tide and aged. On the other side of the hill Yoryis watched a steam shovel widening a lake. A young woman helped his mother with caring for his sisters, Marigho, Vasiliki, and sickly Olga.

Then they were back in Klepá, Yoryis with a brown puppy he named Kanela, Cinnamon. The elections had been lost. Konstandinos came down the mountainside to meet them, hurrying, pushing his crook into the dirt to steady himself. He looked at Yoryis, a lingering palm on his head, eyes filled with tears. Yoryis was surprised, then ashamed: in the greenness of Lefkas, where on its crown he sat and looked all around at the blue Ionian, he had not thought about his uncle Konstandinos once.

71

The villagers gathered happily in the square of Lower Klepá to welcome Yiannis. They listened intently to his account of the politics of the country, feuds in Parliament, crimes of passion, earthquakes and floods, and the quantity and price of the currant, the small seedless raisin that the entire economy of the country depended upon: it was the nation's principal industry and main export.

Yiannis was often escorted over the winding dirt road, across the Great Torrent, dry in summer, knee deep in mud after spring floods when snow melted high up, and to the *platea*, the square of Upper Klepá that was larger than that of Lower Klepá. There he would repeat country and world happenings to the gathered villagers. The men did not go to the fields when Yiannis arrived; their wives and daughters trudged off while they sat, listened, and questioned.

In the evenings men came to ask the judge's advice. Sitting at the room's one window, Yiannis cleaned his metal-rimmed eyeglasses and opened his law books, bound in brown cardboard in imitation of leather: *Romaïkon Dhikaion*—Romaioi, the old word for Greeks, Justice—translated into Greek from the German. The villagers sometimes brought an offering, often a faggot of bracken for kindling; at rare times a small bottle of olive oil to be hoarded for the icon's vigil light and at even rarer times a small sack of wheat.

At the approach of winter the Klepaiotes went down to the towns of Arginion and Aegion and built thatched huts to survive until spring. A few families stayed in the village, snowbound, the icy winds invading rock and mud mortar and keeping the villagers huddled about hearths that voraciously ate the kindling for which women had scoured the mountainside during the summer months.

On nights when the wind tricked them into thinking it had abated somewhat, they walked single file through paths dug in snow drifts. Blankets over their heads, the wind howling at their ears, they made their way to the judge's house. They arrived gasping and frostbitten to sit on the floor, cluster about the hearth where holy oak burned and spit, and, wrapped in their blankets, hear the judge's priest and Karaghiozis's stories. The priest was always illiterate—even Papa–Christos laughed—and Karaghiozis, the cunning hunchback, always got the better of Turks and officious Greeks. Yiannis also told them new stories to add to their communal lore. Yoryis, his hot back to the fire, arms crossed and cold hands in his armpits, listened, his gaze not leaving his father's eyes.

Zaferia brought out treats wrapped in a small white bundle to add to the honeyed walnuts, raisins, and wine of the house: chestnuts given the judge by clients in the village of Kastania; dried apricots from the orchard of his second cousin, the doctor in Kefalovrisson; preserved orange peel from a villager he had helped on Corfu.

After hearing the new stories, the villagers asked for the old ones. "Tell about the gypsy and the mare, Tanga," someone asked, and in the slow, yet terse manner of mountaineers, he began.

> A gypsy was getting ready to see a villager about buying a mare. His young son jumped up. "And I'm going to ride her colt when she has one." "No, you can't," his father said. "It's too young and you'll break its back."
>
> "I will!"
>
> "You won't!"
>
> They argued. In a fury the gypsy picked up a club and struck the boy. No colt, no boy.

"Tell the priest story about the sow!" someone else asked.

Yiannis, true storyteller that he was, began the account of the priest's sow that had dug up an ancient pot filled with gold pieces, looking at his listeners with mock seriousness. After the sow died, the priest made preparations for her funeral while scandalized villagers hurried to the capital of the province to tell the bishop. The priest was eulogizing the sow when he saw the bishop stomping through the doorway of the church. The priest cut short the liturgy for the dead and intoned—here Yiannis in an exaggeratedly deep voice boomed out:

> "Ah yes, this sow was not an ordinary sow. No! She was educated. Before she died she wrote her will. She left one hundred drachmas to the church, one hundred to me, the priest, and she didn't forget our good bishop. To him she left two hundred drachmas." "Ahh, the blessed sow!" the bishop cried out.

73

As heartily and as appreciatively as the first time they had heard the story, the villagers laughed. "Tell about the Vlach and Prophet Elias chapel!"

Yiannis began in an easy, conversational tone of voice. Women had complained to a village priest that someone was eating the food they had prepared and left for travelers in the Prophet Elias chapel in the wilds and not leaving money for the church. The priest hid behind the altar and saw a shepherd enter and eat the *sfongato*, the cheese and eggs. As the man began to leave, the priest rumbled out, "You've been eating without paying. Come back!" Thinking it was God's voice, the villager hastily put a coin on the tray.

"Not enough!"

The shepherd put down another coin.

"Not enough!"

The shepherd emptied his pockets. At the door he turned. "By God, your eggs are expensive!"

With the night wind increasing in shrillness, the gathering sensed the need to return to their houses. Someone began the song of pistol-adorned Grivas and his horse Black who together would "burn" their enemies. Other songs followed of Grivas who would not bow down to the Turkish pasha, of Grivas fomenting insurrections against the Bavarian Othon, of Grivas and his men surrounding the camp of the great Peloponnesian general Kolokotronis and keeping him prisoner until he returned to his widowed daughter-in-law, then the wife of Grivas, her dowry.

The villagers could never hear enough of Theodhorakis Grivas's *leventia*, his manliness; his brashness toward the country's imported royalty gave the villagers continuing pleasure. In King Othon's time, before Grivas led a ragged army of *klefts* against him, he was invited to bring his young wife to the palace. "What's this, Grivas," Queen Amalia said, "an old man with a wife young enough to be your daughter?"

"It's like this, Lady," Grivas answered, "toothless gums need tender chicken."

Distant relatives from deep in the northern mountains were often snowbound in the gray rock house with the family. A first cousin of the judge had come as winter was setting in. Wheezing

74

from the piles of dried corn that Yoryis's mother and sisters were husking for winter storage, the judge answered the night pounding on the door. Nearly frozen from making his way through the mountains, the cousin had come for sanctuary after killing a man in a vendetta. He had been holding his six-month-old son in his arms, he said, when he heard a noise in the snow-filled night. He opened the door and stepped outside. A shadow darted. Throwing the baby onto a snowbank, he fired and killed a traditional enemy of the family.

The cousin lived with them until spring and then went back to face trial. By mountain code it was no shame to kill for family honor. Provincial prisons were filled with men serving terms for crimes of passion, along with the despised goat and sheep thieves. The judge prepared his cousin's case, and in the spring Yiannis, Yoryis, and the mule set off for the provincial capital Lamia. As they neared the outskirts of Klepá, they came upon Papa—Christos. They returned to their house and left the next day: it was a bad omen to meet a priest at the outset of a journey—brother though he be.

The cousin was convicted. His wife, holding the infant Nikos in her arms, and his daughters wailed and beseeched the judge that they were being left without father and husband to champion them, but the judge reminded them that the convicted man came from the Zisimopoulos clan and they were not alone in the world but had many uncles and cousins to stand up for them against sinners who would take advantage of women without men. Yoryis would not see the infant Nikos again until they were man and youth in 1911 in Pocatello, Idaho.

Others could listen to the judge's stories, sing songs about her Grivas clan; her husband could make briefs for a cousin, but Zaferia was consumed with keeping her children alive on the face of Xerovouni. Except for her two family icons, almost all her dowry possessions were gone; she had given her best dress of pink and brown silk to the monastery in Kozitsas as a *tama*, a pledge, in return for her daughter Marigho's cure of lassitude. She would ransom the dress years later for Marigho to wear.

If a goat turned listless, if twigs dwindled dangerously low, when the sacks of corn and beans became slack, Zaferia kneeled before her icons to pray long and insistently. And always there was the anxiety of how to educate her sons to rise above tilling the soil and to provide dowries for her daughters. Whenever elections neared she wrote to kinsmen and reminded them if their party won to remember her husband.

Pericles grew spindly and was always sick; the midwife's cures for Olga seldom worked, nor did the *tamas*, the vows Zaferia made before the icon of the All–Holy and the candles she lighted to Her and to the patron saint of the Church of Saint George help. The saint could sometimes be heard at night riding his white horse over the mountains and through the valleys. On these nights Zaferia and Konstandinos read the Scriptures and prayed.

Olga continued screaming and fainting. Zaferia dreamed one stormy night that Saint George stopped at the door of the house, dismounted, and stood before her. "Enough," he said, "do no more. The child cannot live." Within a few days Olga died.

Dressed in black, a heavy mourning veil over her face, Zaferia sat at the side of the open wooden casket made by Konstandinos and keened the *mirologhia*, the dirges for the dead.

> *What have I done to you, my God,*
> *To take my blossom from me,*
> *To send Charos on his black horse,*
> *To carry my child, my eyes, away?*
>
> *Aieeee, my motherless child,*
> *Alone in Hades, wandering*
> *In the gray mold of the underworld.*

Hour after hour the dirges went on, first his mother keened, then the women of the Zisimopoulos clan, all in black, wailed the laments for the dead little girl, unjustly taken, frightened, bereft of family in the nether world. They called out in strident, undulating singsong to Christ, the All–Holy, God, and Saint George for taking her, a flower in the gray land of life. They asked, demanded, that the mountains, the springs, the flowers weep for her.

The small dead face turned blue, and a smell of moist decay came from the casket. Papa–Christos closed the casket and Konstandinos lifted it on his shoulder. With the priest intoning the hymn for the dead and Yoryis swinging the smoking censer, Olga was taken to the Church of Saint George and then to the graveyard on the edge of the village.

Forty days later Yoryis was sent to Platanos to buy a small sack of wheat. "If you are thirsty," his mother warned, "and have to drink from a spring, say the Our Father quickly three times. Don't tarry if you hear a shepherd's flute. Nereids are there waiting to trick you." Yoryis hurried, saying the Our Father over and over, his hand on a small kitchen knife he had taken when no one was looking. He returned exhausted and kicked Pericles who was watching him from a vantage point on a rock. Pericles murmured and Yoryis kicked him again.

Zaferia boiled the wheat until it became plump, dried it, mixed it with honey, raisins, parsley for the greenness of afterlife, almonds, and the seeds of a pomegranate sent by his father's cousin, the doctor in Kefalovrisson. Wheat, almonds, pomegranate seeds were all symbols of immortality.

The family ate the memorial wheat in great solemnity. Olga, like Christ, had finished her forty-day wanderings and was ready to face God. Yoryis savored the wheat, chewed it slowly. As it was a cold autumn day, the family did not fear the wheat's being spoiled and their dying from it as people sometimes did when the sun burned.

"Now she belongs to God," Papa—Christos said and crossed himself.

Only Yoryis grew strong and was seldom sick, even for a day. Marigho became ill during the Greek—Turkish war of 1897 while Yiannis was in Thessaly; the government had sent him there to oversee supplies for the army. Marigho often went limp for minutes at a time, and Yoryis was sent running for Papa—Christos who came with his Scriptures and consecrated water. Day and night Yoryis crossed the Great Torrent to Upper Klepá and returned with the midwife-witch to dispel the evil eye. More and more often the midwife's arthritic bones kept her housebound, and Yoryis brought Marigho's scarf to be used in her incantations.

While he waited in one of the two rooms of the dirt-floored hut one night, the midwife safely out of sight invoking the Trinity in her magic, he approached a *dhikanon*, a short rifle that he had coveted from the first time he had seen it. The gun was set on a ledge above the hearth. Yoryis quietly took it down and turned it slowly, gazing at its carvings and notches. A thundering blast and he screamed; blood gushed and his index finger, a red-stained thing, lay on the dirt floor. The witch rushed in, stanched the blood, and wrapped his hand. He ran home clutching his wound in terror.

Konstandinos walked to Kozitsas and returned with a doctor who burned the stump with a foul liquid and sewed it. "This has cost a month or more of your father's salary," his mother said after the doctor jogged off on a mule.

Anxious, Zaferia scrubbed the wooden floors until they splintered and whitewashed the walls of the house often, not only for Easter. Every article of clothing was clean and folded neatly on shelves Konstandinos built. When the villagers wanted to attest to the cleanliness of something, they called it "as spotless as Zaferia."

7

The party heirs of Trikoupis won the next election and Yiannis was again sent to Mitikas. His family went with him to live in a white-stuccoed house. Yoryis and Pericles had two more years of school there. Pericles followed Yoryis to the wharves where they looked down at ancient buildings covered by water, watched caiques sailing in the Ionian Sea, their white sails billowing, sat on the seashore and looked across to the island of Lefkas, and once walked three miles to Kandyla where a daughter of Demetrakis Grivas, who had married a naval officer, lived. They walked quickly by her two-storied, white-stuccoed house, Yoryis glancing at it from the corners of his eyes.

Konstandinos had come with them to Mitikas. Yoryis helped him plant corn, beans, squash, tomatoes, cucumbers, and onions. Before it became dark, Konstandinos sent him home to memorize his lessons. Yoryis took the long way through the village square. Men sat there, gossiping about dowries and talking about America. One day a crowd had gathered around a man who had just returned from the United States after six years' absence. Sitting under a plane tree, he sputtered, his face purple, "And in this house where I worked for these rich people who gave big dinners, the women *smoked*! They crossed their knees like men!"

In Mitikas, Yoryis finished the two years of intermediate school; but in the next elections when Yiannis lost his position, he appealed to Demetrakis Grivas's daughter in Kandyla for help in educating his sons. She invited Yoryis and Pericles to live in her house and attend school with her sons. Their clothing tied in a piece of woven black goat hair, Yoryis and Pericles walked to Kandyla. The road was muddy and near the navy captain's house, they stopped and scraped their shoes with twigs.

Even though Demetrakis's daughter was as old as Zaferia and walked with a slow, heavy tread, she seemed far younger to Yoryis. Her serene eyes looked kindly on him and Pericles. Her life was one of inspection: while several young village women worked inside the house and boys took orders from an old gardener outside, their aunt, for so they were told to call her, examined and counted the freshly ironed clothing brought by the washwoman; inspected the cupboards for needed supplies; wrote messages and called one of the boys to deliver them; looked over the vegetables the old gardener brought to her in a cart, selected what she wanted, and divided the rest among the servants. In the evening she embroidered. Her husband was away on duty.

Three times a day Yoryis and Pericles sat at the dining room table, set on a marble floor, with their aunt and her two sons, one and two years younger than Yoryis. The sons wore navy blazers with brass buttons and laughed and talked, competing for their visitors' attention while their mother looked on indulgently. They began each story with the words, "I'll tell you a story—" as if they were speaking to young children. Most of their talk was about their grandfather Demetrios and great-grandfather Theodhorakis; a favorite story was about the campaign against the Turks in northern Greece. They never asked, "Have you heard the story?" Again and again Yoryis and Pericles listened to an anecdote they had heard many times before.

Demetrakis and his father had quarreled about strategy. The general insisted that they occupy houses in the village and ambush the Turks when they entered; Demetrios wanted the men hidden behind boulders and bracken above the village. Theodhorakis brushed his son aside and ordered the men to follow him. Demetrios called out, "Who thinks as I, follow me!" Whereupon all the young, white-kilted *pallikaria* trooped after him. Fuming, cursing his son, Theodhoros descended to the village with the older men. "You'll have to ask me for help," Demetrakis called after him.

The Turks rode in, surrounded the houses, set them on fire, and rained bullets on them. "Demetrakis, help!" Theodhorakis shouted and Demetrios and his men rushed down and routed the Turks.

For two weeks Yoryis and Pericles sat at the well-laden table in their cheap, striped Piraeus pants and scuffed shoes. On Wednesdays they ate chicken, on Sundays lamb. The night of their second Sunday in Kandyla Yoryis opened the bedroom window, crawled out, and he and Pericles walked back to Mitikas.

At the moment Yoryis crawled out the window, he renounced forever any life except that of a laborer. "How will we get dowries for your sisters?" his mother demanded. His father paced the floor not knowing what to do with him. A few weeks later Yiannis sent him north to a monastery where he knew a monk and asked him to teach Yoryis to become a chanter.

The hollow-cheeked monk, his beard a skimp of dandelion fluff, knew from the first day that no incipient chanter stood before him. "Aaaaaaaaaaaa," he keened, his breath, foul from fasting and rotted teeth, wafting over his pupil. "Aaaaaaaaaa," Yoryis sang, his eyes on a patch of sky framed by a small, high window.

Each time the monks censed the smoke-smudged altar screen below—the Turks had left the monastery burning two hundred years previously—the fumes seeped into the cell and swelled Yoryis's nose shut. Then his "Aaaaaaaaaaaa" came out "Ghaaaaaaaaaaz." After a week, Yoryis left behind the monastery with its smell of old sweat, incense, and monks, some of whom could not read but had learned the liturgies by rote, and all of them, he knew, with lice and spiders nesting in their beards.

In despair his father sent Yoryis to northern Xeromero—Dry Place—where he was apprenticed to a shoemaker. There Yoryis slept in a hayloft, was awakened at four in the morning, and worked until ten at night learning to make pomponed *tsarouhia* for men and European-style slippers for men, women, and children. After two-years' apprenticeship, he looked for a shoemaker to take him in and found none. With corn bread that dried and cheese that went stale as he walked from village to village, he looked for any kind of work. At sheep folds, charcoal ovens, shops he stopped, hoping Fate would be propitious. He became desperate. How would he fulfill the ancient expectations of dowries for sisters? How would he help lift the burden from his mother and father?

Again and again he set out with a bundle of corn bread and cheese. He was careful. Whenever he approached two bisecting roads, he made the sign of the cross and said the Lord's Prayer to repel the bad spirits that inhabited such places. He clutched his baptismal cross when he quickly kneeled to drink from streams, alert that at any moment a beautiful Nereid would appear and entice him into madness. Hadn't one of his cousins been lured away from his sheep and been found in a neighboring village dancing like mad at a saint's day festival? At roadside shrines he crossed himself. On mountainsides he stopped at white stone chapels dedicated to Prophet Elias and said a prayer at crude icon screens.

Everywhere he saw ancient ruined acropolises and battlements of the Frank, Venetian, Slav, and Turkish conquerors: sturdy walls and citadels, the history of which he knew nothing. On the way he stayed with distant kinsmen of his father who shamed him with vivacious welcomes because he was descended from the renowned Grivas family and was the son of a jurist. In Aegion where ten people lived in a hut, he was given a bench to sleep on while the others lay on the dirt floor.

He went south as far as Lord Byron's Messolonghi. He went north as far as Vonitsa—this time with Pericles who, nearing nineteen, had to register for the army but as the oldest son of the family was exempt from service. As they walked over a plateau of thyme, reeds, and bracken, a distant keening came to them. On reaching a rise in the land, they looked down upon black-dressed women and children hoeing the rocky earth and keening for their men, all killed in a vendetta.

He could go no farther; he had neither money nor kinsmen in the north, in Epirus. He would have liked to see Arta where, according to a legendary song, the young wife of the master builder was encased in the pillars of a bridge under construction to keep it from falling each night. The great General Makriyiannis was born in Arta. Yoryis did not know then that the general's memoirs would be found, published, and have little good to say about Theodhoros Grivas and his clan. Northwest of Arta was Yiannina where Ali Pasha had imprisoned and poisoned Grivas's father and forced Theodhoros into the *armatoli*, the peacekeeping force of Greeks under Turkish command. When the news came that Bishop Germanos had raised the Greek flag of revolt on March 25, 1821, Grivas and the other young *armatoles* jumped on their horses and thundered south to join the uprising.

Farther north were the Albanians. The upper half of their country had been so thoroughly vanquished by the Turks that in self-interest many converted to Islam and the rest were forced by sword and fire. With time they became traditional enemies of the Greeks where once "there was no distinction made between Albanians and Greeks." Yoryis did not know that a drop or more of Albanian blood ran in him. The Grivas clan had first been heard of in the 1400s; Albanian chieftains, they had entered Greece in pursuit of the Turks and had remained in the magnificent Epirus mountains to marry and live with the Souliots.

As no other Greeks had been able to do, the Souliots harassed Ali Pasha, refused to "bow before him," and met the fate the despot had vowed: their complete extermination. There in the rugged, massive mountains the women of Souli saw below the massacre of their men and rather than be taken to harems and their children sold as slaves, they joined hands and danced a *kleftic* song. As the leader finished a round, she jumped over a cliff with her children. The dance continued until all had fallen into the ravine. The Souli had been destroyed; only several escaped to make their way to the Ionian islands. One or two of the Grivas clan continued to survive down through the years to Theodhoros Grivas and his four feuding brothers.

Yoryis trudged between boulders and scrub oak to villages and towns, portioning out his bread and cheese to last. He noted landmarks on the way: ravines, an unusual twisted fir tree, a boulder resembling an animal, and rivers and streams below, winding, fanning, disappearing; he was careful not to become lost and starve to death. And he was always hungry for something sweet, for something vinegary. Always hungry.

8

Even in old age when her memory was nearly obliterated, Emilia remembered the feast of feasts marking the end of Ramadan fasting in the Turkish villages dotting the Macedonian plain of her childhood. In the early morning she had listened to the distant, joyous din floating with the breeze to her Greek village. In their two-story rock house, her grandmother finished braiding her gray hair with knobby fingers, then tied a worn black silk kerchief over her head. "Are you ready, Emilia?" she asked the nine-year-old girl who had been waiting by the door, watching her grandmother.

"Yes, Yiayia."

They walked to the landing. Suddenly Emilia clattered down the wooden stairs. "Careful," her grandmother said in a loud whisper and Emilia stopped and drew in her breath.

"Say goodbye to your father."

Emilia entered the *sala*, the room once reserved for visitors but now a bedroom for her young father. Propped against pillows behind and on each side of him, a reddish stubble on his cheeks and chin, he lay crookedly. Emilia walked on her toes to him, lifted his freckled hand to her lips and kissed it.

"So you're going to the Turks' great feast?"

"Yes, Father."

"Go well," he said and crossed himself three times.

Outside, Emilia's mother and twelve-year-old Anna were pull-

ing up the last of the flower garden. On a piece of old newspaper
was a pile of broad beans to be planted. "To think," the grandmother said, "our flowers once filled the church on feast days and we
cut them for every wedding and baptism and funeral in the village.
But Fate, Fate." She let out her breath noisily and added, "Kismet,
Kismet." She often punctuated her Greek with the Turkish
equivalent.

Emilia's mother stood up and crossed herself with dirt-smudged
hands. "Go well," she said and stooped to her work. Anna smiled
and crossed herself.

In one brown-splotched hand the grandmother carried a small
white bundle holding a bottle of water, two thick slices of brown
bread, and on top of these a bowl of sugar-dusted butter cookies.
Her other hand was free and Emilia moved away from it, but her
grandmother said, "Give me your hand." She relinquished it when
they passed the yellow stucco church to make the sign of the cross,
then snatched it again.

The grandmother nodded to three old men in black kilts and
brown fezes who were sitting outside the coffeehouse. "Give the
Turkesses our regards," one of them called, and all three laughed at
this sally of a Greek, or any man for that matter, sending greetings
to the veiled women.

When they were well on the outskirts of the village, Symbotnik
its Turkish name, the grandmother let go of Emilia's small, sweaty
hand. Emilia skipped down the dirt road, twirled, and chased a
white butterfly with a black spot on each wing. Her grandmother
smiled.

The plain lay ahead, a faint green with sweeps of red, yellow,
blue, and white spring flowers brushed over it to the borders of the
Turkish villages. In each far-off cluster of brown and beige squares,
a domed, mud-colored bathhouse squatted and a slender minaret
rose. Beyond the villages on a distant, fir-covered mountain, a
white chapel of Prophet Elias glinted.

The road was wagon rutted. To the right, lumps of golden gorse
and broom hid the gently flowing river in places. The plain looked
deceptively flat, but it descended into little hollows and over small

hillocks; and the sweeps of solid colors became scattered flowering clumps on the earth. Faint acrid and flower scents were in the air, and white butterflies hovered in the clear coolness. While Emilia chased butterflies, her grandmother hummed and sang French ditties. She stopped abruptly when far off a small gray cone appeared on the plain.

A hundred yards or so off the side of the road, the pyramid of stones was near the spot where the red-haired brother of Emilia's father had been shot by a Turk as he ran onto a Moslem's land after a runaway cow. Under moonlight Emilia's godfather and father, walking on the outer sides of his feet and wincing with each step, had erected the cairn just short of the Turk's boundary.

Emilia took her grandmother's hand as they walked among small plants and flowers to the cairn. They made the sign of the cross three times and then, although they were not hungry, sat down and ate the two pieces of brown bread and drank from the bottle. They stood up, crossed themselves, brushed the dirt off their skirts, and walked back to the road. After a considerable distance in silence, the grandmother said in a low voice, as if the plain were peopled with Turks, "Barbarian Turks! When, when, dear little God, will you give us back our lands?" Their feet scuffed over the hardened ruts. After another long silence, she said angrily, "It's the men, the men who commit these crimes!"

The sun grew hot and the grandmother walked more slowly. Several times she and Emilia stopped to rest under a clump of broom that gave little protection from the heat. Emilia looked sullenly at the village, still too far off, from which waftings of drum and pipe music came. Her grandmother tried to wipe the perspiration from Emilia's forehead, but she leaned away from the brown-splotched hand. Her grandmother sighed and slowly got to her feet.

The music grew louder, the village closer. In a little hollow at the outskirts Turkish women were congregated. Eyes rimmed with black, fingernails painted red, they crowded close together with their children, eating, laughing, and shrilling to warn men of their presence and that they might be unveiled. Three young women caught sight of Emilia and her grandmother and ran to meet them, adjusting their veils over their faces. Their orange, pink, and golden holiday dresses over silk trousers were like clouds of sunset to Emilia.

One of the young women took Emilia's hand, the other two linked arms through the grandmother's and with gay little cries brought their visitors to the hollow. Calling out greetings in Turkish, the women stood up. They and the grandmother touched their fingers to the ground, to their knees, their heart, their lips. Emilia looked at her grandmother with fear that she would fall when she bent over. Too late she saw the flash in her grandmother's eyes, but everyone had risen and she was afraid she would be laughed at if she salaamed tardily. "Come here, little hanoum," one of the old women, in black like her grandmother, beckoned and pointed to the plates of meats and sweet delicacies on an embroidered tablecloth spread over the ground. "Eat! Eat!" Little girls clustered and knelt about Emilia, picked up one plate after another, and offered her sweets.

"Tsourekia, Emilia!" her grandmother said, smiling encouragingly, pursing her lips at the same time to hide the gaps at the side of her gums where her teeth had been pulled out. "Your favorite." Emilia blushed as the black-rimmed eyes looked at her.

"Take a tsoureki, little hanoum." The matriarch, sitting cross-legged, nodded vigorously and exclaimed over Emilia's little fingers that turned in like her grandmother's.

From the village square the sprightly, lilting music of pipes became louder. The little girls took Emilia to a knoll where they chased each other and stopped a moment to watch through a narrow opening between walls men twirling in dance. The girls ran after each other until they were panting. They devised a game: each girl would choose a color and pick flowers of that hue while they counted to one hundred. Emilia could not count that high in Turkish, but she hurried to gather bluebells while voices came from various places on the plain: "Bir, iki, utch, dort, besh, atli, yedi—" A short distance from the hollow, flowers grew at the base of a gray boulder. Emilia ran toward it and stopped. A man was peering at the women from behind the boulder. She screamed.

The voices in the hollow were silenced, skirts rustled, feet pattered. Dropping the blue flowers, Emilia ran, glimpsing the man bolting from behind the rock and streaking toward the village. She sat down, close to her grandmother. The women were hushed, frantically bringing their veils over their noses, huddling, drawing their children to them. After a time of listening, their startled eyes moving from side to side, the women slowly began speaking again but in muted tones, the gaiety gone. They talked of what Fate, Kismet, had done to their lives.

"Kismet, Kismet," the women sighed, sorrowful noddings accompanying their doleful litany as Emilia and the little girls began again chasing each other—but closer to the hollow. When they tired, they sat by the women and ate candy, which Emilia never had at home, and honey-nut sweets. Her grandmother rocked back and forth as she talked about a war that had left her a widow, her sons dead, and no one to care for her property; about having to come to live with her daughter who lost her two older sons to the epidemic; and about her son-in-law with a broken back, unable to tend his land and small *pandopoleion*, where he had once sold a little of everything.

Some of the women had also lost sons in the smallpox epidemic that was still talked about with awe. In the Greek village not one girl had died, only boys.

On the way home the grandmother carried a bowl filled with the Turkish women's pastries and tied about with a dish towel. Emilia held a large, braided sweet bread she was saving to share with her sisters and brother. They stopped for a moment on the road, looked in the direction of the cairn, and crossed themselves. The grandmother's lips moved in silent prayer. "If the Turks would only give back our land," she said aloud. "There is no reason for men to die on their own land."

A yellow and orange sunset tinted the plain as they walked. Emilia wanted to catch little insects that whirred from plant to plant, but she glanced at her grandmother and walked quietly at her side. After a while her grandmother looked down at her and began singing in a clear, high voice.

Three days before Easter Emilia's godfather came from Thessaloniki with a pouch of tobacco, a sack of white flour, a bottle of ouzo, a box of loukoum, and a pair of shiny black shoes for Emilia. A row of buttons went up the sides of the shoes; the family exclaimed over the new city fashion of tops barely covering the ankle.

The godfather's Easter visit was the talk of the house for weeks before he arrived in a high, narrow wagon like those of gypsies but painted a plain sky blue without the vivid birds, flowers, and trailing vines of the *tsighani*. Emilia's mother whitewashed the house and the dirt path through the garden; the grandmother mended, washed, and ironed curtains; the children were constantly at chores. Anna took Emilia and Faní to the riverside where she cut winterdead willows that the godfather, Christos, would use to barbecue the Easter lamb. Anna brought her sisters along to prevent gossip for going about by herself; their grandmother stood on the outskirts of the village where everyone could see her, head up, peering at her granddaughters.

Afterwards at home Anna supervised her sisters in picking up twigs and brown, matted fig leaves that had lain on the ground all winter. As she swept the hard-packed dirt yard, Anna said in imitation of their mother, "We want your godfather to see that we are prepared for Easter. We don't want him to think we are gypsies."

Immediately on his arrival, Emilia's godfather made preparations to repair the roof, first crossing himself and asking forgiveness for having to work on a most solemn day of the year, but "Our God understands. He's not Allah." For the past three years Christos had haphazardly repaired the roof. Not having the twenty drachmas the village carpenter asked, Emilia's father had climbed a ladder on the sides of his feet, the sores on the soles made worse by the drip of kerosense prescribed by the midwife. As he reached the top rung and tried to climb onto the roof, his hands slid from the broken tiles and he fell backwards into the garden.

"Emilia!" her grandmother had screamed, "run to the coffeehouse!" The *kafetzis* and the schoolteacher ran back and carried her moaning father onto the floor of the *sala*. He was well over six feet tall and broad in the shoulders. The men looked at each other, at the narrow stairs leading to the second floor, and then brought down the carved wooden bed and set it up in the *sala*.

As Christos climbed the flimsy ladder, everyone congregated in the yard: the grandmother leading two-year-old Yiannis by the hand, the mother, and the three girls. While Christos daubed a mortar of mud and straw and placed the broken tiles over it, the grandmother continually made the sign of the cross, her wrinkled lips moving in prayer. When he climbed down, smiling broadly at the completion of his yearly patchwork, the children clapped, forgetting for a moment that it was Great Thursday and Christ was condemned to be crucified.

Several times during Great Saturday Emilia went upstairs and looked at her new shoes and Easter dress. Her grandmother and Anna had remade the brown wool dress from one that had been in the dowry of Emilia's mother. The dress had faded, but the underside was still a deep brown color. Anna had pulled out all the stitches and ironed the pieces flat. On them the grandmother had placed a pattern cut from old newspapers, and under her direction Anna sewed a pleated skirt with small, even stitches. From the enormous bow at the back of her mother's dress, the grandmother fashioned a short jacket and lined it with gray satin from a shirt she had brought with her to the village years ago.

Emilia passed her palm across the fine wool and rubbed her fingers back and forth over the satin lining. Her face burned at her secret enjoyment while Christ still lay in the tomb. She rushed out and stopped before the icon of the All–Holy and Christ on the wall at the landing. On the shelf under the icon the vigil light was not burning because Christ lay dead. It would not burn again until the Resurrection at midnight when her mother would attempt to bring the candle flame proclaiming Christ's immortality from church. Emilia hastily made the sign of the cross and asked forgiveness.

Outside, the twigs and charcoal had burned to gray ash and red coals, and over the searing heat Christos turned the spitted paschal lamb he had bought from a nomad Sarakatsan. The window of the *sala* was open, and Christos carried on a conversation with his bed-ridden friend. The scents of incense from the nearby church, roasting meat, and a fresh coolness from the river were in the air.

Inside the house Emilia's mother was preparing the Easter *may-eritsa*, the lemony-egg soup of chopped kidneys, liver, and intestines that would end their fast after the midnight Resurrection liturgy. The grandmother decorated the Easter bread with rolled strips of dough forming a cross, red-dyed eggs, and a sprinkle of sesame seeds.

The expectant silence presaging the great happening of the Resurrection was in the house. When the lamb was glistening and brown, it was wrapped in dish towels and set on an old table in the cool shed attached to the house. With everything ready for the breaking of the forty-day fast at midnight, her mother said, "Emilia, come into the sala."

Faní and Yiannis followed their grandmother and mother, but Anna held them back. In the *sala* Emilia's father and godfather were talking in low tones. They stopped abruptly when Emilia entered.

"Come here, Milia," her father said. He called each daughter after a tree in the garden: Emilia—Milia, after the apple; Anna—Kástanna, after the chestnut; and Faní—Dhafni, after the laurel.

Her father, shaved and his hair unevenly cut by her godfather, smiled. "Don't look afraid. You haven't done anything wrong." With her mother and grandmother on either side of her, Emilia waited. "Your godfather knows of a good family in Thessaloniki who are looking for a girl to help in the house. Would you like to go?"

"Yes! Yes!" Emilia turned to her mother and grandmother for their permission. Her grandmother's eyes were blurred with tears; her mother's eyes were dry but her face was stony. Perplexed, Emilia looked from one to the other, then both gave a nod. She hurried out of the room to tell Anna and Faní.

The next day, while the village resounded with the singing and dancing on the square, Emilia's grandmother took her by the hand and they walked to the church of Saint Demetrios. Behind came her mother and sisters, Anna holding Yiannis. Several neighbors joined the procession.

The church doors were open, incense exuding through them. The grandmother gave Emilia a shove toward the two icons, bordered for Easter with spring flowers, one the All–Holy and Child, the other Saint Demetrios, namesake of the church, on his rearing brown horse. Emilia crossed herself before the icons and slid the *karto* her godfather had given her earlier into the wooden slot under a tray of new orange beeswax candles. While her grandmother nodded, Emilia lighted a candle from one of the many burning tapers inserted into the tiered, circular candelabrum that had been cleaned of wax for Easter.

Again her grandmother gave Emilia a push, and they all padded over hand-loomed rugs strewn down the aisle. Before the icon screen, shiny with the blaze of Easter candles and festooned with greens and sweet-scented flowers, her grandmother prodded Emilia from one icon to the next to make the sign of the cross.

Emilia lay awake for a long time staring at the watermarks in the corner of the bedroom ceiling. On other nights, the light of the icon coming from the landing made shapes out of the many hues of brown; sometimes they were like the designs of the Turkish rugs the grandmother had brought with her from Thrace but which had disappeared; at other times they were what she imagined the *kalikanzari* were like, the mischievous human-animal forms that tormented people. Then Emilia burrowed under the bed covers. That last night, they were merely watermarks; she could only muse on going to the great city of Thessaloniki.

At four in the morning, Emilia's mother awakened her. Shivering, she dressed in the clothes laid out for her the night before and put on her new shoes. Her mother came in again and with cold hands plaited her hair into one braid. "Do what they tell you," her mother whispered giving her head a yank, "and they'll be nice to you. Never, never use the familiar. Understand? Never use the demotic when you talk to the master and mistress or any older person. Always use the katharevousa. Never talk back. Never gossip. Don't drink water in the evening or you might wet the bed. Always serve a glass of water with a plate under it."

Her mother tied her braid with a blue ribbon. "And someday," her mother said hurriedly, "you will have monthly troubles. Don't be afraid. Go to the kyria and she'll tell you what to do. Come and eat now."

Her grandmother put a bowlful of hot goat milk and floating pieces of anise-flavored Easter bread before her.

"You must eat," her mother said. "You have a long way to go."

"Have you gone to the privy?" her grandmother said. "Finish and go to the privy!"

Her face hot with anger at her grandmother for shaming her with such talk, Emilia hurried down the cellar with its horribly smelling, stone-lined hole in the dirt floor. "Wash your hands! Wash your hands!" her grandmother shrilled when she returned and as if she were too young to do it herself, wiped them for her.

The family congregated in the *sala*. Her father beckoned to Emilia. "Go well," he said and made the sign of the cross three times. Emilia kissed his hand. In silence everyone made the sign of the cross and went out to the high wagon with the tall, slender wheels. Emilia's mother kissed her on both cheeks; her sisters and little brother were pushed forward for the strange ritual—no one from the family had ever left the village before—and then her grandmother pressed her wrinkled, soft lips on her face, eyes frantic. Emilia's mother and godfather kept talking: her mother wanted Emilia to look proper when she arrived. The grandmother screeched at her, "Have you relieved yourself?" Emilia held a handkerchief in which she had tied a few coins. A German, who said he was a professor, came every spring to the village and paid children a *lepta* or two for shards plows had unearthed.

The mule lurched forward. Emilia looked back and waved at them, grouped at the gate of the white stone house. Slowly they also waved, and as the wagon rolled through the mud, they moved as one to the edge of the road. In the quiet of early morning, the stone houses with their Easter whitewash were tinted a faint blue. As the road curved, the houses began to obscure Emilia's own house. The grandmother stepped into the mud and waved her black kerchief. Emilia's mother took hold of the grandmother's arm and pulled. The mule clopped down a hollow. The house disappeared; Emilia's face froze.

They passed the church and made the sign of the cross. The wagon creaked past the store that was also coffeehouse and post office, the yellow-stuccoed two-room school, then more houses. Christos reined in the mule, jumped into the mud, and leaped toward an old woman standing in a doorway. He kissed his mother's hand. "Go well," she said and called out blessings to Emilia.

The wagon skidded down another dip and rose again. A short distance from the road was a small graveyard with three slender cypress trees growing close together in the center, the watchers of the dead. Christos crossed himself three times and Emilia crossed herself. On Great Monday she had been sent to the neighbors for sprigs of geraniums to add to bunches of basil and with her grandmother had gone to the graveyard and laid them on the graves of her two brothers who had died of smallpox. She had lighted a candle under her grandmother's direction and placed it in the wooden enclosure at the head of the common grave. Then they had gone to church and crossed themselves over a box of skulls and bones of grandparents and great-grandparents she had never known, except for one, her father's father, the priest. Because he had been a priest, he had been buried sitting up. Just before the liturgy for the dead, her mother had herded the children into the *sala* where her father now had his bed, and each of them was instructed to approach their sitting grandfather, lean over, and kiss his dead hand. The bowl used to wash his body with wine was placed on the room's mantel.

The road went up a small knoll. Below, an ancient plane tree, Old Man Plane, spread tall and wide, its branches just coming into leaf. Water gushed between exposed, giant roots. Christos stopped the wagon, jumped down, and held up his arms for Emilia. "Let's drink from the Old Man."

The plain spread far ahead. At a shrine to Saint Paul, marking his journey towards Athens, sprigs of basil surrounded a burning votive light. The gray of the sky faded into blue, and from the east pink feathered clouds spread to the west. She had once gazed at such morning skies with infinite delight.

Paralleling the road was land that had once been Greek, then Turkish, and was now abandoned, gone back to thyme, holy oak, and gorse, piles of rocks the only testimony that it had once been cleared and tilled. Farther back was the plowed land of the Turks, the *tsiflikia*, that had been taken from the Greeks centuries before. Several minute figures of women in trousers and veils were stooped over, planting tobacco. The pink, feathery clouds disappeared and the blue of the sky brightened. At times the sea glittered far to their left.

The wagon rolled through an awakening village. A man drove two cows to pasture, and farther off a girl with a long willow guided three goats toward a clump of green. An old woman looked up from making a fire in an earth oven and smiled toothlessly.

The wagon went on. Throughout the plain of scrub oak, wild currant bushes, and plowed strips of earth ready for tobacco planting, men and women were driving their few animals to pasture. Black-dressed and cowled women, each surrounded by several grazing goats, worked spindles of gray wool. At times, a ragged woman grazed but one goat. At the sight of people, Emilia's godfather talked continually and sang snatches of songs. At wayside shrines, fresh flowers wilting, votive lights flickering, he crossed himself dramatically and droned the Lord's Prayer.

The number of people dwindled as the greenness became sparse, until only one wiry man remained on the plain. He was pushing a wooden plow hitched to a bony mule and an emaciated cow. Unearthed rocks lay where they had been thrown at the side of a small patch of plowed ground. "Wretched man," Christos said, but in a moment his old exuberance returned. Farther on, in black, moist earth among patches of green and strewings of gray rock, stood a blackened cone like a solitary burned tree trunk. As they neared, the cone became a nomad in a black, stiff goat hair cape that came to a peak over his head, and the gray rocks turned into a flock of sheep. The nomad Sarakatsan stood far off the road, leaning on a shepherd's crook. Between the black peaked hood and black mus-

96

tache, black eyes glared. "Poor man. If only I had a bird to put a cigarette in its mouth to fly it over to him."

Christos lifted his hand and waved, and after a moment's delay the Sarakatsan slightly lifted his arm. "They're wary," Christos said and repeated what he had heard about them: people said they smelled because they never had a bath after birth; they had fled to the mountains when the City fell to the Turks and stayed there for four hundred years. Christos had come face-to-face with them in 'ninety-seven, four years ago, during the thirty-day war with the Turks. The Greek soldiers in retreat, starved and shivering, had come across a band of Sarakatsans taking their flocks from the low-lands to summer pasture in the mountains. They had no home— here, there, somewhere else a month from then. The Turks could never catch them. The Sarakatsans saw the soldiers' wretchedness and killed lambs to feed them. And why shouldn't they? They never had to do their three-year stint in the army. The government couldn't find them in the first place, and in the second place they couldn't read or write. They would be a burden. They would die, like eagles in captivity. But they didn't smell any worse than other humans.

Christos sang a nomad song about Annoula, the Sarakatsanissa, abducted by three lovesick boys to the mountains. The wagon dipped and rose with the muddy road into the Land Soaked with Blood. The sea there had provided an easy anchorage for barbarian ships, and no mountains rose to hold back the hordes.

Emilia and her godfather came upon a ruined village. The church stood gutted by fire, and black stains streaked its shell. Beside crude animal shelters, women were cooking over outdoor fires. They looked up as the wagon passed, smiled, and nodded, their teeth blackened stubs. In front of a coffeehouse, no more than a storage shed, a white-bearded priest sat wearing a faded hat and robe. He also smiled showing black stubs and gave them a blessing, his thumb and third finger touching. At the well, ragged girls turned to smile, hands across their mouths.

"There! That's the work of the cursed Bulgarian Komitadjes!" Christos exclaimed.

97

Beyond the village the godfather stopped the wagon and untied a dish towel that held a few chunks of Easter lamb, a piece of goat cheese, thick slices of brown bread, and four dark red Easter eggs. "Come on, now, eat. You'll be all right. They're good people. And you know the proverb, 'We feed our grief.' That means food also."

Emilia took phantom bites of the goat cheese, holding her breath not to smell it. Afterwards, her godfather walked toward a clump of willows. When he returned, he gave her a piece of torn newspaper and told her to relieve herself also. Shame curled in her as she walked to the willows. When she returned, she sat in the bouncing wagon weeping at this shameful intimacy. "Now, why are you crying?" "My shoes are muddy," she answered. Yet she made no effort to wipe them with the torn newspaper at her feet.

In the evening they stopped once more to eat and then Christos told Emilia to lie on a blanket in the back of the wagon. It was night when he carried her into a house and up three flights of stairs. Emilia opened her eyes long enough to see she was being put on a cot; she felt the brush of a mustache on her forehead.

9

In 1902 in Mitikas, when Yoryis was almost sixteen and well over six feet tall, his father was without work. At the side of a small rented house, Konstandinos, who had come down from Klepá to help the family, Yiannis, Yoryis, and Pericles planted corn, squash, and beans for the coming winter. The time came when they had so few drachmas the family would have starved without the help of Zaferia's brothers and sisters.

Zaferia's oldest sister was married to a *tselingas*. When he brought his flocks from the highlands to winter grounds, he sent a lamb to the family and another when he left for summer pasture. When he was near enough on name days and festivals, he dispatched a shepherd with a piece of lamb for them. Zaferia's sister Olga was well off but stingy. Among her husband's properties was a bakery; every morning at four Zaferia arrived to knead dough to be baked in the earth ovens in return for her family's bread. Her brother Theodhoros gave her the use of a vineyard that provided them with grapes, wine, and raisins. Another brother, Spyros, lived far from Mitikas and sent Zaferia a little money from time to time.

Occasionally, Yoryis was called to work by a shoemaker when he could not fill all his orders. Through the open door of the shoe shop, he saw his mother at the seashore waiting for the fishing boats to come in. The men threw away the small fish caught in their nets, and these Zaferia gathered to cook for her family. As she stooped on the shore one day, Yoryis pounded on a piece of leather, overwhelmed with pity for his mother and anger at himself for forsaking an education that might have helped his family. A customer slyly got his attention, addressing him as Kravariti, the pejorative for villagers of the Kravara, the mendicants who in generations past had walked across the Balkans as far as Siberia, begging on the way. It had come to mean more than a beggar, a man living off the toil of others.

Yoryis flew out the door and to the outskirts of town where his father was hoeing beans. "I'm going to Klepá!" he shouted. "I will not live here one more day! I will not be called a Kravariti! I'll go to Klepá and open my own shop!"

He shook his head at his mother's entreaties and his father's attempts at logical dissuasion. Their belongings wrapped in bundles and a modest supply of leather, Yoryis and Pericles walked over the mountains to Klepá. From a cousin of their father, they rented a small room off the village square of Lower Klepá, and Yoryis taught Pericles the rudiments of shoemaking.

In cramped misery they lived with one of their father's sisters. The house was filled with mulberry branches, and the shushing sound of the silkworms' gluttonous devouring kept Yoryis awake. He fell asleep staring at his aunt and her daughters unwinding threads from the cocoons to dry and weave for the girls' dowries.

Zaferia and Yiannis mourned their sons; the separation was unbearable. Zaferia's brother Spyros gave them fifty drachmas, but it was not enough to make the move to Klepá. The night of his visit, Zaferia dreamed that Saint George tied his white horse outside the house, entered, and said to her, "Why are you sitting here and don't go to your house?"

"I don't have the money to go."

"You do have the money," Saint George said and disappeared.

When she awakened, Zaferia hurried to the small chest where she had put Spyros's fifty drachmas. With it was a one hundred drachma note and a few *kermata*. Quickly Yiannis, pregnant Zaferia, their daughters Marigho and Vasiliki, and Konstandinos left by boat with the family mule, a goat, her kid, and household possessions for Nafpaktos. There they loaded the goods on the mule and walking, began the journey into the desolate mountains, to Xerovouni and to Klepá on its exposed face.

With his Uncle Konstandinos, Yoryis planted crops; his father lay on a bed of sheep pelts, phlegm rattling in his lungs. Yiannis's vision, like Konstandinos's, began to worsen. Following the midwife's advice, he cut into the crook of his knee and inserted a garbanzo bean, to no avail.

Even before the sky lightened Konstandinos and Yoryis walked the long distance to the family plots, tearing off pieces of heavy bread with their teeth. Yoryis's fierce dog, Kanela, trotted at their side. As they dug and hoed in the clear, cool spring mornings, a shepherd's flute awakened the villagers. The shepherd was a Zisimopoulos cousin, and his poignant call glided down to the two men working silently with the arid dirt. The young cousin had just returned from Nafpaktos where a doctor had cut out a growth on his chest. "If it grows back again," the doctor said, "don't come back. It won't be any use."

Yoryis, with Pericles under his direction, made pomponed *tsarouhia* and belts for men, slippers for women. His first pair of shoes were for his priest-uncle Papa Christos, a gift. To get supplies he left at four in the morning and followed the river to Nafpaktos or the mountain trail to Platanos, made his purchases, and returned late at night. He bought only enough for two or three shoes. On his fourth journey he was well on his way when he heard a rustle of holy oak and turned to see Kanela, tongue hanging sideways, pattering behind him.

Too soon Yoryis found there was no money in the village to buy his *tsarouhia*, which the old men preferred to European shoes. Everything was barter: a piece of lamb promised for Easter, a length of homespun, a vial of olive oil for the family icon.

He was in his shop but two weeks when he took a pair of shoes to an aunt. The family was seated around a warped wooden table—father, mother, and children, the oldest a girl near his own age. In the center of the table was a pot of beans. A metal spoon was passed from one to another to dip into the pot.

"Stay, Yoryi, my eyes! Stay! Eat with us!" his aunt shrilled.

He threw the slippers on the floor and stalked off, cursing them that they did not cut off a branch of *pournari* and whittle a few spoons. Then he knew he was trapped. He had forced his parents, sisters, and brother to the hell of Xerovouni. How would he ever get his sisters dowries? How would he live the rest of his life in Klepá, on desolate Xerovouni?

He worked by the light of the window every day except Sunday. Voices, shouts, screams dinned in his head to remind him that he was trapped, that he had made a terrible mistake in bringing his family back to the village. For three days he worked while the screams and pleadings of a young mother in labor stilled even the talk of the old men and idlers on the village square. The half-blind old midwife screeched at her patient; the women prayed for her in the churches. The midwife pulled out the baby in pieces, but still the mother died. A villager returning from the fields looked in at Yoryis and said, "Still doing battle with shoes, Tango-Yoryi?" Yoryis rushed out and felled him with a fist.

The talk of the men gathered at the square interrupted Yoryis's thoughts while he sat pounding and scheming to escape the village. He never heard the old man Wolf say anything but knew he was there, huddled on the periphery of the group. Wolf had spent his boyhood, manhood, and old age near the top of the red mountain peak called Kokkinia. During long years he hardly ever saw a human being in the summer, and in winter, when he took the sheep he tended for others into the valley, he lived in a mud and wattle hut at a distance from other Klepaiots. Wolf had slept surrounded by his sheep. In his youth he had been awakened in the moonlight by the bleat of a lamb. He jumped up, hand on the knife at his reach. A wolf had clamped its jaws into a lamb's throat. The shepherd grappled the wolf, killed it, and wore its pelt over his black goat hair cape in winter. Bent over, Wolf sat on the ground of the square in all kinds of weather, probably listening, never speaking.

The men on the square talked at times about America, rumors of plentiful work, of great wealth. The old man, Yero—Mitros, with a scanty, yellow-stained mustache knew a villager from Arahova who had gone to America and had sent enough money to his father to dower five sisters. The men spoke in proverbs, told stories of illiterate priests, villagers, and nomads, and on the approach of days marking battles during the Revolution, recounted epic legends of lore and fact. Yero–Mitros was "one of the old." In a sonorous voice he recited long, convoluted stories which sometimes had to be concluded the following day. Among the old men, wearing below-the-knee *foustanellas*, *capotes* thrown over their shoulders, was Stathopoulos who, Yoryis fumed, should not have been given the courtesy of a nod, let alone allowed to talk.

Many years before, Stathopoulos had taken his two young sons down to Nafpaktos, across the water to Patras, and boarded a ship that skirted the Peloponnesos and sailed on to Alexandria, Egypt. There, he rubbed his sons' arms with a caustic and made the rounds of Greek merchants on the wharves, showing the festering sores, fake tears flowing, begging for money to take them to a doctor. He returned to sit on the village square sipping ouzo, his legs crossed leisurely, and talking endlessly about his successful journey and of his cunning.

One afternoon Yero–Mitros was retelling the story of the great Karaïskakis while children were singing Solomos's "Anthem of Liberty" in preparation for a commemoration of the anniversary of the Revolution. Karaïskakis, the son of a nun and a *kleft*, for reasons no one knew, had not been killed under the primeval law of death to bastards. He had risen to become a fierce *kleft* leader. To survive he played both sides: his prick, he said, could play either the Greek trumpet or the Turkish *toubelekia*.

Yero–Mitros was deep into the battle of Arahova near Delphi. One of the Grivases had served there under Karaïskakis and been killed alongside him. Stathopoulos interrupted Yero–Mitros several times. Yoryis rushed out, gave him four backhands that jerked his head back and forth. Stathopoulos did not have the *filotimo* to stay away. Two days later, face still swollen, he was sitting with the old men.

On the feast day of the Apostles, Yoryis was in his shop writing in a record book. Women were setting tables on the square while men hacked at a roasted lamb and filled glasses with wine. Tsarpalias, a man whom Yoryis had known since childhood, looked in at the door and said something to him teasingly. Yoryis bounded over, picked him up, and threw him into the square. Tables, chairs, food, wine, children shot in every direction. What Tsarpalias had said the villagers never knew: no one dared ask Yoryis, and Tsarpalias would not repeat his sally.

All the village and even his mother feared Yoryis. One day, the sky dark, she stood at the window. "Here comes Yoryis," she said in a hushed, fearful voice. A villager beat his wife and Yoryis beat him. A big villager knocked a puny young man down the mountain and Yoryis sent him sprawling down the same path.

When the detested corn, fit only for animals, began to tassle, a neighbor's sheep twice broke down the rock wall Yoryis had put up and were eating when he came upon them at dawn. He beat them off with sticks. "I'll shoot them," he warned his neighbor, "if I find them there again. We aren't going to starve this winter to fill your sheep's bellies." The third time he found the six sheep in the corn, he took the family gun and killed three. Aghast, the villagers raved among themselves: to kill a family's livelihood! To disgrace his family name, stain the Zisimopoulos clan's *filotimo*!

Soon after, a cousin of his father, General Gravianis, came to the village to visit his aged mother. She had given birth to him on the way to winter on the plains. There was nothing to wrap the newborn, so one of the men in the company tore off his shirt sleeve to cover it. General Gravianis had stayed in the army after the compulsory three-year service to assure himself of beans and lentils and had risen from private to become the pride of Klepá. He was immediately told of Yoryis's crime.

In a bemedaled army uniform, a sword at his side, the general appeared at the stone house. Before the entire family, including Papa–Christos, the general shook his finger in Yoryis's face and lectured him on blackening the clan's name, of his disregard for the family's *filotimo*: "And when it is time to give your sisters in marriage, it will not be forgotten that you took a gun and destroyed a family's food and wool! Your sisters will suffer forever for your caprice!"

Yoryis looked down on the general, angry and guilty, yet would say no word of remorse, not ask to be forgiven. Nor was the family ostracized. When the pile of beans and corn were dried, the village girls came to rub the pods between their hands and cut the kernels from the dessicated cobs while they sang of spring violets and mountain streams. To get away from their inane singing while his brain was in foment on how to escape the village, Yoryis walked all over the mountainside. Wheezing from the chaff of dried bean pods, his father sat with Konstandinos on the village square, bundled against the cold, in long, earnest dialogue as if they had not seen each other for years.

Winter came early. Many families left the mountains for Agrinion, Aegion, and Nafpaktos to build reed shelters. The harvest had been poor, and the winter supply of food was scanty. Each morning the family looked at the sky hoping for snow.

When the first snow fell, Yoryis, his father, and Konstandinos loaded the family guns. Through the stillness of snow and deserted mountainside, they searched for the few rabbits that had survived centuries of relentless hunting. The dog, Kanela, ran wildly, ears alert. Just as they despaired of finding one, they saw the small pad and three circles of a rabbit's paw prints. Excited, but careful to make no noise, they followed the tortuous trail until they glimpsed the rabbit in winter-white fur, among the holy oak, standing on its hind legs, motionless, nose twitching. Kanela raced after it.

Konstandinos fired first and missed. Yoryis shot next, and the ping of the bullet was followed by his father's gunblast. The rabbit flew, blood dripping on the snow, crying like a newborn baby. The three men ran around the scrub oak and boulders, keeping to the trail of blood, Kanela frenzied. The cry came closer as the rabbit slowed. Yoryis climbed a boulder and saw the rabbit run in a circle to put them off the trail of his nest and then jump toward a hole among the gnarled roots of holy oak. It pushed ahead a few inches and lay dead.

That evening the family gathered about a bowl of rabbit stew, gave thanks to God for the gift, ate the scrawny rabbit with a thorough sucking of bones, and dipped corn bread in the sauce of vinegary wine. At the other end of the room, the goats chewed on willows. The family crossed themselves again at the end of the meal while Yiannis asked God that they have successful hunts during the winter and that their bullets would last.

In late winter Zaferia went into labor. Yoryis did not go to his shop. His heart beating heavily as he remembered the young mother whose baby had been pulled out in pieces, he stood for warmth close to the mule while it snorted little clouds of steam. Because Yoryis's father was in Platanos that day, the midwife ordered Konstandinos to pin back Zaferia's arms. A woman was delivered standing up, and if the husband was not there to keep her from flailing about, a rope was tied under her arms and thrown over the wooden supports of the roof. Zaferia hardly made a sound; it was against her nature to cry aloud at pain and misery.

Hidden under the patient's skirts, the midwife delivered a baby girl and cleaned her with olive oil. She called Yoryis, gave him a pan of bloody afterbirth, and told him to bury it below where the mule was kept. While he was digging, he found five old Turkish coins. He gave them to his father who allowed him to keep one and used the others for olive oil, salt, candles, and wool cloth that he gave to a Papa–Christos nephew, a newly fledged tailor just returned from his apprenticeship, to make Yoryis a suit. Yoryis wore the suit on feast days and avoided sitting down to keep from wearing it out.

Besides the Turkish coin, Yoryis would add two drachmas to a small leather pouch, the only money he had earned the first year in Klepá. On his way to trade a pair of *tsarouhia* for a piece of leather, Yoryis saw a strange animal in a sapling on the rim of a ravine. He ran home for a gun, expecting to find the animal gone when he returned, but it was still there and he shot it. His father looked at it wonderingly. "This kind of animal has not been seen in these parts for many years. It's not for eating, but its pelt is worth something."

Yiannis skinned the ermine and tacked it on the door of the house to dry. A passing merchant offered Yoryis four drachmas for the fur; Yoryis gave the money to his father who returned two drachmas to him. From then on, whenever he passed near the ravine, he took along his gun and looked carefully for another of the strange animals, but he never saw one again.

With winter having come early, the family hoped that spring was imminent. It was late, and the twin kids at the far end of the room bleated day and night from hunger. "Let's go," Konstandinos said to Yoryis one night when the howl of the storm could not drown out their cries. With blankets pinned about their shoulders and their heads and faces wrapped with homespun, leaving only their eyes exposed, they walked to the edge of the village. The sheets of wind-driven snow blinded them, and they were almost frozen within minutes of leaving the house. They had scoured the slopes often enough to find fodder for the weaned kids. There was only the thorny holy oak. Konstandinos hacked at it with a yataghan. They returned with their arms filled and laid the branches before the kids. "Christ and All–Holy," Konstandinos said, making the sign of the cross, "don't let their little mouths bleed."

Spring came; they had survived the winter, and the dandelions were growing everywhere, tender and wonderfully tart with vinegar. The yellow on their faces disappeared. Water from melting snow rushed down the Great Torrent, taking with it the top story of a house and drowning two young men in it but miraculously leaving the animals in the pen below alive. Flowers bloomed, but there was not a bird in the sky. The villagers let nothing live. They would kill a lone sparrow. On the edge of the ravine they found a bees' nest, rushed down, and destroyed it. Not even a mouthful of honey for each one of them. "They won't let anything live!" Yoryis raged.

That spring, Konstandinos walked to Aegion and found work in a vineyard. With his wages he bought a bolt of muslin from which Zaferia sewed underwear for the entire family She also made his monk's robes. In threadbare clothes, carrying his cassock, Konstandinos walked off to the monastery of Ambelakiotissa in Kozitsas to become a monk. His eyesight almost gone, he left his share of his patrimony and corn for the new child. In Ambelakiotissa, named for the Ail-Holy of the Vineyard, Konstandinos took the name of Konstándios, an obscure saint. Because monks had to leave all, including their names, behind, he chose one as close to Konstandinos

107

as possible. So ascetic did he become that he never again ate meat. Once, after a long fast, he did not awaken to the four o'clock morning *semantron* calling the monks to prayers. He dreamed he heard footsteps coming down the cobbled hall and a voice said, "Konstándios, get up. I am the All-Holy." He jumped up and hurried to the chapel.

When Konstándios first arrived at the monastery, he heard furtive whisperings about the *ighoumenos*, the abbot. Sounds came from his quarters at night, and several monks swore they had heard a woman's voice. Konstándios lectured the monks on their timidity in allowing an unclean man to head their holy institution. He devised a plan by which they could catch the *ighoumenos* in his sin. Several monks would hide in the bushes under the abbot's window, and he, with several others, would take up their station outside his quarters.

On the second night of their watch, the most destitute man in the nearby village and his young wife came out of the blackness. The *ighoumenos* was the godfather of one of their three children. The villager carried a ladder which he set against the wall and steadied while his wife climbed up it and through the window. The monks waited until the *ighoumenos's* puffings and groanings ceased, coins tinkled, and the woman came down the ladder. The monks below and above pounced on their quarry. Before morning the *ighoumenos* had slipped through his guards with the treasury of the monastery. The young mother was stoned and chased out of the village, and there on the outskirts she starved to death.

Summer, fall, another miserable winter and Yoryis wrote his father, then on the island of Corfu, for money; he was going to Alexandria, Egypt, to look for work. "We'll die in Klepá if I don't." Wearing his suit, fifteen drachmas in a leather pouch pinned inside his shirt, he bundled his few pieces of clothing in a black, goat hair bed-covering. He walked to Nafpaktos, crossed the water to Patras in a caique, and took a ship for Alexandria. He stood on the crowded deck most of the way to save wear on his suit and slept, sitting up, when fatigue overcame him.

In Alexandria he was one of a swarm of searchers. He lived in a

Yoryis's uncle, the monk Konstándios, in the monastery of Kozitsas where the bones of the martyred bishop of Smyrna, Polycarpos, were kept.

dirty Arab hotel for two months and every day walked the crowded, filthy streets and alleys around the wharves looking for work. Greek merchants whose families had lived in Alexandria since ancient days, others who were recent immigrants shrugged. "Do you know how many relatives and villagers beg us for work?" they asked.

He left Alexandria. On the ship hundreds of Greeks, Arabs, a few blacks, East Indians, Turks, and Persians were on their way to America. In the day they talked themselves into a frenzy; at night they rested their heads on bags and bundles. Some slept; others lay curled up, eyes wide open under the moonlight.

At Patras, Yoryis got on a boat to Corfu and restlessly paced the deck. In the doorway of the courthouse he looked at his father, bent over a sheaf of papers, holding a thick magnifying glass on the top page and slowly bringing it up and down.

"Father."

"Yoryi!"

Yiannis rented a carriage, and they drove throughout the green island and around the foothills of the great mountain Pantokratoras, named for Christ, Ruler of All. They stopped at the Church of Saint Spyridion and looked at the mummified saint and his shoes that were changed every year because he wore them out on his nighttime travels. "What do you have to tell me?" Yiannis asked as they left the church.

"I'm going to Ameriki."

"No, no," his father said.

"Give me some money to buy supplies to sell to villagers on the way home and to build a new house. The house is ready to fall. I can't go to Ameriki without leaving the family in a new house."

"Wait. Wait."

"If I wait, I'll be taken into the army. And the pay is one cigarette a day!"

Yiannis gave Yoryis two hundred drachmas. Yoryis had not expected so much. He would not know for many years that his father had taken a discount on his future salary to provide the money. In Nafpaktos he bought carefully: what he could not sell would be of use to the family. With two bundles tied on either end of a pole resting on his shoulder, he walked from village to village. In some he sold nothing but traded a spool of cotton thread, a bottle of kerosene, and leather thongs for bread and cheese, chestnuts, frankincense, and a piece of brown silk sent from America. He returned to another winter on Xerovouni.

Two other young men were preparing to leave for America, Pericles Amarantos and Spyros Papachristos. Their families were pooling their money to pay for their passage and a suit of clothes for each. Yoryis asked Yero—Mitros to write a tailor in America for help in finding work for him, Pericles, and Spyros and the mayor of the Klepaiot province to get the official immigration permit.

During the spring and summer Yoryis saw to the building of

the house. He also cleared a patch of ground on a slope called Skambouli and planted grapevines. It would take five years before the vineyard would bear fruit.

He decided to leave after August 15, the feast day of the *Kimisis*, the Falling Asleep of the All–Holy. Soon after the feast day he would exchange the wedding crowns for his oldest Papa–Christos cousin, then be on his way.

Women and girls rushed to help Yoryis with the house. He lined them up the mountainside to a point high above where he had unearthed and piled a mound of rocks. With himself at the head, he and the women relayed stones and flat pieces of shale, for roofing the house, down the slope. They began in early morning and listened while they rhythmically handed the stones downward to the shepherd's flute heralding the new day. Several more growths had appeared on the young shepherd's chest; every day Yoryis thought he would leave his work and climb the mountain to see his cousin but did not. When the flute was still and goat bells tinkled, the women and girls sang chaste songs of violets and love and of young men who pined for a glass of water from a beloved.

In return for the family mule and a small sum of money, an older Zisimopoulos cousin, a carpenter, built the house with Yoryis and Pericles's help. The family slept and cooked under the sky while the old house was dismantled and its stones used to finish the new one. Zaferia sat at her loom in a cove of holy oak a short distance away. She worked until dark weaving a *kelimi*, a goat hair cover of white and a dark red dyed with pomegranate juice. After completing the weaving, she embroidered the *kelimi* with many colors of thread. It would serve to wrap her son's belongings and to cover him while he slept.

When the lower part of the house was ready, the family moved into it; the upper living space was without a floor and would be until Yoryis sent money from America to buy planks.

Just before the forty-day fast for the *Kimisis* of the All–Holy, Yoryis's shepherd cousin sold two of his sheep and invited the villagers to the square to drink ouzo until the cask was emptied. For a few more days the flute was heard; then the mountains were silent in the cool dawn, and ten days later the young shepherd was buried in the ancient graveyard.

Following the feast of the *Kimisis*, Yoryis, his Papa—Christos and Zisimopoulos cousins, his friend Kostas, Pericles, and Spyros combined their coins, mainly good-luck pieces given them at birth, to celebrate Takis Papa—Christos's wedding and Yoryis, Pericles, and Spyros's leaving for America. They climbed to the red mountaintop Kokkinia and gave the money to a shepherd who slaughtered a lamb, cooked it over a spit, and played his flute for them.

The shepherd was ecstatic at seeing people and getting a little money for a lamb. Each spring when he came to the village, people gathered in the square of Upper Klepá to bid on a lamb leg, a shoulder, entrails. If he thought he was not getting enough, he returned to his flock with the lamb.

The young men ate their fill, told priest stories, danced the ancient *syrto* and *kalamatiano* on the slanted rocky slope, and sang the old *kleft* songs. They sang of the Souliot women of Zalongo. They sang of the Roumeliot deacon Dhiakos caught by the Turks, tied to a pole, and roasted over coals, singing until he died, "Live on high mountains, little canyons, and rivulets"; and of Kitsos's mother who told him to come back with his precious guns or not at all. They finished with Grivas who was late, perhaps captured by the Turks, of Grivas and his horse Black who talked to each other like two human beings, of Grivas who would not come out of his *vilayet*, his province, to "bow down to Ali Pasha." Their voices echoed over the valley with Grivas's answer:

> *As long as Grivas is alive, pasha I will not bow to.*
> *For pasha Grivas has his sword, for vizier his gun.*

And another:

> *Cry, country and villages, villages and vilayets.*
> *Cry, for the General Theodhorakis Grivas.*
> *Neither in Patras has he been seen, neither in*
> *   Athens.*
> *They told us some lies, they told us some truths.*
> *They told us he died down in Messolonghi.*

> *They're weeping over him, the troops and all the*
> *vilayets.*

It was the highlight of their lives.

When the festivities for the wedding began, the village burst out of its brown cocoon, vibrating with laughing and reminiscing. A young man was ready to become a *nikokyris*, a respected house-holder, three *leventes* were going to America. With flowers woven in their braids, girls sang traditional songs while bread for the feast was kneaded and baked in the houses of the bride and groom. The hilarious laughter of the villagers at the dough fight between the men of the bride's clan and those of the groom's, a vestige of bride-stealing days, echoed across the valley.

While Yoryis and his cousins tendered invitations to each vil-lager with a bunch of flowers and a drink of liqueur, the girls sang and embroidered the silk flag, the *flamboura* that the bride's young brother planted on the roof of her house. They clustered about and sang at the Saturday ceremonial haircutting and shaving of the groom, the honor of barbering going to Yoryis, the *koumbaros*, the best man.

On the day Yoryis left, he took a book of his father's which his mother wrapped with his clothes in the *kelimi*. "As many strands as are in this *kelimi* that many blessings I give you," she said. Yoryis kissed her hand and she immediately went into the house. From that day she "never had a kind word to say to her daughters." Vil-lagers whispered that she had changed into a female janissary: in spring when water rushed down the Great Torrent, the watermaster made his way tentatively over irrigation ditches. Zaferia grabbed him one day and threw him into the water for damming the stream to her family's garden plot.

Older women and friends accompanied Yoryis, Pericles, and Spyros down the village paths, their friends as far as the river. Clutching his homespun bundle, Yoryis, leading the way, did not look back.

When the men in the village saw Yoryis safely across the old bridge, they suddenly began to sing and dance on the square. They celebrated for hours, relieved that he was gone. He had beaten up almost every man in the village. But his dog howled throughout the day and night. "Kanela is crying for Yoryis," an old woman said, "and we're crying too." When Kanela kept howling, Yoryis's mother asked one of the neighbors to shoot her. Several days later, one of the girls, who had husked corn and rubbed dried bean pods in Yoryis's house and sung during the week of wedding preparations, threw herself into the ravine. A passing villager heard her moaning, "Yoryis, Yoryis," and rescued her, bleeding and limp. Which of the girls she was, Yoryis could not recall when he heard about it years later.

IO

Emilia opened her eyes and did not know who she was, where she was. Then, frozen, she remembered who she was and that she was now a servant in a stranger's house. She sat up, smoothed her dress, put on her shoes, and after several attempts succeeded in buttoning them. She patted her hair and pulled on her braid. On a small dresser, the only other object in the room besides the cot and a chair, were a comb and a small mirror. She did not move but sat looking at the top of the shut door for the giant woman who would appear there. After a long time the door opened and a woman, far younger than her mother, smiled at her. Emilia jumped to her feet. "You're awake," the woman said, her teeth oddly small. "I've forgotten your name."

The lady, the *kyria*, showed Emilia the apartment, the odor of stale cooking smells throughout. The *sala* was small, heavy with tapestries and velvet draperies; the dining room was smaller and windowless. The crowded bedroom was opulent to Emilia: a ceiling high, dark wooden wardrobe, an unmade, ornate bed, and a large chest of drawers on which were silver-chased brushes, combs, and boxes—carved, painted, round, square. In a smaller room, a hanging vigil light burned before an icon on the wall. The carpet, patterned with flowers and palms, was like one Emilia had seen somewhere.

The kitchen, too, was small and dark with a door that led to a landing from which wooden stairs descended. The *kyria* stepped onto it. Emilia drew back at being so high up, then she saw the dried mud on her shoes. Her heart beat faster, but as the *kyria* was waiting and watching, she stepped on the landing. Far down was a court paved with cobblestones and lined with a row of privies. "The third one is ours," the *kyria* said. "Be especially careful when you go downstairs to empty the night jugs. Use both hands."

Emilia's stomach heaved. In the few seconds they stood there, voices came from the second story below them and a shrill cry from farther down. Tears streamed down Emilia's face: strangers lived under one roof.

In the kitchen the *kyria* brought out a new enameled pan from under a metal sink and told Emilia to wash herself morning and night. She pushed up and down on a small pump, and Emilia watched water stream from a strange contraption, a tap. There would be no work that day, the *kyria* said. "Wash the tears off your face, eat a koulouraki, drink a cup of coffee, and we'll be off."

Emilia sat in the dimness and chewed the *koulouraki* because the mistress had told her to. From her bedroom the *kyria* called Emilia to wear her Sunday dress. Emilia drank a swallow of bitter coffee to force down the paste in her mouth and hurried into her bedroom. She opened the old carpetbag, took out the icons of the All–Holy and Child and Saint Demetrios and clutched each to her for a moment before putting it on the dresser. As if the comb were a contamination to the icons, she quickly hid it in the empty top drawer of the dresser. Through tears she looked at the wrinkled brown dress her grandmother and Anna had sewed. She wavered over whether she should wear the dress as it was or ask the *kyria* for an iron to press it. "Come, Emilia," the voice called with a faint sharpness. Panting, Emilia put on her Sunday dress and tried to smooth out the wrinkles with her palms. She brushed back her hair with her fingers and tucked stray wisps into the braid, afraid to take the time to comb and replait it. As she walked out of the room, she thought she would bring the *kyria*'s attention to the wrinkles and in this way the mistress would know she was not unaware or careless.

But the *kyria*, wearing a suit with a brown fur collar, was at the door. Emilia followed her down marble stairs to the second floor where they stopped at a plain wooden door. A large girl invited them in. As she closed the door after them, she smiled at Emilia. "My name's Hrisoula," she said, holding her lips together.

The *kyria* laughed. "She hardly talks, only cries."

Emilia lowered her eyes and waited to be told whether to sit or not. The *kyria* pointed to a straight-backed chair. On one wall of the bare room were tintypes of army officers and a big portrait of a fat man in a bemedaled and epauleted uniform wearing a fez.

A thin, gray woman with pince-nez like the schoolmaster's in Emilia's village came into the room peering. Emilia was afraid of her. The eyes, enormous behind thick lenses, gave Emilia a few seconds of scrutiny.

Hrisoula beckoned Emilia to follow her into the kitchen. Quickly the older girl had the tray ready: crocheted cloth, two glasses of water, and a dish of pink, shredded quince preserve. While water for Turkish coffee simmered in a brass *brik* on the charcoal stove, Hrisoula brought Emilia onto the landing, undid her braid, and taking a brush from a wooden shelf where a pan was turned upside down, untangled and plaited her hair. Emilia remembered Anna and fresh tears spilled out. "We all cry at first," Hrisoula said, "but we're lucky. I have a good mistress and so do you. Mine has never beaten me. She even tried to teach me to read and write, but I didn't have the brains." With a wet rag she wiped Emilia's shoes.

They returned to the kitchen. Hrisoula measured coffee into the *brik*. It rose, foaming, but it did not bring Emilia the old pleasure. Hrisoula took the tray into the *sala* while Emilia sat weeping for her family, remembering her father's asking if she wanted to go to Thessaloniki and she with such foolish glee, had said "Yes! Yes!"

As Hrisoula came back to the kitchen, the old mistress called out that if Emilia did not like the quince, she should be given a *tsoureki*. Recalling the *tsoureki* that she had eaten at the Ramadan feast of feasts in the Turkish village, Emilia wailed silently for her grandmother. She ate the *tsoureki* for comfort, but it had no taste.

Hrisoula called her "little bird" and told her to pray to the All—Holy and soon her homesickness would be gone. She smiled showing black stubs of teeth like those of the people Emilia had seen on her way to the city. Hrisoula then pressed Emilia's dress while she sat in her petticoat in shame.

When her mistress called, Emilia knew at least that she was proper with her hair brushed, her dress ironed. The gray-haired *kyria* rested a claw on Emilia's head and told her she was always welcome in her house. She smiled; her teeth were false, grotesque.

Emilia's *kyria* hurried down the steps to a ground floor apartment where a pretty girl with pink cheeks and glossy black hair opened the door. A stout young woman came into the *sala* quickly and handed a fat baby to the smiling servant girl, Nitsa. Emilia's *kyria* declined a sweet and coffee, saying slyly, with her head lifted toward the ceiling, that they had already been served above.

In the kitchen, identical to the two above, Nitsa held the baby and asked Emilia questions. Emilia thought of her brother Yiannis, and tears dropped off the edge of her nose. Did she have brothers and boy cousins, Nitsa asked, and derisively hooted at Yiannis's age. "Two years old! What can I do with a two-year-old? Fry him and eat him?"

Nitsa's *kyria* shrieked, "Give the girl a piece of ghalatobouriko and you may eat a piece too." When Emilia shook her head, Nitsa placed a forefinger against her lips and ate both pieces. In merry whispers she told Emilia what was being gossiped about in the *sala*: a family across the way was having a hard time marrying a daughter because she was homely. They had sent her in vain to a French school in the city. Now they were trying to get money from a relative in America to increase her dowry. Nitsa moaned over America: if she could only go there.

They left the three-story apartment of yellow stucco with iron grills on the windows. On both sides of the narrow winding street, no wider than an alley, similar yellow and white stucco apartments rose from the cobbled street. Few people were out. As the two went on, the *kyria* ahead, Emilia hurried after her, trying to keep on the two-foot-wide cobbled elevation adjacent to the buildings. More people appeared: small girls like her with baskets on their arms trailed after old men and women. Mistresses walked with servant girls at their sides so that no one could accuse them of being on the streets alone. Country people wearing faded homespun and carrying white bundles bulging with dandelion greens trudged ahead. More tears came to Emilia's eyes.

Myriad sounds swirled and clashed in the air like a *panegyri* on a saint's day. Men called greetings; women screeched to each other; donkeys brayed, blue beads strung around their necks to keep them safe from the evil eye; chickens squawked; carriage wheels clacked over cobblestones. Emilia almost ran to keep up with the *kyria*.

At a roar of thunder Emilia looked fearfully at the sky, but it was still blue and peaceful. They rounded a curve and before them lay the bazaar with its stalls and carts, people screaming and haggling, villagers with trussed chickens hanging from their hands, lambs tied by one leg to a pole, and people with baskets on their heads and at their feet, shouting, "Fish! Artichokes! Figs!"

A woman in patched homespun offered a basket of brown eggs to the *kyria* who swept on without a glance. With Emilia trotting behind, she glided by stalls selling baskets, copper utensils, tobacco, noodles, rice, knives, and rope. In each one men, women, and even children with blue beads on their foreheads were shouting, calling, piping. In one stall a black man, the first one Emilia had ever seen, was wearing a red fez and calling out, not in Turkish but in Greek, "Fresh figs! Just brought in from Smyrna!"

She ran after the *kyria*, but a crowd of schoolboys in military uniforms and caps came between her and her mistress. Emilia ran around them, her panicked eyes scanning the stalls. She bolted a few steps forward, then turned in another direction, and down another aisle of stalls. Ahead two women were talking; a servant girl stood a little apart from them. The woman Emilia thought was her *kyria* was wearing a brown fur collar. Emilia approached uncertainly. As she came up to her, the woman said, "Here is my new little servant."

Again Emilia trotted after the *kyria*, past the bazaar and into a wide, cobbled street of large buildings with miniature trees in tubs on either side of their entrances. Farther out, they walked past domed churches and Jewish synagogues; the *kyria*'s starched petticoats rustled from hurrying.

Houses were larger; trees rose on the other side of walls and grilled gates; several storks stood in big nests on tiled roofs. "These houses belong to wealthy Jews," the *kyria* said, and led the way through the park where brown-fezzed, white-bearded old men sat on benches and leaned on canes. Some fed pigeons. Remembering the village priest who kept pigeons in a row of screened boxes for roasting on his name day, Emilia looked at them lingeringly through tears. Then hurrying, hurrying after the *kyria*, she glimpsed round beds of stately flowers inside rigid circles and fresh tears came.

In the evening under the *kyria*'s direction, Emilia set two places on the table in the windowless, stifling dining room and one for herself in the kitchen. She thought the man, the *kyrios* who would appear at the door, would be large, burly, dark, like the villager who had killed a girl tending goats on the plain.

The door opened and her heart beat horribly at a mustached, pudgy man with gray hair at his temples. He smiled, showing the same small teeth as his wife's, handed Emilia a newspaper-wrapped package, and said her godfather and he had served in the army together.

While sounds of whole-hearted soaping and rinsing and little grunts came from the front bedroom, the *kyria* opened the package of liver. Without scalding it, she floured the liver and placed it into a pan of sputtering olive oil. Emilia looked at her. "Pay attention, Emilia," the *kyria* said, "so I won't have to tell you more than once."

The *kyrios* called his wife into the dining room. His voice was low, patiently reprimanding. The *kyria* returned and said, "Set a place for yourself in the dining room."

Emilia sat eating with the two strangers, chewing and chewing the liver that would not go down. The master told his wife in a kindly way that the liver was overcooked. He told Emilia her god-father had saved his life in the war of 'ninety-seven against the Turks. Emilia recalled that dark, laughing man she seldom saw and wept silently.

Under the *kyria*'s instructions she washed the dishes, put them away, and prepared for bed, hardly able to lift her arms, even while making the sign of the cross at her icons. The *kyria* and *kyrios* talked in the living room about wheat and the *karagouni*, the villagers of the plain of Thessaly. In bed Emilia cried until her body felt dry. The walls of the room came closer.

The next morning *Kyria* Harangoglou, Hrisoula's mistress, came to the apartment and reproved Emilia's *kyria* for not sending her to spend the evening with the servant girls gathered in her *sala*. She herself had gone to matins for Saint George and did not know that Emilia was not with them. The girls were meeting in *Kyria* Karagheorghiou's that evening, she said coldly, and Emilia should be there with some handwork.

After the older woman had gone, Emilia's *kyria* told her to look in a sewing chest on her dresser for a pair of pillowcases. Emilia found them, stamped with butterflies and daisies, one flower half finished, puckered with uneven stitches. Through tears Emilia chose a scissors from several under the lid, a few needles, and tangled colored threads. When she returned, the *kyria* said, "Now why are you crying?"

"It's my father's name day today," Emilia began, but the mistress said liturgy was over by then.

All the while Emilia dusted and swept with the *kyria* pointing to corners where matted dirt had to be dug out by her fingernails, she thought of her family eating roasted chestnuts, drinking blossom tea, her father playing the *tamboura* while Anna sang. On the small table next to his bed, among the tools and pieces of wire with which he repaired villagers' pots and lamps, was the nearly finished wooden bird he was carving for her little brother.

Someone knocked on the kitchen door. The *kyria* opened it, and an old woman grunted a greeting and entered. With one hand she steadied a large basket of folded linens on her head. Her face was a mass of deep wrinkles; her eyes peered to see better. With a "Hup!" she dropped the basket on the kitchen table. Scraggly gray hair escaped from a rust-tinged, faded black, homespun kerchief. Her man's shoes were splattered with mud. The *kyria* exclaimed that she had forgotten Anastasia was coming, and the washwoman would have to wait while she changed the sheets.

"You're the new servant?" the old woman asked in a thick dialect.

"Yes, Kyria."

"I'm no kyria. I'm the washwoman." She cocked her head toward the door and still smiling sarcastically said, "I come every Tuesday, and she never remembers. A Bad Hour to her! All the witches and demons bring her a Bad Hour!" Emilia trembled.

On the cramped landing the washwoman set up tubs and filled them, one with hot water heated over the brazier, the other with cold water from the tap. Up and down the red, deformed hands pulled and pushed sheets against a wooden washboard. Emilia began dusting the dining room furniture.

After the washwoman had rinsed and wrung the first tubful with powerful crooked fingers, she called, "Child! Help me down the stairs with the basket." The two made their way slowly down the stairs, the old woman lifting the basket to take most of the weight.

"Go back up," she said at the bottom. "I'll hang this batch up now."

The *kyria* was waiting for Emilia when she returned to the kitchen. "*Never* leave a worker alone in a room. You never know what they'll steal. Now, go make the beds again with clean sheets."

Emilia finished making the beds and then cleaned and polished the kerosene lamps with great care because she had displeased the *kyria*, but worse she had been disloyal, saying nothing when the washwoman cursed her mistress with the Bad Hour. The smell of kerosene worsened her despair; she thought of her father letting drops fall onto the raw soles of his feet and writhing in silence. Several hours later, Anastasia left and Emilia sat on a kitchen chair; the *kyria* had gone to her bedroom to sleep. For city people it was the hour of the siesta, and no sounds came from the outside. She looked above the brazier to the blackened ceiling for a magic sign that would suddenly take her back to her house in the village. She wept.

In the evening, after she had boiled greens and fried squid under the *kyria*'s watching eyes, then washed the dishes, she walked down the dark stairway with the pillowcase rolled about thread, needle, scissors, and thimble. She stood at the ground floor apartment door a moment.

"Go on, knock," the *kyria* said from above.

The door opened and Hrisoula took her hand and led her into the kitchen. Sitting at a table on which a kerosene lamp sputtered were Nitsa, drinking weak tea, and a girl hunched over, sniffing and cradling her arms. She raised doleful eyes to Emilia, then looked at her untouched cup and sighed loudly. "Enough's enough, Koula," Hrisoula said sharply. "'Even God gets tired of too much Kyrie, eleison.'" She poured a cup of tea for Emilia, taking over the duty of Nitsa, the servant of the house. "If you'd do your work properly, you wouldn't get beaten for eating a sweet. Furthermore, you should never take anything without being given it. Now, drink your tea."

Koula jutted her lips belligerently but lifted her tea cup. In a moment she joined plump, pretty Nitsa in questioning Emilia: Was her *kyria* pregnant yet?

Emilia thought of her brother Yiannis whom she had watched while her mother hoed. Her mother had screamed at her when he fell and bruised himself. Now it was Fani who tended him and Fani who was hoisted up and into the enormous woven basket in the cellar to scoop up a pan of wheat. She, Anna, and Fani had slept on straw next to the great basket when the grandmother had filled every room of the house with planks and covered them with mulberry leaves that the silkworms ate voraciously. The dresses their grandmother had sewed from the silk she had spun, dyed, and woven were folded in a large chest in the room where Emilia's father lay—for Anna's dowry.

The girls jostled her to come to attention, to forget her homesickness, to hear their gossip. A servant girl had received passage to America from an uncle there. Nitsa and Koula moaned, "Ameriki, Ameriki." Hrisoula told them a secret: her *kyria* had saved enough money from her pension to have her teeth fixed.

The next morning, while the *kyria* slept, Emilia prepared coffee for the *kyrios*. He insisted that she eat bread and honey with him.

When she was small, she had begged to go with her father to a hollow tree to gather honey. She stood a short distance away while her father lit a cigarette and blew smoke into a hole in the hollow. "This will stun them," he said, "and they won't sting." She had marveled as he took out the heavy, gourd-shaped cone, his bare hand covered with seething bees. Her mother used the white honey, which was the best, for making sweets for visitors and put the brown honey on the table for the morning bread. Emilia's grandmother strained the darker brown honey for wax to make candles.

It was a special day when they had honey. Her mother or Anna made *katsamaki*. In a large pan of barely boiling water they carefully added flour and salt and pierced holes in the center and around the edges of the dough. The *katsamaki* simmered for a long time, water seeping into it until it was thick. "Watch carefully," her mother said to Emilia, standing on a chair. Her mother tested the *katsamaki*, pricking it with a two-pronged fork from time to time to see if it was cooked through. Then she and Anna took turns stirring the dough until it thickened even more. The grandmother poured in a cupful of honey; it swirled in golden circles and disappeared. "Ready!" their grandmother said, and the children rushed to the table.

A clicking on her plate: the *kyrios* was speaking. "Emilia, dry your tears. I know about homesickness. 'Homesickness has no cure,' the proverb goes, but I can tell you it fades after a while. I was sent away to school, seven years old. I cried myself sick. My salvation came from the few books I had. Whenever you feel melancholy in the evening, look through my books."

After the master left, Emilia went to the glass-front bookcase in the *sala* and quietly, with glances toward the *kyria*'s closed bedroom door, selected several books and quickly turned a few pages of each one. Of imitation leather and yellowing pages with smudged print, they recorded accounts of ancient gods, the Greek–Persian wars, the fall of Constantinople, the City, the Turkish occupation, and the perfidy of the Great Powers after parts of Greece were liberated. But she did not feel any different.

Emilia often awakened in the morning knowing she had dreamed and sensing it was about her family. She tried to will the dreams back to her. In them she would learn of a happening at home that would bring her back to the village. She tried desperately to remember and grieved for her lost dreams.

She often dreamed she was going back to the village, but she became entangled in the aisles of the bazaar; after a long time of hurrying up and down, avoiding people and carts, she was walking rapidly down the narrow streets, the *soukakia*, but she took many wrong turns that brought her to the Turkish section of the city where silent, veiled women gazed at her through latticed windows. She had to come back to the same alley again and again. Never did she reach the outskirts of the city.

She coveted the *kyria*'s dream book. It would tell her the meaning of her dreams, but she was afraid to ask her permission to look into it. She bided her time until the *kyria* was in one of her gay moods and then approached her. "If you have all your work finished," her mistress said.

Emilia began her work in the entrance hall where an ornate vase in the corner sprouted a bouquet of dusty peacock feathers. Next to it was a coat stand where a pale linen coat the *kyrios* wore on warm days hung. The odor of must and stale sweat lingered in the space, and Emilia held her breath as she shook the peacock feathers and wiped the vase. Then she cleaned the doorknob. "You're going to wear out the doorknob," the *kyria* trilled on her way back to her bedroom with an Athenian magazine. Emilia looked angrily at the cleaned doorknob thinking of the *kyrios*, kind and quiet-spoken, who picked his nose and increased her work. Every day she wiped the doorknob and any drawer pulls she had to touch because of him. She washed her plate and cup first and stored them in the cupboard, the dish under the stack of plates, the cup behind them. This way, the *kyrios* could never use her plate and cup. She was always washing her hands.

When the *kyria* had eaten and gone to her bedroom for her siesta, Emilia set the kitchen in order, waited a few minutes, then tiptoed into the dining room, took the dream book, and almost ran into her bedroom. Keeping the door an inch open to hear the *kyria* if she called, Emilia turned the pages of the dream book. Under each letter of the alphabet were words and sometimes a drawing: an eagle, a book, a letter. She saw how it was and turned to the *T*'s for *taxidhi*, journey. She read slowly under a drawing of a carriage with two pairs of horses.

> *If you see yourself traveling toward the sea, the dream shows you are thinking of traveling always, and courageous undertakings, if completed, will bring you a multitude of rewards. If you see others making a journey, the rewards that should be yours, will be awarded to other hands. If you travel in good weather, your progress in your business endeavors will be good, but if the sea is rough with storms, it portends unfortunate results. If you are traveling by carriage, it means you are tormented with vain and secret dreams that after great sorrow, you will find remain impracticable.*

She turned the pages still trying to find the kind of dream she had been having, but she did not know under what word to look. *Lost,* she thought, and turned the pages, searching. Charos: the word stood out on the page. She closed the book, her heart beating loudly.

On the last Friday of each month, the *kyrios* sat next to Emilia at the dining room table and under the light of the kerosene lamp she wrote the same lines to her family.

> *Greetings, my respected grandmother and parents. I hope you are all well. I am in good health. The kyrios and kyria are well. I attend church every Sunday. I fare very well. I kiss your hands, grandmother and parents. I kiss my sisters and brother.*
>
> > *Your daughter,*
> > *Emilia Papachristou*

The *kyrios* read the letter swiftly, correcting spelling and accent marks, pointing out mistakes to Emilia who reddened and hung her head. "Now, Emilia, you must pay more attention to the accent marks. I've explained them time and time again." The *kyrios* then inserted a money draft into the envelope and sealed it with a flourish. From his vest pocket he brought out a bank book and showed her the other half of her earnings deposited for her future dowry.

καλὴ θέσις, ὥστε ὠφελήθητι τῆς περιστάσεως. Ἐὰν εἶναι πλήρης ὕδατος, θὰ κερδίσῃς ἀπὸ τὰς ἐπιχειρήσεις σου χρήματα. Ἐὰν εἶναι κενή, θὰ χάσῃς τὰ κεφάλαιά σου· Ἐὰν τὴν σπάξῃς, κακὸν σημεῖον.

Λαγώς. —Ἂν ἀπλῶς τὸν βλέπῃς, σημαίνει ὅτι δεικνύεις διαγωγὴν ἀξίαν περιφρονήσεως, πολλὰ δὲ ἀκόμη θὰ πάθῃς ἕνεκα τῆς δειλίας καὶ τῆς ἀπειρίας σου. Ἂν βλέπῃς λαγὸν νὰ τρέχῃ,  κέρδος καὶ μεγάλαι χρηματικαὶ ἀπολαύσεις· ἂν δ' ἐνῷ τρέχει τὸν καταδιώκῃς, σημεῖον ὅτι μεθ' ὅλας τὰς προσπαθείας σου δὲν θὰ κατορθώσῃς ὅ,τι ζητεῖς. Ἂν φονεύσῃς λαγόν, θὰ πάθῃς ἕνεκα τῆς σκληρότητός σου πρὸς ἄνθρωπον, ὁ ὁποῖος δὲν σὲ ἔβλαψεν· ἂν δὲ τρώγῃς τὸ κρέας του, θὰ διαδοθῇ φήμη ὅτι εἶσαι δειλός.

Λάδι. —Ἂν βλέπῃς ὅτι τρώγεις λάδι μὲ τὸ φαγητόν σου, χαρὰ καὶ ἀγαλλίασις· ἂν ὅμως χύνεται κατὰ γῆς τὸ λάδι, στενοχωρίαν μεγάλην σοῦ προμηνύει καὶ ἀγανάκτησιν διὰ τὴν ἀργοπορίαν τῶν ὑποθέσεών σου. Ἂν βλέπῃς ὅτι πίνεις λάδι τῆς μουρούνας ὡς φάρμακον, ἴσως θὰ διεκινδύνευες τὴν ζωήν σου. Ἐὰν ἴδῃς ὅτι λάδι ἐχύθη εἰς τὰ φορέματά σου, μεγάλας ζημίας θὰ ὑποστῇς καὶ ἀνεπανόρθωτον συμφοράν. Ἂν ἀλείφεσαι μὲ λάδι ἢ κοινὸν ἀρωματικόν, ματαίας ἐπιδείξεις τῆς καλλονῆς σου κάμνεις καὶ ὁ κόσμος ἤρχισε νὰ σὲ ἀηδιάζῃ. Βλέπε καὶ ἔλαιον.

Λαγκάδια. — Ἐὰν βλέπῃς λαγκάδια ἐκτεταμένα ἐνώπιόν σου, διὰ τοὺς νέους καλὴν πρόοδον σημαίνει, διὰ δὲ τοὺς γέροντας εὐτυχῆ καὶ ἥσυχα τέλη ἐν τῷ μέσῳ τῆς οἰκογενείας των. Ἐὰν ἴδῃς ὅτι εἰσῆλθεν εἰς λαγκαδιάν, τῆς ὁποίας δὲν εὑρίσκεις τὸ ἄκρον νὰ ἐξέλθῃς θὰ μάθῃς ὅτι ἐναυάγησε κάποια ὑπόθεσίς σου.

Λαϊκός. —Ἐὰν βλέπῃς ὅτι κληρικὸς γνωστός σου ἔγεινε πάλιν λαϊκός, κακὸν τὸ ὄνειρον· Ἂν δὲ λαϊκὸς γνωστός σου παρουσιάζεται ὡς κληρικός, θὰ σοῦ γίνῃ καλὴ καὶ εὐτυχὴς ἀπόδειξις μεγάλης εὐνοίας καὶ ἐμπιστοσύνης ἐκ μέρους τῶν φίλων ἢ τῶν ἀνωτέρων σου.

Λαίμαργος. —Ἐὰν ἴδῃς ὅτι εἶσαι λαίμαργος ἢ ἀπλῶς ὅτι ἄλλος σὲ κατηγορεῖ ὡς λαίμαργον, σημεῖον ὅτι ἀταξία μεγάλη βασιλεύει εἰς τὰς πράξεις σου, ἡ ὁποία θὰ σὲ κάμῃ νὰ μετανοήσῃς ἀργότερα.

Λαιμός. —Ἐὰν βλέπῃς ὅτι ἔχεις ὡραῖον καὶ ζηλευτὸν λαιμόν, τιμὰς καὶ προβιβασμοὺς θὰ ἔχῃς ἐκ μέρους τῶν ἀνωτέρων σου. Λαιμὸς λευκὸς καὶ κομψὸς σημαίνει αἰφνίδια πλούτη ἀπὸ

A page from Emilia's dreambook. "If you see a rabbit running, you will receive gain and a great amount of money."

127

Emilia's father answered in the purist, the *katharevousa*, the words in beautifully elaborate penmanship, with a pressed basil sprig or yellow white anise blossom inside. Sometimes her grandmother wrote her blessings, also in the purist, but her hand was shaky, the words almost illegible. Emilia's mother added a few lines once. The words were hardly better written than Emilia's own. Emilia remembered her bustling mother whose hands were rough, the palms black lined like the washwoman Anastasia's. The village women, washing and pounding their clothing at the riverside, boiling them with ashes over open fires, and draping them on bushes to dry had called Emilia's grandmother *grammatismeni kyria*, educated woman. While waiting for their wash to dry, they sat around her and asked questions which Emilia's grandmother answered like a sweetly talking schoolmistress. Emilia wondered about her mother: why was she not a *grammatismeni kyria*? And she wept with pity for her mother's black-lined palms.

She smelled the basil and anise again and again and read her father's letter over and over to see if there was some word she had overlooked.

> *Our dear daughter Emilia, we are all well and give thanks to God that you are well also. We know you are a good girl and are obedient and respectful to Kyrios and Kyria Papadimitriou. We send them our greetings. It is the season for heat now. We kiss you on both cheeks. Greetings from all the family. Your parents Gheorghios and Eleni Papachristou.*

Emilia wept throughout the day, and whenever the *kyria* was in her bedroom or visiting below, she ran to her room, opened the dresser drawer, and holding the precious letter to her nose, breathed in the piquant scent.

One evening while she was frying slices of veal, the *kyria* spoke sharply to her. "You've cried enough, Emilia. No more tears."

That evening in bed, her eyes dry, she felt her head was swelling. She thought of her grandmother and Anna remaking her mother's brown dress into a Sunday dress for her. She thought of her father calling her in to ask if she wanted to go to Thessaloniki to become a servant girl. She saw how it was: it had all been planned—her godfather's visit, the dress ready. It had been talked about, and they had said nothing to her; *they* had decided.

Each Sunday Hrisoula's *kyria* herded the servant girls to church. For three hours they stood trying to whisper and not be noticed by the sharp-eyed *kyria*. At each intoning of the names of the Trinity and the All–Holy, the *kyria* crossed herself laboriously, leaned forward, and looked to see if the girls were following suit.

On the way home they stopped at the *zaharoplastis* shop, and the *kyria* bought them a piece of Turkish *loukoum*. In the afternoon while their masters and mistresses slept, they visited in each other's kitchens or on good days accompanied the grayed *kyria* to the park where she sat on a bench and read a newspaper with great attention, chewing her thin lips, adjusting her pince-nez, and glancing severely at the girls from time to time to admonish them for talking too loudly.

On some evenings only Emilia and Hrisoula were together. When cloddish Koula was kept in as punishment beyond her regular beatings, Emilia was relieved that she would not have to be alert to her teasing. Sometimes Nitsa would fail to come and would give no reason when they met the following night. On these nights Hrisoula's *kyria* spent much of the evening with Emilia's handwork. "You have the talent," she said, and showed her how to baste a piece of tissue paper over a design, take small "running" stitches to outline it, and then fill with overlapping stitches and cover with small, even ones until the motif became raised and solid.

Hrisoula smiled showing her new gray teeth while she crocheted. "My hands are too big for such fine work," she said with no envy. Hrisoula often recited her good fortune in serving the *kyria*, who was educated and had taught embroidery in a girls' school for the daughters of rich Jews, almost all of them furriers.

Emilia's *kyria* turned irritable and tearful, and Emilia knew she could not leave in the evening to enjoy herself while her mistress was unhappy. On those nights bile rose to her throat as she thought of herself, a stranger living with strangers whose blunted voices came through the wall: the man, who picked his nose, spat morning throat clearings into handkerchiefs for Anastasia to wash; the woman dropped soiled drawers in a puddle on the floor; their nighttime urine swished in the white pottery pail painted with pink roses as she carried it down the back stairs; the musty clothes that came off the strange man's body hung on the coat stand.

She dreamed one night of the *kyria* screaming, the *kyrios* shouting. In the morning a midwife was in the house; she walked sprightly from the kitchen to the *kyria*'s bedroom with cups of camomile tea and broth kept simmering on the brazier. The midwife gave Emilia orders not to go into the *kyria*'s room. "She's had a miscarriage and she's of a nervous constitution anyway."

In the evening chestnut vendors cried out on the street. The servant girls were laughing on the balcony below among pots of basil, marigolds, and oleander. Emilia pined to be with them, to hear their voices, to be with people. The small room with the red carpet drew her night after night. She thought someone she knew would be standing there. The room was always empty, and she stood staring at the familiar looking carpet. One night she knelt with a lamp in her hand and passed her palm across the carpet until she came to a round deep burn. Her father's pipe had fallen there. He had called, but by the time Anna had run into the room the burning tobacco had made the hole. She caressed the burn, thinking, "Now strangers have my family's possessions."

Each night from then on she found an excuse to enter the small room. It was ten days before she felt it was safe to meet with the servant girls again. She wanted to tell Hrisoula about the carpet, but it was shameful to talk about personal matters as Koula did. She knew Hrisoula's *kyria* could explain it to her, but to talk about her mistress! Be disloyal! Even risk being beaten by her if she found out!

The girls had missed her, they said. "We couldn't tell you our dreams and find out what they meant."

A year later the *kyrios* announced at the dinner table that they would be moving to the City. The *kyria* smiled to herself, and the *kyrios* pulled down his vest as he did whenever he was pleased with himself. Emilia told the servant girls that evening. "Constantinople!" Koula squealed and Hrisoula made the sign of the cross. "Our holy City," she said. "Some day it will be Greek again and in Ayia Sophia the Orthodox liturgy will be heard."

Koula hugged her arms and rocked back and forth moaning over Emilia's good fate. Nitsa burst into tears and ran out of the room. Two days later she disappeared, and Hrisoula said her *kyria* had been told that she was pregnant. Koula maintained Nitsa's *kyrios* was the culprit; she had seen the two of them on the stairs one day, and he had a look in his eyes.

Emilia remembered seeing Nitsa's *kyrios* in the gloom by the privies saying something to her. They stepped away when they saw her, and the *kyrios* said in a loud voice, "Be sure to finish your work in the kitchen," a strange order reserved for mistresses.

Koula said she expected Nitsa's brothers would kill her and wished they would kill the *kyrios* also; Hrisoula hoped Nitsa had gone to a nunnery to dedicate herself and her child for the rest of their lives to the service of God. Koula scoffed: Nitsa would put the baby on the steps of an orphanage and take to the streets.

Yet Nitsa's master, the seducer, came and went as before. Behind their apartment door his wife hissed and screamed. To the neighbors she smiled as always and complained of a cold in the head. The neighbors brought teas made from boiled herbs and wine simmered with cloves. The gray *kyria* offered to cup her and had the water glasses heated and ready to place on her plump back when *Kyria* Karagheorghiou suddenly got up from her bed and hurried out of the room.

When Emilia met Nitsa's *kyrios* on the stairs, she looked him in the eye and said in a hard voice, "Good day, Kyrie Karagheorghiou," so that no one could say she had not greeted him properly.

Hrisoula's *kyria* gave a party for Emilia and a present of six white and blue satin ribbons, the colors of the Greek flag. Koula gave her a small comb and Hrisoula a little blue and gold money purse she had embroidered.

Emilia said goodbye to them on a Sunday evening. Early the next day they got into a carriage that would take them a hundred miles and more toward Bulgaria. Emilia felt cold at the word *Bul-*

garia—the Bulgarians hated the Greeks as much as the Turks did. "God is giving light," the *kyria* said and crossed herself as dawn fell over the plain of thyme.

Emilia looked to the right of the road. Somewhere farther toward the sea, she thought, was her village. She gazed until her neck hurt. All the while, the *kyrios* was explaining to the *kyria*, like a schoolmaster, the history of the Orient Express that they would board near Adrianople for Constantinople. The tobacco he smoked was grown in Adrianople.

II

Far ahead of Pericles Amarantos and Spyros Papachristos,
Yoryis followed the almost dry riverbed. With a branch stripped of
twigs, he slashed at bushes and bracken to keep his suit from being
snagged. When the sun grew hot, he took off his coat, folded it,
and draped it around the crook of his elbow. From time to time he
sat on a rock and scraped the mud off his shoes. After several hours,
he came upon a young, ragged charcoal maker. They sat under a
plane tree, Yoryis on his bundle, and shared their food. The charcoal maker devoured Yoryis's lamb, clutching it with grimy hands;
and with relish Yoryis ate the stranger's small, bruised apricots,
obviously picked off the ground. "Where you going?" the charcoal
maker said, when nothing remained to be eaten. He spoke the Roumeliot dialect, as thick and clipped as the speech of the nomad
Vlachs.

"Ameriki."

The ancient, "Ach," came from the stranger.

They parted, raising their hands in two-fingered salute. Yoryis
picked up his bundle, coat, and stick while the charcoal maker
gazed at him with envy. "Go well," the stranger said at the last
moment.

In mid-afternoon Yoryis, with Pericles and Spyros close behind,
arrived in Andirion, to the narrow gulf separating Roumeli, central
Greece, and the Peloponnesos. Boats and caiques, white sails
against the blue sky, were bouncing over the churned-up water

toward Rion. In them sat young men, some of them mustached, all holding bundles and homespun bags, their eyes on the opposite shore. Other boats and caiques were returning to Andirion, emptied of passengers. Yoryis motioned Pericles and Spyros into the first caique that reached them and gave an old boatman his ten *lepta* fare. He sat on his bundle, folded his coat over his arm, and fingered the lining where his money was sewn.

Two brothers of about fourteen and sixteen years of age and their old father in white kilts, who took a long time to extract the fare from a pouch, took places about Yoryis. Two older young men holding new cardboard valises got into the boat hastily, causing it to sway. They stared at Yoryis and the other occupants.

The boys chattered, amazed eyes darting here and there; they had never gone beyond their mountain village before. "Plug it!" their morose father barked at intervals.

The two young men sat, pensive, frowning. A greenish cast illuminated their faces, and the skin was black under their eyes. The boys' father pulled on his thick gray mustache and watched the young men with cold eyes. As they headed into the mass of boats and buzzing humanity on the shore, the old man said, "Listen to me, lads, you're not going to fool the officials and you don't have enough money to fill their pockets. And if by some miracle you get to Ameriki, one glance and they'll see the malaria burning you up. So save your precious bit of money. Go back to your little mothers."

The young men did not move, only looked at the old man with narrowed eyes. Yoryis kept his left hand with its stub of finger under his coat. Reaching the shore, he jumped out, ignoring the carriage drivers who called out their fares for the long walk to the port of Patras. With Pericles and Spyros, he joined the straggling line of men walking to save a few coins. Fear grew in him as he walked: for a foolish act when he was a boy, he could be denied passage.

The wharf teemed with emigrants: men sitting at small tables exchanging Greek money for American; *hamalidhes*, the human beasts of burden, bent over with bales, trunks, and boxes on their backs; tradesmen shouting their wares; men cooking entrails, fish, bits of meat, and chestnuts over smoking charcoal in braziers. The smell of cheap olive oil, of fat sputtering on charcoal rose with blue fumes to hang thickly over the wharf.

Crammed with hundreds of emigrants into a barren room, Yoryis stood for hours to show the document secured by the mayor of Klepá and was then examined by a small fastidious doctor who made no comment on his missing finger. Yoryis hurried out lest the doctor should call him back. He stood on the wharf looking at the ships coming into the gulf where they anchored at a distance; he scrutinized each boatload of arrivals being rowed to shore. As time passed and the sun went down, he became afraid he would miss his ship and have to take another the following day. Pericles and Spyros also looked anxiously across the water and then left to find food. Toward evening the ship from Corfu entered the gulf, and Yoryis saw his tall, thin father getting into a boat. As the boat neared, his father nodded solemnly to acknowledge that he had seen him. The judge's face was pale from a recent attack of asthma, and he held his shoulders turned inward.

They shook hands, quickly made their way to the ticket agent, and bought Yoryis a third-class ticket. The judge then wound through the crowd to a seafront restaurant where they sat inside, away from drafts. The meal was a banquet: mullet, bread, and wine and sliced cucumbers, tomatoes, and onions in olive oil and vinegar. The judge and Yoryis ate with ravenous hunger.

When they finished, the judge took out his pocket watch, laid it on the table, and asked questions about the family and the village. "Is it time?" Yoryis interrupted. They walked out and stood on the wharf where boats were tied, ready to take passengers to the Italian-Austrian ship bound for Naples. The judge looked from side to side anxiously. His eyeglasses clouded. "Don't go! I'll never see you again!" He took off his glasses and wiped them. Tears flowed from his ruined, peering eyes. "Don't go!"

Yoryis shook his head. "In three years, five at the most, I'll be back."

The tears ran into the judge's mustache as he emptied his narrow leather purse into Yoryis's palm. With the money sewed in his coat lining and the coins in his palm, Yoryis quickly calculated that he had the equivalent of twenty-three American dollars, three dollars above the twenty dollars "show money" United States officials usually required for admission. He exchanged the drachmas at the nearest moneychanger's table, glaring at the man who quickly counted out the correct number of dollars.

The judge and Yoryis shook hands. Yoryis sat facing the great ship and did not look back as the crowded boat swayed over the waters. The boat was maneuvered parallel to the side of the ship, and Yoryis climbed up the ladder. His feet firmly on board, he turned to the huddle on the wharf. His father in his worn suit was looking across the water. They lifted their hands to each other.

In Naples the passengers were forced to wait for one of the larger ships steaming back and forth over the Atlantic. For a week Yoryis, Pericles, and Spyros were jammed with twenty or more boys and men in one of many rooming houses, in a stink of unwashed bodies. Harried men and women servants brought food in pails which they ladled onto tin plates. It was odd food—clams mixed with spaghetti, snails, soups made with a peculiar kind of meat, neither goat nor lamb. In the waterfront waiting room the Greeks searched each other out, sat in circles in the odor of sweat, urine, tobacco, and flesh and talked of their villages, families, and what they had heard about America. Men now, away from their families, they decided to grow mustaches. They speculated over the polyglot people swarming about. A group of Serbians wore karakul caps; two of their women with scarves tied about their blonde hair sat a little apart from them, their hands on possessions tied in sheets. The Greeks eyed and were eyed by several Bulgarians, traditional enemies even though they were both Orthodox. More Italians were in the hall than any other emigrants, some with wives and crying babies. Enemies also, they had split the True Church; they revered their pope as if he were Jesus. All, except Yoryis, who had seen Negroes in Alexandria, were amazed at the few blacks sitting together, red fezes on their heads. The young Greeks wondered if the Syrians and Armenians were clansmen of the gypsies who wandered through the mountains and valleys of Greece to play clarinets, flutes, bagpipes, and drums at weddings and baptisms and to steal a few sheep at every opportunity.

When a ship arrived from America, they pushed aboard into three weeks of fetid, flea-bitten misery. With each heaving of the great ship, a queasy, bone-sapping nausea brought bile up Yoryis's throat. It stifled his panic over the dangerous examination awaiting at Castle Garden. He ate bread when he could eat anything at all; the sight of strange meat in gray juices was repugnant, and its smell brought new surges of nausea. After a week the sickness abated somewhat, and Yoryis climbed to the deck and sat with a company of Greeks. A sixteen-year-old Peloponnesian played a *laouto* and sang songs of *xenetia*, songs of exile in far-off places. One song was centuries old, sung from the time the Turks swept through Greece and a vanguard of Greeks fled to Italy, pining for Greek earth:

> *In foreign lands wear black*
> *That your clothes match the burning in*
> *your heart.*

The boy wept; others wiped their eyes. Then, animated, they began talking about America. The Peloponnesian showed again a picture of three cousins who would meet him in Ellis Island: three young men wearing white hats, pants, and shirts against a painted backdrop of a baronial house and grounds. "See, they don't grow mustaches in Ameriki," he said. A week before the ship reached Ellis Island, Yoryis, his village friends, and the other Greeks shaved off their incipient mustaches.

After the Peloponnesian had wrapped his *laouto* in a piece of gray homespun, the Greeks sat in an island of silence amid the polyglot cacophony. Then they blurted out their worries: "Just because he had a few sores on his head, this man from my village was turned back!" "We better watch ourselves not to catch cold. They'll send us back. Say we have tuberculosis. It's happened!"

They conjectured over bribes and how they would know into whose palm to put their coins. The talk grew frenzied. Their heritage of a thousand and more years of Byzantine past, of Turkish rule spilled out: Would the satraps take all their money? They cautioned each other to hide it, although they all had their money skillfully sewn into waistbands or the linings of their coats by black-cowled mothers and grandmothers whose lips had moved without stop, cautioning them to take care, to be ever watchful, to have four eyes, already seeing their men-children pounced upon and tricked by wily men, the *keratadhes*, the horned ones, and led, entranced, by bewitching women—Nereids in disguise. America was full of them.

One of the men aboard ship was called Grivas. Short-legged and big-shouldered, he was also nineteen and running away from army duty. Yoryis thought he had found a relative, but the Peloponnesian was not of the old guerrilla clan. His grandfather's right arm had been cut off as had Grivas's son Demetrakis's. From then on people took to calling him Grivas, and the family name was no longer used. Grivas often brought out a letter from a villager and read again instructions to the Tripolis Coffeehouse in New York.

The ship entered the harbor on a foggy day, the Statue of Liberty rising awesomely, the immigrants cheering. The throng moved down the gangplank with their assorted belongings, babies, and children. Yoryis stood in a line of men to take a shower, to have kerosene rubbed in his hair, and to have his clothes sprayed with a horrible liquid. He approached the American doctor with pounding heart, but the bald, mustached man saw his hand and said nothing. He passed through.

At a cubicle an officious Greek seated at a desk spoke to him in terse *katharevousa*, the purist language, looked at his letter from the tailor in Pawtucket, Rhode Island, and sent him on with a tag to tie in the lapel of his coat. "I've written your name down as *George*. Do you hear?"

A young Greek led him, Pericles, and Spyros through a buzzing crowd to a counter and told them to give a half-dollar for a paper bag of food. The young man pointed toward a small steamer. Yoryis boarded it looking around for Grivas, the Peloponnesian, but he had lost him. Packed tightly into the steamer, the mass of people gazed, now subdued, at the great Statue of Liberty and the tall gray buildings rising into the fog.

The steamer docked. A man in uniform read each immigrant's lapel tag and pointed in various directions. Yoryis followed the man's pointed finger to a line of people buying railroad tickets. Pericles and Spyros ran to keep up with him. When Yoryis reached the window, a man wearing a green eyeshade glanced at his tag, sold him a ticket, and pointed to doors through which people were hurrying. At the doors a man in uniform looked at his ticket and pointed to another uniformed man standing outside a train with steam hissing through black wheels. Yoryis hurried to the man who directed him to another track and to another uniformed man.

Then he boarded a coach filled with screeching, wild-eyed immigrants clutching bundles and bags, straw or canvas suitcases, one or two of them with small, wooden-slatted trunks at their feet. Babies screamed. He found a seat in the middle of the coach; Pericles and Spyros sat in the back. Almost an hour later the train jerked out of the station. Soon it was moving slowly past blackened brick buildings with large chimneys expelling dark gray smoke, and past rows of smudged brick and frame houses, and finally into hilly farmland. Only then did he think of the humiliation of the shower rooms and the smells of the kerosene and the fumigation, of the ridiculous Greek at the desk speaking the purist to villagers. Later, he opened the paper bag and examined the strange lunch of white bread, rubbery orange cheese, and a new kind of suspicious meat, its smell revolting. He ate the bread. He had eaten white bread in the house of his mother's cousin where he had been sent for the schooling his pride rejected. The bread reassured him: in America even the poor did not have to eat coarse corn or black bread.

Just before each stop a fat uniformed man looked at the tags on the immigrants' clothes and herded several at a time to the front of the car. Through the dirty window Yoryis looked down at the crowd of people waiting on the station platform, craning their heads, and wondered what he would do if the tailor was not there to meet them. He was. A nervous little man, he said he had found work for them in a factory that manufactured screws. At the back of the tailor's shop in a dim, dank room, Yoryis was given a cot alongside another newly arrived Greek, Zacharias from Messolonghi. On a small coal stove, the tailor kept a pan of dried beans or lentils simmering. Yoryis carefully hung his suit on nails driven into posts in the unfinished walls, the old wood lath showing, and put on his everyday pants and shirt.

With food bought from a Greek grocer several stores down—bread, feta, and olives in paper sacks—Yoryis, Pericles, Spyros, and Zacharias, lanky and blue-eyed, walked through the iron gates of a blackened brick building and into the whine of machinery driven by that miracle, electricity. At the door they gave notes from the tailor to a Greek interpreter who explained what they were to do and left them. With a horrendous clatter in their ears, they fed long rods of brass into small holes in the machines. Ten hours later a whistle sounded, and moving along with a crowd of workers, they escaped into a cool evening.

A roar stopped them, but they were pushed roughly from behind. Outside the gates a crowd of men, women, and children were shouting, screaming, and shaking their fists. The workers ran, holding their hands about their heads to protect them from flying rocks. Yoryis and his friends streaked through the streets and into the heart of Greek Town. Gasping for breath, they slowed and looked at each other in bewilderment, for all in the mob were *xeni* like themselves—Italians, Poles, Slavs.

The tailor explained what strikes and scabs were. Sitting near the window to catch the light, his fingers working rapidly, he told them he had got their jobs through a Greek labor agent who was proving his worth to the factory by recruiting Greeks as scabs. "Otherwise you would have had to pay for the job," he said. "And if you stay on after the trouble is over, you'll have to pay him."

Yoryis was astonished that American workers had the effrontery, the courage to demand rights of employers. After eating a bowl of lentils, the four walked past Greek stores selling the dried fish, Turkish coffee, and olive oil of the fatherland, past restaurants where men were huddled over their plates, and to the Roumeliot coffeehouse.

The labor agent, sitting near the window smoking a *nargileh*, was not much older than Yoryis. A diamond glinted on his little finger, the nail long to show he did not work with his hands. They went inside and ordered a demitasse of coffee from a sad-faced boy. Men older than the labor agent came with cap in hand to ask for work. A dish towel tied around his waist, the *kafetzis* welcomed the newcomers and called others from their card games and *tavli*, backgammon, to introduce them. The men were laughing, in good spirits because at last they all had jobs at the screw factory. For protection they would meet in the mornings at the coffeehouse and go to work in a body.

On the fourth day, Yoryis, Zack, Pericles, and Spyros went to the factory and collected their wages. The Greek interpreter tried to convince them to stay. "We didn't come to Ameriki to get killed over a few dollars," Yoryis said. At the coffeehouse men off shift clustered about them and advised them to return to New York; sneak into the Pawtuckett rail yards around six in the evening when the detectives got careless and gathered at the lunch counter in the station; find an empty freight car; and, if caught, allow themselves to be arrested and pay the vagrancy fine. "The railroad *detectives*," they spoke the word in English, "are Ameriki's Turks, with their fingers on the trigger." When the freight train slowed to enter the New York rail yards, they should jump off to avoid the swarm of detectives stationed everywhere. They should walk until they found the nearest policeman and say, "Greek Town?" He would point the way.

12

In New York they walked the cobbled streets in a freezing winter, the year of the panic of 1907 when even Americans could not find work. Neither Yoryis, Zack, Pericles, nor Spyros had an overcoat. They folded newspapers over their chests and backs to protect their lungs and wore their homespun stockings, one on top of the other, their two pairs of pants, their caps pulled as far over their ears as they would go, and walked. At the back doors of restaurants and stores they knocked, made signs with their hands, jumped out of the way of pails of dirty water and garbage, learned what the words *dirty foreigners* and *dirty Greeks* meant. They met other *patriotes,* also walking, searching, and like them eating dried beans to stop the gnaw of hunger. "Romaios are you?" they asked, stopping each other on the streets.

In the evenings they went to the Roumeliot Coffeehouse. Priests, labor agents, and other *patriotes* wrote their names in little black notebooks and on the backs of envelopes. At night they slept at the ice cream tables, their heads resting on their bent arms, their belongings under the chairs, Yoryis's still tied in his mother's red and white *kelimi.*

In the Atlantis Book Store in Greek Town they bought small, gilt-edged, Greek–American dictionaries and studied them while *nargilehs* bubbled and waiters with trays of Turkish coffee held high skirted shouting men who flailed the air as they upheld factions in Greek politics. "Listen! Listen!" they demanded, and read from the royalist *Atlantis* newspaper published in New York.

Greece was mired in bankruptcy, yet the young men shouted for its army to fight the Turks again under the old banner of the Great Idea, the recovery of their centuries-lost lands. "The City! The City! We must win back our holy City! Constantinople, Ayia Sophia must be Greek once more!"

"We're starving and they're talking about fighting the Turks," Zack complained.

Yoryis quoted the proverb, "'What are fifteen whacks on someone else's ass?'"

One evening the men were clustered about a portly, red-cheeked priest, sitting regally in black robes and tall priest's hat. "Yoryi!" The *kafetzis* beckoned him from the door. "Father," the coffeehouse owner said, "this is Yoryis Zisimopoulos from your part of the country."

The priest stopped smiling, slowly raised his hand to his gray black beard, and Yoryis knew he was looking at the abbot over whom a young mother had been driven out of a neighboring village to starve to death. With a hasty nod, the priest got up and hurried to the door. "A Bad Hour to you!" Yoryis called after him.

The *kafetzis* and the young men lashed at Yoryis. "No! Lies! He's a good priest. He's done so much good here!"

Yoryis, Zack, Pericles, and Spyros rented a small stable for six dollars a month and slept in the stalls, making small fires to warm their frostbitten hands and feet. Almost every day Yoryis stopped at the Tripolis Coffeehouse to see if Grivas had sent him a letter. Grivas was working on a railroad gang somewhere in the West— Ghouest, the dictionary pronounced it. One morning as Yoryis pulled on his frozen shoes, they broke into pieces. He and Zack then took turns going out to look for work wearing Zack's shoes. They were too small for Yoryis.

In January Yoryis found a job washing dishes in the Regis Hotel for ten hours a day. As part of his dollar-a-day wages he was allowed as much soup and bread as he wanted. With his first money he bought, not an overcoat, but a "six brothers," a gun he could clutch as he walked through black, silent streets. He would keep a gun pushed behind his belt until he was eighty. The others found a job of sorts. In return for a room above a saloon they and Yoryis were to run at the sound of a broomstick thumping on the ceiling below to break up fights.

In February a Greek labor agent came to the Roumeliot Coffeehouse to sign up men for a railroad gang in Iowa. They each gave the agent ten dollars from their first wages. The next day they were on a train coach, traveling on a railroad pass. They called across the aisles to each other, jubilant. They were finally going to the America they had heard about, finally would be sending money to their parents for their sisters' dowries. A few Americans, smoking cigars, looked on with amusement and made comments to each other.

The train stopped on a flat, snowy plain of dried grass. A line of railroad cars, wooden slatted with one door and three windows each, stood on a siding. An American railroad gang was quartered in them. The Greeks were housed in both railroad cars and tents. Those not housed in tents slept on platforms on either end of each car and cooked and ate in the center of it. A Greek interpreter slept on a cot in one of the cars. He wore a suit, tie, and rubber boots.

The men were set to changing rails from narrow to standard gauge, following directions the interpreter relayed from the Irish foreman. With crowbars they lifted up the old rails and wooden ties and carried them to one side. They leveled the roadbed, placed oiled ties on top, and on these the rails. Those who volunteered to pound in the spikes with sledgehammers were paid an extra ten cents a day. Yoryis took up a sledge. The ring of hundreds of sledges on steel pinged through the cold air and the rails hummed over the earth.

The Greeks in each car took turns cooking. One of the older men, Vasilis, showed Yoryis's group how to bake bread. He dug a hole in the side of a dip in the ground, filled it with bits of paper and twigs, lighted them, and covered the opening with a piece of rusted metal. When the twigs had burned to ashes, he threw in a ball of dough and replaced the metal sheet. The men ate the bread, ashes and all, along with the daily stew of meat and potatoes that Vasilis taught them to cook. In their quarters they grumbled against the Americans who had a cook and one entire railroad car in which he prepared their food, another car set with tables and benches for eating, and other cars fitted with bunk beds. At night

145

the Greeks played cards, talked, sometimes sang old *kleft* songs, and then went to bed, those living in tents reluctantly. Yoryis and his friends took turns sleeping in a tent. Within a month they had almost reached Des Moines.

When the paymaster arrived with their wages, the labor agent was on hand to take the ten-dollar commission from Yoryis and his friends. The entire gang of Greeks walked along the tracks to the city, while several handcars passed them, filled with American workers, the Greek labor agent and the interpreter on one of them. The interpreter met them at the post office and charged them a dollar each to make out money orders for their families. Yoryis sent fifteen of his remaining twenty dollars to his father.

The men then followed the interpreter to a coffeehouse where several Greeks who worked at the railroad roundhouse invited them to come to their *bekiariko,* bachelor house, for dinner. Most of the men went off to a house of prostitution, a nattily dressed pimp leading them. Carrying bottles of American beer, sacks of potatoes, and a lamb that cost them a dollar fifty, Yoryis and the others walked to the nearby bachelor house of four rooms with bare wooden floors, several cots, a table, and assorted chairs. When the men realized there were thirteen of them, one of the bachelors went off to bring back another guest to insure against bad luck.

In the backyard the lamb roasted on a spit. Inside, the men prepared the potatoes, sliced a cabbage coarsely and doused it with olive oil and vinegar. Throughout the night they ate, drank, sang, and were interrupted at four o'clock in the morning by officers who marched them to the police station where they were fined five dollars each for disturbing the peace. Yoryis and Zack looked at each other, taken aback; they were left with only a few coins in their pockets.

At the railroad camp the interpreter told the men he was leaving for Kansas City and would have work for them there. The American gang would finish changing the rails. Most of the men went with the interpreter to take a coach to Kansas City. Yoryis, Zack, Pericles, and Spyros climbed a freight. "How will we know when we get there?" Yoryis asked.

146

"Open the door and the smell will tell you," the interpreter answered.

Even before reaching the Kansas City rail yards, the stink of the stockyards penetrated the freight car. While the train slowed and came to a stop, Yoryis looked through a slit in the doors. Railroad detectives were walking around with billy clubs in their hands, guns in holsters. The freight rumbled on and arrived the next day in Oklahoma City. Near the rail yards outside a decrepit employment agency, they came face to face with two countrymen. "Romaioi are you?" Yoryis asked them.

They nodded gleefully. The men were from Crete, one short, the other thin, both with curled-up mustaches. They had just signed on to dig a sewer and were living in a shack in the black section of town. "Better come with us. There's no work anywhere else," they said.

The two-room shack was empty except for an old coal stove and a battered washtub; old newspapers covered the windows. In the backyard was a water pump; one of the Cretans worked the handle while the other washed a panful of intestines he had scavenged from a slaughterhouse. After cutting the intestines into pieces with a pocketknife, Andonis, the short Cretan, put the pan on to boil. "If it weren't for the slaughterhouse garbage," he said, "we'd have croaked long ago." They sat on the floor to eat, the pot in the center, and dipped into it with misshapen spoons.

Early the next morning, they began digging with a gang of blacks who joked and laughed at them. The gang worked on two platforms to dig a twenty-foot-deep trench. Those on the lower platform, Yoryis among them, shoveled the dirt up to the top platform; the workers there threw it out of the trench. Some of the dirt fell back on the men below. Seepings from the old sewer had moistened the earth, and the foul smell enveloped them within the walls of the trench. That night the men sat on the splintered floor of the shack, pulled apart a loaf of bread each, and lay down to sleep with their clothes on. "We came off the ship with fleas," Andonis said. "We'll be scratching again." Yoryis covered himself with his mother's red and white *kelimi*.

At the end of the week, ashamed of their odor, they went to a nearby grocery store, bought soap, and began heating water in the washtub. They took turns boiling more water, washing their hair, bathing, and left their dank, wretched clothes on the floor to rot. Yoryis smelled the *kelimi* and dropped it on the floor also. The men gathered at the window, pulled off the newspapers, and talked of what they should do. A few blacks passing by on the dirt street looked at them. The Cretans had village friends working in the southern Colorado coal mines and mulled over going there. Yoryis tried to convince them to go to Chicago's Halsted Street where Greek labor agents circulated.

As they talked, an old black came down the street, walking slowly, one hand clutching at his chest. A white policeman sauntered by and said something to the man who continued walking. The policeman took out his pistol, aimed, and shot, and the old man fell to the sidewalk. Blood ran beneath him.

The policeman stood looking down on the black. People ran out and gazed at the dead man. "Either the black didn't see him or didn't hear him," Andonis said. "The law in this part of the country says if a black doesn't resist, the white man is fined five dollars. If he resists, he isn't fined anything. Horned ones!"

In Chicago Yoryis wrote to the Tripolis Coffeehouse in New York, asking if a letter had come for him from Grivas. Within a week he received a two-month-old letter with a railroad coach ticket to Pueblo, Colorado, where Grivas had found work in the steel mill of the Colorado Fuel and Iron Company. Pericles and Spyros spent all they had on coach tickets for themselves.

When they arrived in the arid terrain of sagebrush and scrub oak, much like the thyme and holy oak of Greece, there was no work. An Italian labor agent, who traveled regularly to Italy at the company's expense, had just returned with a gang of peasants. Such contract labor was illegal, but bribes to immigration officials allowed it.

Pueblo swarmed with Greeks. They had recently built a small church of red brick where the priest, black bearded, his long hair twisted into a knot at the back, conducted liturgies on Sunday, alone. The men went to church on Christmas, Easter, the Kimisis of

148

Pueblo, 1908. The first picture sent back to the village. Yoryis seated right. "In between his foragings for work he lives with Grivas and five other Greeks in a chicken coop surviving on beans and lentils."

the Virgin on August 15, on their name days, and for the liturgy of the dead when one of their *patriotes* was killed. Holy Week, Easter, and his name day came and went, and Yoryis, scouring for work in Pueblo and in the coal towns south, had not attended church once.

In between his foragings for work, he lived with Grivas, Pericles, Spyros, and three other Greeks in a chicken coop and lived on beans and lentils. A Greek butcher told them to charge a piece of meat at least for Sundays, but they owed him almost twenty dollars and refused. Only Grivas had work at a dollar seventy-five cents for a ten-hour day. "I'm well off," he said. "The Romaioi who have jobs are getting fifty cents a day. In Greece I made charcoal six days a week, sixteen hours a day for two dollars a month."

To heat the coop the men lay in wait on the outskirts of town where freights bringing coal for the mill's furnaces slowed around a big curve. With agile jumps the men were up, on the cars, and throwing down lumps of coal. Practice increased their skill until by the time the engine completed the curve and picked up speed, enough coal was strewn at the side of the tracks to last several days. One of the men had swept floors in a saloon for a time and had learned a few American words. He stood off at a distance from the tracks and shouted at enraged firemen and engineers, "Bastards! Sonabitch! Whorelicker!" and was rewarded with a shower of coal. Having spent his early years tending goats on mountains and jumping from boulder to boulder, he leaped expertly out of the path of the speeding coal with triumphant jeers.

At the mill overhead vats of molten steel snapped a cable and turned, spilling on the men working below. Piercing screams, and white flesh with blackened skin lay grotesque, arms, legs, skulls, consumed. At the screeching of the whistle, Yoryis and his friends rushed to take the jobs of the dead, but hundreds of Italians, Greeks, and Slavs were milling about the company offices ahead of them.

They returned to the chicken coop. Grivas was huddled on his improvised bed. His face was swollen with black pocks oozing blood from the splatter of the liquid steel. The men pooled their money, and Yoryis ran to a saloon for a pint of American whiskey that would "cut the pain." One of the men, remembering a village midwife's remedy, broke eggs into a hot frying pan, burned them to a black powder, and covered the wounded flesh.

Grivas did not go back to the mill. He paced the dirt floor of the coop, making the sign of the cross, and mumbling. He joined the priest in the empty church, lighted candles to the All–Holy and Christ and made a *tama* to them for having saved his life: he would build a wayfarers' church to Prophet Elias on the mountain slope beyond his village.

Yoryis and a Serb he met in the coffeehouse decided to hold up the mill's paymaster. On payday they walked to his office; at the door they stopped, looked at each other, and without a word turned back.

Pericles Amarantos and Spyros returned to Chicago's Greek Town on Halsted Street to look for labor agents. A week later Yoryis and Grivas met the black-robed, black-hatted priest and a labor agent on the street, They gave the agent all but fifty cents of their silver, caught a freight, and traveled one hundred seventy-five miles out of Pueblo to work on a steel gang.

When they reached the few bunk cars and tents in a wilderness of sagebrush, the American foreman said he had not asked for men. It was night. They were hungry and shivering from the desert cold. While they walked up and down and stamped their stinging feet, the steel gang ate under hanging kerosene lanterns inside one of the railroad cars.

Hours later a freight came by, slowing down while bundles and heavy gunnysacks were thrown out. Yoryis and Grivas ran over the ties, grabbed onto a flatbed car stacked with enormous culvert pipes, and climbed aboard. Crawling inside one, they made a small fire with every bit of paper in their pockets. The wisp of flame barely warmed their stiff fingers and was gone. After hours of excruciating pain they got out, their feet like wood, into strange rail yards, not Pueblo's where they knew a few countrymen. "Greek Town?" they asked the ticket agent who yanked his thumb to his right. In a Denver coffeehouse, Angelos Raekos, a Roumeliot, jumped up at the sight of them and took them to a Greek baker. Every day the baker cooked a huge pot of food for hungry, wandering Greeks.

Again they frequented coffeehouses. Employment agencies had few signs chalked on blackboards: cowboys, cooks on ranches. The labor agents brushed them aside; their labor gangs were filled.

151

It was Holy Week and in the bachelor houses, in the *bekiarika*, and in Greek restaurants, men were cooking the lenten foods of beans, lentils, and greens, the regular food for most of them anyway. Well-dressed labor agents, cardplayers, and the "flesh merchants," who brought over village boys and indentured them for years in shoeshine parlors, ate meat openly, as if Holy Week could only be celebrated in *patridha*, the fatherland.

On Great Friday as Yoryis left the church, Raekos introduced him to a white-haired man. "He's from a good family," Raekos said. As they shook hands, the old man put something in Yoryis's suit pocket. It was a five-dollar gold piece that kept him and Grivas fed for a month.

Roumeliots sent them to Greek foremen of section gangs in Colorado Springs, Cripple Creek, and Glenwood Springs. While working near Glenwood Springs, they were approached by a tax collector who demanded three dollars from each of them for a head tax. They had been warned by *patriotes* of this harassment of immigrants. Three dollars were almost a week's wages; they refused to pay it. Before the tax collector had time to return with the sheriff, they made arrangements with the paymaster to send their checks to Leadville and caught a freight to avoid that worse harassment, jail on vagrancy charges.

They arrived in Leadville on a gray, rainy evening. No work and no Greeks were to be found. They went in and out of the post office, in and out of the depot for a moment's warmth. They tried to sit on the benches of the depot, but railroad detectives sent them out. When the detectives wandered off momentarily, they hurried in for a second or two and out again into the deepening cold.

For three days they asked at the post office for their pay. They had not eaten since they left Glenwood Springs. At night they went into the snow-dusted sagebrush and built small fires, taking turns trying to sleep and guarding each other. On the fourth day their pay came. With a loaf of bread each, they got on a boxcar going to Salt Lake City to find the labor agent Skliris. At four stops they were discovered by railroad detectives and forced off. Three days later they arrived in Salt Lake City and walked into the Greek section of town that surrounded the rail yards. Hundreds of young men were in the coffeehouses looking for work, waiting for labor agents.

The labor agents were henchmen for Leonidas Skliris, whom the Americans called the "Czar of the Greeks." Besides his labor agency and office for the Austro–Italian steamship lines in the heart of Greek Town, he owned considerable stock in metal mines. Hardly any of the laborers had ever seen him. He had come to Salt Lake City just before the turn of the century; and although he was not much older than the wandering Greeks, he had made pacts with railroads and their coal companies and with copper mines to supply them with immigrant Greek labor. Rich and powerful, Skliris lived in an American hotel beyond Greek Town. After a Cretan had tried to kill him, several Greeks who took care of his hiring and payroll sat at desks in front of his closed office door.

In the Cretan coffeehouses, the Paradise and the Open Heart, Yoryis asked if anyone knew the Cretans he had met on the Oklahoma sewer gang. "They've passed through," someone said. It was an expression Yoryis would hear regularly in the next quarter of a century. Others told them of a Roumeliot from his own mountains who worked on a Denver and Rio Grande Western section gang.

They hurried south of the yards to the railroad cars the company allowed their laborers to live in during the two winter months when it was impossible to work. Yoryis knocked on the door of the second car. It opened and stocky, wide-faced Nikos Mouyias of Upper Klepá stood there. The two slapped each other on the shoulders, shook hands. "Moré! Ti hambaria?"—You! What do you know?— Nikos shouted in thick Roumeliot dialect. Yoryis, who did not ordinarily speak the dialect, answered in kind, laughing at the familiar red face and benevolent smile.

Nikos invited them to sleep on the platforms in the car along with himself and four others. Out of money, he had not kept enough for himself and had sent too much to his parents. Yoryis was silent with shame.

And that is how it was: the young men sending back money from America to provide dowries and help to parents; schooling for younger brothers raised the quality of life there, and those just being born and those who would come after would never know the horrible, debasing poverty that had sent the young immigrants into voluntary exile. The south Europeans sent more than the north Europeans, the Greeks most of all.

In the morning Nikos walked to the outskirts of the city and dug up dandelion greens on the edges of fields and irrigation canals. The Greek restaurants paid him twenty-five cents a gunnysack. Others were also out digging: Serbs, Bulgarians, Italians, all uprooting the spring delicacies that the whole of the Balkan and Mediterranean people throughout the centuries, wan and yellow-skinned from their winter diet of corn bread and beans, awaited with festive expectation.

Except for a sixteen-year-old, the men went through Greek Town every morning in search of rumors of work. The young man lay on a cot next to the coal stove, his knees drawn up. Although he had drunk a quart bottle of American medicine, he had stopped eating. He strangled with a coughing that left him blue in the face and his shirt soaked with sweat. Yoryis looked at the bottle of medicine. The label was printed with a skull and crossbones.

Nikos returned from a Greek restaurant, his ruddy face alight with smiles. A restaurant had allowed him to wash a sack of dandelion greens which he put on to boil. "This will fix you up," he told the boy turned toward the wall, "young dandelions and plenty of olive oil and vinegar." He brought news that a Greek woman had just arrived and was living in the mill town of Magna fifteen miles west. She was a midwife and had used folk cures to save the leg of a worker whose knee had been crushed. His friends spirited him away before the company doctors, "those fuckers of the All–Holy, those horned ones, cut off his leg."

Nikos dispatched one of the men to take a freight to Magna, find the midwife, and explain the boy's sickness. In the evening the man returned with a gallon can of goat milk and a flour sack filled with supplies. The midwife, the *mami,* had sent clean rags and a bottle of egg whites, mustard powder, and flour mixed together for a plaster. Two quarts of chicken broth with homemade noodles were

154

also in the sack. Nikos followed the midwife's directions for applying the mustard plaster and fed the boy hot goat milk and chicken
soup. The courier was excited about seeing a Greek woman. Her
husband had a *boardinhowz,* he said, and if they needed her, her man
would get a horse and buggy and drive her to the rail yards. If the
boy didn't get better, the *mami* thought he might have the evil eye
and she would come over and loose him from it.

The men asked what the midwife looked like, how many children she had, where she came from in Greece, what kind of man her
husband was. She was little and handsome, the courier said, and
already had four children. She was from Ahladhokambos—Pear
Valley—in the Peloponnesos, and her man was not even Greek! He
was one of the Slavs who had come to Greece when the government
began to build the roads the Turks had let go to ruin. The Greeks
didn't know how anymore, and foreigners like him had come in.
The *mami* was a fourteen-year-old girl, clearing rocks out of the
road, when he married her. The men called the Slav a devil, jealous
that he had a woman to take care of him.

The midwife's cure worked, and her patient joined others in
walking through Greek Town and into the city looking for jobs.
Greek Town comprised several streets around the rail yards. Pockets
of Lebanese, Italian, Japanese, and Slav stores and houses infiltrated
its borders. The neighborhood had been Mormon once; immigrant
converts from Scandinavia, Germany, and Holland had moved farther east as they prospered.

Yoryis learned to know each Greek place well: restaurants with
warped wooden floors and bare, scarred tables, the kitchens small
and steaming with great kettles of food that the immigrants examined before making their choices; grocery stores crowded and
pungent-smelling with goat cheese in barrels, cured meats, dried
gray octopi and yellow *bakalaos,* codfish, hanging from twine tied to
pegs in sooty ceilings, and a small assortment of Turkish delicacies
on their shelves—tobacco, coffee, and powdered-sugar *loukoum;*
bakeries, the fragrant scent of baking dough wafting over the
streets, their windows stacked with rings of bread that the young
men carried in the crook of their elbows to their rooms; shoeshine

155

parlors where boys were spending years of what was left of their childhood to work out their passage fare, many times inflated by the flesh merchants; and the coffeehouses—The Parthenon, Open Heart, Paradise, Athena, Corinthos, and Liberty.

Basil plants grew in dusty cans on the window ledges of the restaurants and coffeehouses; men broke off sprigs to put in their lapels and from time to time brought them to their noses and breathed in the piquant scent. "Ach, patridha, patridha," they said. Day and night the men off shift from the surrounding rail yards, mills, and smelters and those without work sat at the ice-cream tables in coffeehouses, drank demitasse cups of Turkish coffee, read aloud the latest Greek newspapers published in America: *Atlantis* of New York, *Ellinikos Astir*, "Greek Star," of Chicago, *California* of San Francisco, and *O Erghatis*, "The Worker," of Salt Lake City. They argued and pointed to large, fly-specked maps on the walls. Next to the maps, Greek and American flags were crossed above the photographs of King George and Eleftherios Venizelos, the Cretan premier of Greece.

From time to time showmen from Greece brought puppet shows that the young men hooted at, slapping their thighs. Behind white sheets the puppeteers manipulated *Karaghiozis*, the hunchbacked Greek villager who always got the better of Turks and officious Greeks—just as the men expected. Troupes of musicians came by playing their *laoutos, lyras*, and *santouris*. At times a woman dancer or two in faded dresses rattled tambourines and sang songs of *xenetia*, laments for their lost country. Then the youngest of the Greeks cried with "that homesickness that has no cure." Immediately, though, the women sang songs of the seaports that brought bursts of salacious laughter that the young men joined in loudly.

The dancers were given space in back rooms if they were *poutanes* as well, but women, American prostitutes, were plentiful in Greek Town. All that was needed was money. The Salt Lake City Council had moved one hundred prostitutes out of the commercial district in the center of town and into Greek Town, which, they said, the immigrants had ruined anyway.

156

The mayor had brought a well-known madam from Ogden, forty miles north, to form a real estate company to build a "stockade" of one hundred "cribs" and six parlor houses. The stockade, enclosed by a brick wall, and a three-story hotel across the street owned by the mayor were designed by a member of the city council. Respectable citizens could enter the stockade with less fear of being seen there than uptown.

The young Greeks went to the stockade as regularly as they could afford it: a man could get sick if he kept his semen in too long; at least every six weeks he should reinvigorate himself by visiting the prostitutes. A Greek doctor set up an office near the stockade and prospered by treating gonorrhea and syphilis until an immigrant told him, "I'm tough. Give me a double shot of 606." The doctor injected the 606, fluid arsenic for treating syphilis, into the man's vein and he fell, dead. Eventually the doctor turned to making whiskey in his examining room to keep alive.

When the coffeehouse palled for the men, when too many of them were without work, when they had told and retold priest jokes, when no *Karaghiozis* cavorted behind a sheet to slap their thighs over, no women with tambourines, no money for prostitutes, groups of them walked to Main Street to watch American women go by. They eyed them, making obscene remarks. Women sometimes glanced at them with faint smiles for their good nature, their zest. The men laughingly elbowed each other, choosing among the women's feathered hats—"I'd like to shit in that one"—and the women themselves—"I'd like to fuck her front and back."

Every day men left for Chicago. The Greek colony there had, like New York's, grown into a small city. Former Greek laborers were opening up chains of candy stores, restaurants, flower shops, shoeshine and dry-cleaning cubbyholes, a fur factory. The men talked about working as dishwashers or waiters by day, attending school by night, and becoming insurance agents or store owners. They boasted of the large dowries they would give their village sisters that would bring them doctors or generals for husbands. Yoryis thought of his parents and sisters waiting for his letters, hoping for

157

dowry money inside. Fifteen months had passed and he had been able to send only twenty-five dollars. He gnashed his teeth in his sleep, Nikos said.

Nikos Mouyias, who could neither read nor write, received a letter from his brother in January—he had been given a lunch-stand concession in the Chicago rail yards. Nikos left the railroad car, lifting his hand in the two-fingered Greek salute.

13

In late February the Czar of the Greek's henchmen
began making up labor gangs for the Western Pacific, Denver and
Rio Grande Western, Oregon Short Line, and Union Pacific railroads. The Czar's men were all Peloponnesians and first chose immigrants from Skliris's village near Sparta, then Spartans, and then
men from surrounding villages. Next, his agents who were from
Tripolis and nearby mountain villages signed up immigrants from
their area. Needing more, they went beyond to men from Argos and
Nafplion. Their relatives were taken on first, from brothers to cousins far removed, then the relatives of relatives, the *koumbari* of each,
and the relatives of *koumbari*. Though Grivas was a Peloponnesian,
he came from a village near Olympia, far beyond the circle of the
preferred.

Labor agents arrived from Idaho and Wyoming. Leaving their
hotels, they were stopped by clusters of young men on the streets
and had their gangs completed before they reached the coffeehouses.
"We'll bloat from hunger," Yoryis told Grivas. "Let's go to
Chicago."

With two rings of bread each, a gallon of water, a pail of lard, a
bundle of old newspapers and twigs, and a small sheet of rusty
metal, they sneaked into an empty boxcar. For several days and
nights they paced inside the bouncing, rumbling car to keep their
feet from getting numb and swung their arms stiffened from the

cold. On the piece of metal they made small fires to heat the lard and dipped pieces of bread into it.

The freight train was long, and as Yoryis and Grivas had caught one of the last cars purposely to be at a distance from the rail yards where detectives prowled, they were able to get out at several stops through the Rocky Mountains and over the prairies. An icy wind blew over the hamlets and towns and sent them shivering uncontrollably back into the momentarily deceptive warmth of the boxcar after relieving themselves at the side of the tracks. Each time the freight came to a stop, Yoryis looked into his Greek-American dictionary to read the name of the depot and store signs for a clue to Chicago.

It was night when they reached the stockyard stench of the Chicago rail yards. They jumped out and ran swiftly over the maze of tracks and into darkened streets of blackened warehouse buildings and small, unlighted restaurants. The freezing wind took their breath away and penetrated the newspapers folded under their shirts. They ran from one doorway to another for a few seconds' respite from the bitter wind. The streets became brighter with more lights, but stores and restaurants were closed down for the night. Grivas wanted to huddle up in a recessed doorway. "Let me just sit here and die," he said, but Yoryis forced him to go on.

Under a light post a policeman sat on a horse and held a lighted match to a cigar. Yoryis ran toward him, holding his hands up and away from his body as he'd been told. "Greek Town?" he said to the policeman puffing on the cigar, his right hand on the butt of his pistol. Wordlessly the policeman pointed. They walked, hurried, ran block after block, afraid the policeman had given them false directions. They came to stores with Greek signs, closed down for the night, and they were fearful that the coffeehouses would also be locked up. A poorly lighted Peloponnesian coffeehouse was open; several men dozed at the tables. The owner rose from a chair sleepily, brought them to a potbellied stove, put in fresh coal, poured glasses half full with ouzo, made Turkish coffee and served it with a plate of bread and dried *kokoretsi,* grilled lamb viscera. Then fully awake, the *kafetzis* rushed about nimbly, his face melancholy, performing the age-old duties of hospitality. Yoryis said to Grivas, "How many of us has he seen?"

"Stay here," the *kafetzis* said. "The place will fill up tomorrow. Maybe the patriotes can help you."

The next day Yoryis told an interpreter he was looking for Nikos Mouyias. "You'll need a note to get by the railroad detectives," the interpreter said, and wrote one beginning with the words: "To whom it may concern." He charged them a dollar.

On the way to the rail yards, Yoryis told Grivas, "A man works one to three days for a dollar and he scribbles two lines! That's the last time I give a kerata a penny!"

In a sooty dimness under a great canopy of smoky glass, they found the Mouyias stand, a six-by-twelve-foot, flat-topped building. The brothers served coffee and ham, cheese, and beef sandwiches to the rail yard workers. The lunch room had a small stove without an oven; each morning the Mouyiases stopped at a Greek bakery for the day's baked ham and roast beef. A water fountain stood in a corner of the room. In the smoke and steam Yoryis and Grivas ate heartily.

Nikos sent them to a labor agent on Halsted Street, and Yoryis signed with him for a Nebraska railroad gang. Grivas shook hands in goodbye. "I'd rather wash dishes among my people than go out into that Amerikaniko wilderness again," he said.

On the railroad coach to North Platte, Nebraska, Yoryis learned that Zack, Zacharias the Messolonghian, who had worked with him in the Pawtuckett factory, walked the streets with him in New York, and dug the sewer alongside him in Oklahoma, had been killed by a fall of steel rods off a freight car on a Midwest steel gang.

From North Platte the men were taken by wagon to a small tent city far into the prairie. An American and an Arab gang were already at work when they arrived. The three gangs were kept separated by a big Irish foreman whom the Americans, scrawny transients, called "Big Red." The Greeks looked at the Irishman's red hair and blue eyes surreptitiously and whispered the old proverb to each other: "Red beard and blue eyes portend the devil."

In the cold, wet spring the Americans tamped down the tall red grass and filled hollows; the Arabs laid down the oiled ties, and the Greeks far behind set the rails and drove in the spikes. Big Red was jovial. He was more a buffoon than a devil, Yoryis decided. He drank too much with no shame and had favorites among the gangs, men who brought him a pint of whiskey on paydays. While the laborers dropped picks and sledges from their frostbitten hands and little clouds of steam came from their mouths and noses, the favorites lolled in tents around monkey stoves on the pretext they were sick.

The twelve-year-old water boy Kostas looked bewildered whenever Big Red was near. "Kostakis" and "Takis," as the men called him, carried a pole across his shoulders from which two water buckets were suspended. At times the foreman laughed and took the pole from Takis and himself brought the water to the men. At other times he growled at Takis for no reason that the men could see. One evening when Yoryis was teaching Takis to shoot at whiskey bottles set up as targets, Big Red trudged menacingly toward them and grabbed the boy by the collar. The men looked at him, frowning. "Why do you want him?" Yoryis asked, and Big Red mumbled and walked back to his quarters. Takis often cried at night and whimpered for his mother, "Manoula, Manoula."

Yoryis had hardly been on the gang a week when one freezing morning his fingers loosened about the pick, and the sharp point went through his shoe and nicked the side of his foot. He motioned to Big Red and went to his tent where he tore a piece off a shirt bottom and stanched the blood. The pain grew worse with the passing days. Limping, he remembered a fellow villager whose leg had been cut off a year ago and stories he had heard in coffeehouses about company doctors amputating legs and arms and sending the mutilated men back to the old country with a hundred dollars or two.

Yoryis wrote to the village asking his parents what to do. A yellow, putrid pus oozed from the blackening flesh, and red streaks spread up his leg. The *erminéas,* a man from his own province, who arrived weekly to take letters and bring supplies, brought him a salve that did not help. One of the men recalled that he had once gone to a *praktikos* for an infection in his arm and the folk healer had

162

instructed his mother to make poultices of boiled onions and use them until the infection had drained. Others remembered herb remedies, but nothing grew on the prairie, only red grass. Each night the cook gave Yoryis a pan of hot water to soak the wound.

Two months later Yoryis received a letter from his parents telling him to take a tuft of clean sheep's wool, dip it into the film floating on top of a crock of feta cheese, place it on the cut, wrap it, and change the dressing each day. "Sheep, a crock of feta in this wilderness?" he said to the letter sardonically. By then his foot had healed, leaving a thick scar.

When the air turned warm in May, prostitutes came to the camp. Two men in straw hats drove the wagons and pitched tents for the women. The railroad company relied on women to keep the men from sneaking off in the night and from fighting among themselves when the prairie blazed and the night skies were vast. "In our country the skies were close to us," the men said. The pimps talked with Big Red, drank his whiskey, and left.

The prostitutes moved along with the gang. They hung their colored finery on ropes tied between tents to dry and through the long days sat on camp stools to watch the men work. As the sun grew hotter and drew out an oppressive, raw smell from the bowed red grass, the women stayed inside the tents.

Muscles tight and bulging in their arms and shoulders, shirts soaked with sweat, the men lifted rails, put them down, swung sledges, the silences broken at times by calls to Takis for water. Takis hurried with sloshing buckets and clinking dippers.

The men worked into July, visited the women's tents at night, sat around small fires in the siltlike dirt, and played cards. One of the Greeks strummed a *laouto* a quarter of a mile away from the ribald laughing and high spirits that came with relief after the heat of day. Yoryis took the lighted kerosene lamp from the stifling tent where he slept and sat on a patch of dry grass to write letters to coffeehouses, labor agents, and priests whose names and addresses he had put down in a small black book. He needed work, he wrote, for winter when railroad gangs were idle. He pondered the letter to his father; should he send what money he could for Maria's dowry—

163

money the family would without doubt have to use for their desperate needs—or accumulate the necessary amount. Remembering his father standing on the wharf of Patras in his worn European suit, he gave what he had to the *erminéas* for a money order to Greece.

His letter writing finished, he listened to the men's "songs of the table," of fallen heroes, of Fate, of Death. Takis's voice soared above theirs, high like a girl's. His mother, he said shyly, had hoped he would stay in *patridha* and become a priest or at least a chanter. Big Red came out of the women's tents and watched.

The men laughed bitterly at Big Red. He was a blunderer, as much an autocrat as arrogant people of authority in *patridha*. All had stories about the inequities of the fatherland. "If a man has one sheep more than you, he won't talk to you," Yoryis said. An eighteen-year-old who had come from the Aegean coast of Greece and who smiled so seldom that he looked unnatural when he did, told how he had been apprenticed to his mother's cousin to learn carpentry. He lived in a stable for three years, worked until it was too dark to see, and wore his master's cast-off clothes, his shoes tied with string, and never one *lepta* for a cigarette or a fresh fig. An uncle in a distant town offered him a job making furniture with pay. There he worked another three years, asking for his pay and being put off: "When I go to market"; "Times are bad"; "I have my daughter's dowry to gather first."

"Give me some money so I can go home to see my parents!" he at last insisted, and angrily his uncle threw a five-drachma note at him.

He walked to his village, two days and a night, and begged his father to send him to America. A moneylender took a mortgage on the family's small land at fifty percent interest. From one of the many steamship agents combing the mountains and valleys of Greece to supply cheap labor for American industrialists, his father bought him a steerage ticket.

He walked then about one hundred miles to the seaport of Patras. Nearing the port, he came to a plain where yellow flowering bushes grew in patches. His eyes reddened and itched. In Patras he was turned away by an immigration official because of his eyes. Frantic, he found a doctor who told him coldly that his eyes needed rest and charged him five drachmas. He walked home again, through the yellow flowering plain where his eyes swelled almost shut. He ate nothing for the hundred miles. Miraculously, his eyes were well by the time he reached his village. A year and three months later he made the same journey and this time he successfully boarded ship.

"At least we were in our own country," the men said. "Here, who can we go to for help?" They were eager to tell their stories. One of them had come directly from South Omaha where a Greek had shot a policeman who had stopped him on the street and rebuked him for walking with a "white" woman, a prostitute. In the rampage that followed, Greek Town was set afire and burned to the ground. Affidavits were circulated that the woman was a virgin. "Those Amerikani didn't know what they were doing, neither nose nor ass."

Another of the gang said his cousin had opened a candy store in Great Falls, Montana, and been driven out by vigilantes. Two of the men had been with a gang of one hundred Greeks, south of Boise, Idaho, and had cleared the land of sagebrush, the roots as thick as a man's leg. The night before they were to be paid and leave, fifty or more masked men on horses drove them from their tents and down the tracks, clutching their belongings. "They were afraid we were going to use their women! Unsalted people! White hair, their lashes like a roasted goat's!"

The sun scorched down day after day. Even with visits to the prostitutes the men grumbled. They had not seen one sod house in several weeks. The flat land of red grass swishing with a dry hiss in the hot breeze, the endless whitish sky, and the sameness of each day dulled the men, sporadically brought alive by angry curses over accidental bumpings and careless handling of tools. As they moved rails, as their sledges rang down and were about to be brought high again, they looked over the plain for some sign of life and to the sky for the occasional blackbird or jay.

Big Red stalked the rail bed angrily. The smell of whiskey seeped from his sweaty skin. The engineer who came by weekly spoke sharply to him, and the paymaster looked at him in silence.

The first week of August, one of the pimps who had brought the prostitutes to the camp returned with three women and a large dog. One of the women was black; the Greeks glanced at her often. "Big show tonight," Big Red told the men, walking from group to group along the tracks. Yoryis and the other Greeks went to the show, telling Takis he was too young to come along. They knew they would witness the kind of shows they had heard sailors frequented in seaports. When the dog was led in, Big Red stood up in frenzy, shouting, "Git the kid in here! Bring in the kid!"

Big Red lurched out of the tent. Some of the Americans clapped and shouted in singsong, "Bring in the lil Greek! Bring in the lil Greek." Yoryis and the Greeks went after Big Red; several Americans followed in curiosity. "No. He's a boy. Too young," Yoryis said. The Greeks and several Americans shouted, "Too young, Big Red. Let him alone!" Takis came out at the noise and stood in the lighted opening of the tent. Big Red bellowed at the Greeks, "I'm the foreman here and what I says goes, you goddamn black Greeks." In the next instant Yoryis and Big Red clashed with fists swinging. Greeks and Americans stood still a moment, then rushed at each other and rolled in the dust, grunting and cursing. Prostitutes, pimps, and the dog looked on. Within a few minutes Big Red lay on the ground, beaten, moaning. The fighting subsided, and the Greeks returned to their tents, excited, unable to sleep.

The next day Big Red and Takis were gone. "You're the boss now," a scruffy American said admiringly to Yoryis. Until the engineer came by on his weekly visit, the men worked docilely under Yoryis's direction, the Greeks chattering continuously of what they would do if they ever found Big Red. When the engineer arrived, he said without surprise, "So, you're the boss now?" and smiled. "Bigger fists." The engineer gave Yoryis an old gray ledger, each lined page written with a heading: Supplies, .Hours, Wages. Yoryis was astonished to see he would be paid fifty dollars a month, twenty more than he had been getting swinging sledges. In the evening, while the men visited the women or listened to the *laouto*, Yoryis sat in Big Red's old tent and using his small, gilt-edged, Greek–American dictionary and Greek–American method book, learned to write well in English and to keep books.

Yoryis drove the men to finish laying the track before winter. At dawn a dullness presaging a sweltering day was already in the swiftly vanishing coolness. The sun's heat poured down, and the odor of the men's unwashed bodies was thick in the still air. In the distance heat waves shimmered; mirages of blue lakes lay over the plain. Throughout the long days the men swore at the heat, their shirts sweat-splotched. The swearing and the clang of steel on steel reverberated over the plain. The water in barrels and canvas bags was warm, never satisfying. The men looked up at red-winged blackbirds and magpies, their white wing patches like snow, and when crows and hawks soared by. Nothing on the earth moved except black crickets; the clang of steel had driven away lizards, snakes, and prairie dogs. Each day the men awoke to red grass, often fenced on both sides of the rails with barbed wire, and the muscle-sapping heat.

The men complained to Yoryis that he was driving them hard. "For the first time in your life you've got meat to fill your bellies," he told them. "The next person who opens his mouth will get a beating from me that will make the priest look like a donkey to him!"

The food was dry, tasteless. "Put plenty of pepper on it," Yoryis said. Pepper had been such a luxury that some of the men had never tasted it before coming to America.

The men talked constantly of the water in their part of Greece, which often had to be carried a long distance over rocky trails, how cold it was, its special taste, its curative qualities, how its fame was known throughout the province and people came from afar to drink it. They spoke the names of waters with reverence: Kefalovrissi—Head Springs, Palaios Platanos—Old Plane Tree, Mahi Topos—Slaughtering Place, Nyfi Peplos—Bride's Veil, Nerolithari—Water Rock.

By the time frost silvered the red grass, the rails had been laid and the job was finished. The *erminéas* had brought Yoryis several answers to his letters, none with news of work: dishwashers and shoeshiners were a glut everywhere. In North Platte, Yoryis sent his father a money order for one hundred dollars and bought a small, wood-slatted trunk and American clothing to put in it: an overcoat, two sets of underwear, two shirts, work pants, new gloves, and an American hat. Then, with most of his men crowding the street, he led them to a public bathhouse the paymaster had recommended and they washed off ten-months' dirt and sweat. He returned to Salt Lake City where railroad gangs out of work for the two winter months filled the coffeehouses.

14

On Stavrou Street in the City
just off the wide, cobbled Galatea Way and across from the Holy
Trinity Greek Orthodox Church, the apartments were built of gray
stone with marble facing around heavy wooden doors. Two marble
steps led from the street to each entrance. Until late at night the
voices of Greek, French, Italian, Spanish, Albanian, and Jewish
inhabitants vied with the cries and noises from the surrounding
soukakia, crowded, winding cobbled streets, no more than alleys,
where shops displayed vegetables, fruits, dates, figs, copper utensils, tobacco, and liqueurs.

Down Galatea Way and into the City proper the noise increased
into a roaring cacophony: horse-drawn streetcars, shouting vendors,
booming whistles from the great ships in the Sea of Marmara, wailing phonograph music from coffeehouses filled with men smoking
nargilés and fingering *komboloyia* beads, hawkers extolling motion
picture theaters, and people talking excitedly. Men wore caftans or
European suits and fezzes of red, black, or brown; others in full
black pantaloons and vests of islanders, and sailors in the uniforms
of many nations. Women of all races moved with the crowd but
only seldom a veiled Turkish woman, for they, like those in Thessaloniki, watched behind the grilled balconies of their gray wooden
houses.

In the first days the *kyria* went everywhere with Emilia tripping
at her side and even hired a boatman to row them to Prinkipa, the

169

largest of the Sea of Marmara islands where the wealthy lived. They walked about the dusty streets and looked at the great houses rearing above rock walls, grilled gates, dark green, pointed cypresses, and flowering lemon trees. The *kyria* breathed in deeply of the fresh piquancy of lemon blossoms, waving a linen handkerchief toward her face to get more of the scent. She hired a carriage to drive them to the top of Pera, the Greek district, and under a pink and violet sky of early evening, they looked over the City of many mosques, Greek Orthodox churches now desecrated with the minarets of the conquerors, Jewish synagogue cupolas, mud-colored bathhouses, and patches of green among the gray and brown wood and stucco houses.

"Ayia Sophia," the driver said and pointed to the church.

"Will we go there?" Emilia asked the *kyria*.

"What!" The *kyria* frowned at her. "To enter our great church and see how the barbarian Turks have plastered over the icons and frescoes and painted their hideous words over them! No true Greek would step there until the City is Greek again and Ayia Sophia is ours once more!"

Emilia reddened. The driver talked on about the great church, but she would not look at him to see if there was contempt on his face for her, a servant girl, thinking only of her pleasure.

The driver said Greeks were allowed to enter Ayia Sophia only on Fridays. When anyone went, he should make his eyes blind to the Koran sayings on the arches. He then embarked on the story Emilia had heard many times in the past and would hear more often in the future: when Turks broke through the walls of the City, the Greeks ran into Ayia Sophia hoping to be safe there, but the Turks, having no respect for Christian holy places, tore down the doors and slaughtered the men, women, and children. A priest disappeared through an altar side door. A Turk rushed after him, but found the door locked. He raised his scimitar, struck the door, and fell dead. Since that day in 1453, the door resisted attempts to open it. It would never open until the City was Greek again. Blood ran out of the church, down the streets, into the bay, and the water was red for forty days.

Later, at the dinner table, the *kyria* complained that the driver insisted on telling the old story even though she had told him she and every Greek knew it and that he charged her more than he should have. The *kyrios* mildly asked if she had haggled over the fare beforehand, then told her one place she could not go without him was the great bazaar, Kapaiikarsi, because it was filled with thieves. A person had to have four eyes.

On an evening when Emilia had been sent to stay with a servant girl of the Jewish family, the Namiks—*Kyria* Namik pretty, always smiling—the *kyria* and *kyrios* also went out and returned with several newspaper-wrapped packages. Flushed, the *kyria* spread the contents on the dining room table: a gold ring with a purple stone, a linen dresser scarf embroidered with spring flowers, a small icon of Saint Demetrios, and a pair of rose damask bedroom slippers. The *kyrios* took out a small pin in the shape of a fish and, smiling, handed it to Emilia. They did not say where they had been, but Emilia knew they had gone to the great bazaar, alleys and alleys, she'd heard, both open and covered over, with goods from all over the world. She knew, also, that she would be trotting often after the *kyria* in the great bazaar.

In the dungeon of the apartment house several women, one large and old, washed for the families above. The women worked six days a week under a kerosene lamp's muted light, the air thick with smells of strong soap, lye, and a cobwebbed mustiness; their lethargic children were kept behind a barricade of old boxes and planks.

The first time Emilia took down a bundle of wash, the old woman was scrubbing with her back to the door. Breathlessly Emilia ran to her, then crestfallen, looked into a plump, wrinkled face. She ran upstairs, ashamed of her foolishness for thinking old Anastasia, left behind in Thessaloniki, would be down in the dungeon among the gossiping washwomen.

A French dressmaker came often. The dining room table was cleared and the birdlike woman measured, cut, pinned, and sewed the fabrics. The *kyria* sat at the table and stroked the satins and brocades. Although everyone who came to the house and who waited on customers in shops spoke Greek, the *kyria* used her nun-taught French with the dressmaker. Sometimes the dressmaker forgot and answered in Greek.

Neighbors visited briefly in the mornings wearing serviceable, dark cotton dresses or old visiting dresses of silk smelling of perspiration. The *kyria* especially enjoyed the visits of *Kyria* Namik, and soon Emilia's Saturday ritual began with her going to their first-floor apartment to light the brazier for the Jewish Sabbath. One Friday evening Emilia's mistress sent her with a small package to the Namiks. What was in it, the *kyria* did not say. *Kyria* Namik opened the door, her round face red and shiny from her seder preparations. Her black hair was coiled on top of her head, and she was wearing a fringed black Spanish shawl printed with full-blown, dark red roses. *Kyria* Namik smiled cheerfully at Emilia. Behind her the seder table was set, ready.

To *Kyria* Namik she ran with the letter from her village. When she had opened it, no scent of dried anise or basil escaped. Her fingers prickled. Your grandmother, her father wrote, has died, her soul is at rest. Tears streaming, Emilia ran to *Kyria* Namik and blurted, "My yiayia is dead!" *Kyria* Namik led Emilia to the *sala* and sat next to her, talking softly and stroking her cold hands. Afterwards, Emilia and her *kyria* went to Holy Trinity and in the cool dimness lighted candles and crossed themselves.

Women callers came in the afternoon. They sipped liqueurs and Turkish coffee, ate preserved fruits and honey-nut sweets, and carried on vivacious conversations in high-pitched visitor voices. They dressed in shining dark colors, and their hats were of velvet with sweeping feathers of white or gray.

Once, sometimes twice a month, the *kyrios* and *kyria* gave dinners. A stolid, methodical cook, a white dishcloth tied about her head, came to take charge. Emilia was at her side, standing on a stool to beat and stir as she was told, also with a dishcloth tied about her head. "It would be a mistake," the cook said with serious admonition in her gray blue eyes, "for someone to find a hair in his food." "It would be a mistake," she said, "for a guest to eat fish with curdled mayonnaise." "It would be a mistake for a guest to find lumps in the ghalatobouriko."

While Emilia and the cook worked in the kitchen, the *kyria* set the table, hurrying back and forth from the chest that held her dowry linens to a glass-fronted china closet, to the window, calling down, "Taki! Taki!" Takis, the errand boy, ran up the stairs and, looking at the *kyria* with mean black eyes, listened to her orders, held out his grimy hand for the coins, and ran down the marble stairs. The *kyria* came into the kitchen many times to whisper, "How is the food coming along? Do you have everything you need? If not, Takis can be sent for it."

The cook looked at Emilia one day and with a rare smile said, "The more important the guests, the softer she whispers."

The servant girls gathered in the evenings, but not nightly as in Thessaloniki. Besides the dinners, which every family gave constantly, all of them, except Emilia's, had children who took up the girls' time. On their masters' name days when many people were expected, they helped each other, excited at the brilliantly dressed women talking and laughing, the men portentously discussing politics, the clinking of liqueur glasses, the music of the gramophone.

At rare times, Turks came but without their wives—some had as many as four. On these nights the *kyrios* bent so low over their hands that he looked ready to kiss them. Because it was not a Moslem custom, the *kyria* did not sit at the table. She became a silent servant going in and out of the dining room to fill glasses and bring in platters and bowls. Whenever Turks were expected, the *kyria* unnecessarily reminded the cook that she would be cooking veal or lamb. "Because, of course, the Turks do not eat pork."

"And no one else should either," the cook said grimly. "Pork is filthy."

For several months there were no dinners. The *kyria* was sick, and Emilia dreaded going into her room where the odor of vomit made her retch. Breathing through her mouth and trying not to look into the pan, she hurried down the outside wooden stairs to the backyard privies to empty it. She hoped she would see a servant girl, even snappish Aristea, in the courtyard or on the landing to talk with for a few minutes.

The vomiting and languishing stopped suddenly, and the *kyria* and Emilia walked everywhere again. As in their first days in the City, they always ended in the neighborhood of the great houses, shaded and secluded from the outside.

The French dressmaker made new dresses for the *kyria* with adjustable hooks for her ever-expanding waist. When the last hook was reached, the *kyria* paced the floor. Just before the *kyrios* came home, she went to bed and began crying. He entered obsequiously; at the *kyria's* screeches and sobs, he lifted his fat arms and let them fall helplessly.

One night Emilia sat at the bedside of the *kyria* who screamed, "I'm going to die!" and clutched an icon of the All–Holy to her. Emilia gazed at her: it was a puzzle that it mattered so much to the *kyria* whether she lived or died.

On a bleak winter evening, the baby was born amid the screams of the *kyria* and the running about of midwife, doctor, and *kyrios*. The baby was a boy who would be named Achilles after the *kyrios's* father. Emilia went back and forth with trays while a wet nurse thrust a nipple into the baby's mouth every time it began to cry.

When the forty days were over and the *kyria* took the baby to Holy Trinity to be blessed and her uncleanliness dispelled by the priest's reading over her, she was peevish at the *kyrios's* protests that he had dinner obligations to fulfill. The *kyria* spent all her time with the baby while the cook and Emilia looked to every detail. When the dinner was served, one of the neighboring servant girls sat in the *kyria's* room, rocked Achilles asleep, and fed him a bottle of camomile tea when he awoke. The *kyria* went in many times during the evening to peer apprehensively into the baby's plump, sleeping face.

Whenever Emilia rocked the baby, she thought of Yiannis, her own brother, and hugged the baby to her. At times she called him Yiannis, forgetting. One spring evening while she was rocking the baby and singing to him on the balcony, the scent of lemon blossoms came from far off. She looked over the City, over the minarets, the Jewish temple cupolas, the Greek church domes. In the bay swaying caiques surrounded the great ships. On the quay, with boxes and bales larger than they on their bent backs, small

figures, the *hamalidhes*, the lowest of the squalid, loaded and un-
loaded the ships.

Emilia gazed at the quay where the *kyrios* worked in an office.
His talk at dinner was always about currants from the Peloponnesos,
silk from the East, rugs from Anatolia, cotton from Egypt, tobacco
from Thrace, figs and dates from the interior. A deep, blaring whistle came from one of the ships; black smoke billowed from its big
stack; slowly it moved out of the harbor toward the west, toward
America.

The *kyrios* had no books on America. One of the businessmen
who came to dinner had been to America. He had sputtered,
"Amerikanidhes are as free as men! They go about alone, even on
trains. Overnight! They have no respect for anyone." With a savage
thrusting of his cigar he shouted, "They stop right on the street and
talk to men. Supposedly respectable women! They have no respect
for anyone! They cross their legs like men!" He never came again to
the apartment; he had returned to America.

Emilia rocked on, watching the *hamalidhes* load the ships. That
night she dreamed of a barefoot young man bent over with a bale on
his back. His face was hidden, but when she awoke, she sat up
quickly and knew that the *hamalis* was her brother Yiannis. With
trembling fingers she turned to the *h*'s in the dream book. The
dream book did not have everyday words in it; she turned to the *l*'s
but there was nothing about a brother's being a laborer. "If you see
others working, it is a reproach for your indolence." Emilia knew
instantly what the dream meant. If she did not exert herself, her
brother would join the miserable, despised *hamalidhes*. Her brother
must learn his lessons well, she thought, and someday she would
ask the *kyrios* if he would give him work. She added an extra line to
her monthly letter: "I hope Yiannis is learning to read and write
well to help him get work when he is older." The *kyrios* read her
letter but said nothing.

The next time Emilia sat on the balcony and watched a great
ship move out of the bay, a profound, intense longing to be on it
going away, away, overwhelmed her.

Whenever the *kyrios* and *kyria* went out, her mistress told Emilia over and over what to do, that a neighbor would drop in several times and that she must not let Achilles cry because boy babies could develop hernias. Emilia closed the balcony doors if the salt breeze brought odors of decay and filth. She lighted all the lamps and said her prayers at the icon of the All–Holy, not only at her own, but at the *kyria*'s as well. Holding the baby in one arm, she made the sign of the cross in sets of three. The baby smiled, but Emilia was too afraid to play with him. She sat in a rocker, her eyes on the door that at any moment would be broken down by a fleeing young Turk or a Bulgarian *Komitadjis* looking for sanctuary after setting off a bomb. She prayed that even Aristea would come to sit with her; she had hoped Aristea would be like Hrisoula in Thessaloniki, but instead she was an ugly, angry girl whose uncle went to South America, promised her a dowry, and was never heard from again. Emilia was more afraid of being alone than of being with her.

Aristea told the girls the same stories repeatedly: her sister's wedding night horrors; a young aunt's death in childbirth; seduced girls sent out of their villages to starve; men in the apartments who had lovers, their wives fooled; and one *kyrios* whom she came upon in the dungeon washroom kissing the baker's apprentice! The first day Aristea met Emilia, she took her to the balcony and pointed north of the quay. "That's where men go," she said, her eyes glittering, "for prostitutes, even little girls and boys! Men go crazy and can't be stopped!"

Many nights Emilia lay awake a long time, her head hurting, thinking about her brother and how she would make him the salvation of the family.

Try as she did, she sometimes could not remember her people's faces.

It was more than two years before Achilles reached, as the *kyria* said, the age of reason and would sit on a little chair with a pot under the hole in it. No longer did the washwomen greet her with, "So, presents for us again, eh, girl?" as they took the pail of reeking diapers from her.

Emilia recited French and Greek poems she had learned from

her grandmother to Achilles and his solemn, moon face lighted up
at her singsong:

> *Snow is falling in the yard.*
> *How very cold it is.*
> *My nose reddens*
> *I run into my house!*

And with that she tweaked his nose and he laughed showing little
rabbit teeth. Now that Achilles had reached the age of reason and
slept through the night, afternoon visiting and entertaining began
again. Emilia rushed about, preparing trays, serving the women
who talked rapidly in Italian, French, and Greek. Light came in
through the linen-draped windows, breezes from the open doors of
the balcony. The excited voices rose to crescendos; laughing left
shimmers in the room. Emilia hurried to the kitchen and back,
smiling, to pick up pastry crumbs Achilles dropped wherever he
walked.

After the women left and while she washed the dishes, she still
smiled, remembering some of the stories and anecdotes the women
related. Aristea's mistress told *hodtzas* stories about the Turkish
teacher and sometime priest with a flinging out of her arms to emphasize the *hodtzas*'s slyness. Almost every time women met,
Aristea's mistress had a new *hodtzas* story, and afterward Emilia
reviewed them several times to herself so she could repeat them to
the other servant girls.

The girls knew many *hodtzas* stories themselves. Emilia's favorite *hodtzas* was Nasrentin who, acting as a judge, caught criminals
in cunning ways. The girls vied with each other in telling the stories. Aristea guffawed over irascible *hodtzas* like one who convinced
a baker to sell him the mayor's goose. This led to several tragedies
that the *hodtzas* took care of in an arbitrary fashion, and then he ate
the goose. Emilia countered with her stories. Two men came to
Nasrentin for his judgment on who was lying. One had given the
other a sum of money to keep for him while he went on a pilgrimage
to Mecca. When he returned and asked for his money, the other

denied he had been given any. There were no witnesses; the transaction had taken place under a tree. To the complainant Nasrentin said, "Go to the tree and cut a limb off it and bring it to me. It will tell me who is lying." The man was gone a long time and Nasrentin said, "Why is he taking so long?" The thief replied, "Because that tree is a great distance from here."

Early one morning Emilia awoke in pain. "Sit down from time to time," said the *kyria,* who spent two days of each month in bed. From then on the *kyria* looked down the stairwell on Saturday mornings when Emilia went to the Namiks to light their fires. The *kyria* told her she could no longer attend liturgies unless one of the mistresses went along with the girls, even though the church was across the street. "You'll go when I go," said the *kyria,* who attended liturgies only on Christmas, Holy Week, the Kimisis of the Virgin on August 15, and her husband's and child's name days. She now stood behind Emilia when the charcoal seller's apprentice brought the week's supply of fuel or a tradesman's errand boy delivered a package.

Between Emilia's fourteenth and fifteenth year, when she had become as tall as her mistress and took charge of all the cooking and housekeeping, talk of brokers and markets stopped at the dinner table. The *kyria* no longer went out to gaze at the mansions. Achilles was listless. The *kyria* and Emilia spent hours cajoling him to eat. A new errand boy had replaced the old one who had disappeared on the wharves; perhaps, Emilia thought, to join the *hamalidhes* bent over their great burdens. Emilia sent the new boy to the market for ingredients she needed to make delicacies for Achilles. Her mistress kept a small money purse in her dress pocket and counted out the money. The *kyrios* saw to it that the Turkish coins in varying denominations were always available. For Achilles, Emilia cooked rice-stuffed squid, goat cheese pastries, rose-petal jam, honeyed *tsourekia, soudsoukakia,* cumin-flavored meat rolls, and candied, preserved eggplant no bigger than the boy's thumb. When he looked at his mother and Emilia, his eyes big in his pale face, and tried to eat to please them, the *kyria* and Emilia clapped and encouraged him with cries of "Bravo, Achillaki!"

The *kyria* began attending Sunday liturgies, then all church holidays and feast days. She consulted practitioners of folk medicine: the Greek *praktiki*, Turkish *hodtzas,* and a kindly, shabby Syrian in a dismal, dark alley near the wharves. Emilia placed her icon of Saint Demetrios on the shelf above his small bed alongside the *kyria*'s All–Holy and Christ.

The *kyria* pinned amulets of garlic inside her son's undershirt. One of her sisters in Egypt sent her a sliver of the True Cross. Emilia wrapped it in a bit of cotton, sewed it within a square of blue satin, and crocheted for it a chain as a necklace for Achilles. He already wore a blue bead on a silver chain to ward off the evil eye.

The *kyria* often took Achilles to church and had the priest read over him; at intervals, she summoned the priest to the apartment and with incense and chantings he exorcised it of some unknown uncleanliness or sin. The sharp odor of the frankincense Emilia burned on the brazier after the rooms were made clean for Sunday hung heavily in the draperies and air. The one or two amber pieces she had once used increased under the *kyria*'s orders. The *kyrios* fumed and complained of his nose swelling and of gasping for breath. "No!" the *kyria* said, "you will not open a window or the door!" Meekly he sat with Achilles on his fat knees and pulled the boy's head to rest on his big stomach.

Often while she worked or lay in bed, exhausted, yet unable to sleep, Emilia thought of Anastasia, their washwoman in Thessaloniki. One morning on the pretext of lighting a candle for Achilles, she hurried down the marble steps and across the street to the church of Holy Trinity. She glanced over her shoulder, but the *kyria* no longer stood at the top of the stairs to watch her until she entered one of the apartments or looked out of the window while Emilia searched the street for the errand boy.

Her heart pounded at being closed up with the dour old priest in the small confessional. While he looked at her with gray-filmed eyes, she quickly told him that the old washwoman in Thessaloniki had cursed her *kyria* with the Bad Hour, and she was afraid Achilles's illness was the result of it. "And what power has the curse of an ordinary person?" The priest leaned forward as Emilia leaned backward. "Only the clergy and the Holy Ones have that power. Nonetheless, light a candle before the icon of the Trinity and say your prayers. Women and their petty concerns!"

Emilia clattered over the marble floor in her haste to get away from the priest. She wanted to tell *Kyria* Namik about him, but her neighbor was in turmoil over her husband's going to America. She remembered the priest with hate when the *kyrios,* who had often boasted that he had not gone to confession since he was ten years old, said he had that day. "For Achillakis I went gladly. We had a nice chat, the priest and I. A little deaf, but a good little old man."

"And what did you confess, Sophocles?" the *kyria* asked.

"Eh, what did I confess? That I didn't like Zarangoglou. I couldn't think of anything else."

During this time, tradesmen, dressed in Sunday suits, too large or too tight under the arms, celluloid collars choking their throats, began coming to speak to the *kyrios* about marriage arrangements between Emilia and their godsons or nephews. Emilia kept to her room or when Achilles was awake, rocked him and played with him in his little room where the *kyria* now slept on a cot at the side of his crib. Other men also came, better dressed than the tradesmen, to discuss business matters, for the *kyrios* no longer met them in coffeehouses; he had become infected with the *kyria*'s anxiety for their son and spent every moment outside office hours at home.

Kyrios Papadimitriou with his thumb in his vest armhole called Emilia in after each tradesman left and explained the marriage offer. Emilia answered with a shake of her head, and the *kyrios* smiled in relief. The *kyria* kissed her. A miserable restlessness took hold of Emilia. The *kyrios* chided her. "What's this, Emilia? You're not eating. You're looking so glum. Look at Achillakis. He understands. You're making him feel bad."

Late one evening after a tradesman had gone, Emilia stood on the balcony watering plants. The din of the city was far off. A breeze floated over her, bringing the scent of lemon blossoms. She put the can on the wooden floor and went into her room. Even there the lemon scent from the land of the conquered Greeks entered through the small, high window. She crossed herself at the icon of the All—Holy and spoke silently: "Help me to have my own home, my own linens on the bed, on the table. Don't let me stay here trapped forever." Back on the balcony, she looked at the great ships in the harbor and crossed herself: she would go to Ameriki, even if alone. She would take her dowry money for passage. She would go!

She recited the Creed and the Our Father, then marched into the living room where the *kyrios* was reading and tsk-tsking over more bombings by the Bulgarian Komitadjes. "Kyrie," she said, "please, no more people coming with proxinyes. I don't want any more of it."

The *kyrios* nodded, said, "Very well, Emilia," and returned to reading his newspaper.

On the following Saturday, Emilia went as usual to the Namiks' to light the Sabbath candles. In the hallway was a small trunk, new, of wood buckled with leather straps. *Kyria* Namik stood at Emilia's side, looked at her husband's trunk with fearful eyes, and wept that she might become one of the white widows like *Kyria* Piacitelli and *Kyria* Romanoff who never heard from their men again. America swallowed people.

"*Kyria* Namik, let me go with you!"

They whispered and then parted. "I will find you a husband in Ameriki," *Kyrios* Namik told her the next day.

As often as she could without arousing the *kyria*'s suspicion, Emilia visited the Namiks. In her dark room at night, she pondered how she would arrange her leave for America. She would, she told *Kyria* Namik, first have to go to her village to see her parents, but she would not tell them of her plans because they might not give their permission. Then she would have to tell the *kyrios* and *kyria* that she would take her wages in lieu of a dowry to buy her ticket to America. "They'll try to keep me," Emilia said, "but I will not stay! No, I will to go to Ameriki!"

Two months later *Kyria* Namik received a letter: a passage ticket from her husband would come after he had paid back what he had borrowed from a Jewish immigration society; the only work he had found was in a factory. Make ready and come, he said.

When Emilia asked permission of the *kyrios* and *kyria* to visit her village, they gave it readily. "Now don't desert us and stay there," the *kyria* said, wagging her finger and handing Emilia a flowered silk scarf. It was a week before the *kyrios* could make the proper arrangements to send Emilia by rail and horse carriage. He had to have assurances that she would be in the company of reliable travelers and trustworthy drivers and that the carriage would be protected from renegade *klefts* who descended from mountains to rob and even kill passengers.

Emilia's sister Anna and her husband lived at the other end of the village with his parents. The rooms of the narrow, two-story rock house were smaller and even more bare than her parents' home. In a corner of the *sala* where Anna and her husband slept, a cradle at one side, the silk dresses her grandmother had woven and sewed for her hung on pegs in the whitewashed wall. A bed sheet covered them.

On the third evening of her visit to the village, Emilia sat under a plane tree in the dirt yard and picked bits of chaff and rocks from a tray of lentils. Seated next to her, Anna sewed a shirt for the baby she was expecting and at intervals gave the cradle a gentle push to keep her son from awakening. Anna's husband had come from the fields and was washing his face and hands in a basin placed on a bench by the kitchen door. Grunting, he rubbed his face vigorously, then sat on the doorstep, untied his shoes, took off his homespun stockings, and put his feet into the basin. Anna reddened: washing one's feet had been done in private in their family. Two young men with hoes over their shoulders walked past and called out pleasantries. "Wash your feet good," one of them shouted, "or she'll throw you out of bed."

Emilia and Anna bent their heads lower. Everywhere Emilia had gone, to church, to the graveyard, to the neighbors, young men like them, wearing village caps or brown fezzes, stood looking at her and trying to appear they were not. Talking loudly, they slapped each other on the shoulders to draw her attention. She tightened her mouth: she would never marry any of them, never stay in the village.

"A husband can be found for you here," Anna said in a low voice.

Emilia yanked the ends of the flowered silk scarf her near-sighted, finely wrinkled mother had ordered her to wear. ("What immodesty is this? Bareheaded! Showing off your hair!") "I don't want a husband here!" Emilia said. Then in remorse for speaking sharply to the sister she had for years been in awe of, she added, "Not yet anyway."

When she said goodbye to them, she knew she would not be standing in the stucco church for her father's funeral and her knees gave way. She almost burst out her secret, but looking at tall, thin Yiannis she felt strong with resolve. During her six-week visit she had thought of taking him aside and telling him of her plans and that one day he would be receiving a ticket from America—but she would not trust anyone; she could not have her scheme spoiled.

As the wagon passed the charnel shed attached to the church, Emilia made the sign of the cross for her old grandmother whose bones had been dug up three years after burial, cleaned, and stored in a huge basket along with those of generations of her daughter's people by marriage. On the outskirts of the village Emilia dropped a pebble to ensure her never having to return.

15

In late February, Yoryis found Angelo Raekos,
who had helped him in Denver, waiting for him in the Parthenon
Coffeehouse. He had recently become an agent for the Oregon Short
Line, one of three Greek labor contractors, the other two suppliers
also for the Union Pacific. Raekos gave Yoryis a contract to take a
gang of Corinthians to Idaho to change rails from narrow to standard gauge. "I need a fellow Roumeliot to make my orders stick,"
he laughed. For the next six years Yoryis would spend ten months of
the year as a foreman of gangs and two months getting through
winter as cheaply as possible.

While in Heyburn, Idaho, Yoryis sent for Pericles to help with
their sisters' dowries. He arrived frightened, skinny, and as clumsy
as when he was a boy. He complained of the cold. The rails and
sagebrush were brushed with frost; steam escaped from the men's
mouths, and their nostrils stuck together when they sniffed. At the
end of Pericles's first workday, the Corinthian assigned as his partner came into the railroad car raving, "I'm teamed up with a bastard
who can't even hold up his end of the rail!"

Yoryis struck the Corinthian on his frostbitten ear and cut it
open. The other Corinthians jumped forward. Yoryis took out his
pistol, and the Roumeliot cook came forward with a shotgun. "If
anyone touches Yoryis, he dies," the cook said. The men retreated
but sent one of their *patriotes* to Pocatello to swear out a complaint.
A sheriff rode into camp on horseback and fined Yoryis five dollars.

The Corinthians were dissatisfied that Yoryis had not been fired. A Roumeliot, Haralam Sampalis, drove out in a buggy to see Yoryis. He was a florid, handsome man with a thick mustache, and like Raekos, wore a hand-tailored suit. To show his wealth, Sampalis had had his teeth covered with gold and a diamond embedded in a front one. Between his teeth he clenched a fat cigar. Lifting his hand slowly to remove the cigar and slowly to replace it, he straightened out his little finger on which a large diamond sparkled. "The Corinthians have their own coffeehouse in Pocatello," he told Yoryis, "and they've vowed to get you."

Sampalis was one of the labor agents for the Union Pacific and Oregon Short Line, among other enterprises that he spoke of in large, general terms as "investments." An aura of success and daredevilishness emanated from him, success because of the money he had made in America and daredevilishness because he had arranged for an entire prison full of men to escape Greece. He had been a jailer in a provincial capital of Roumeli where almost all of his prisoners had been locked up over vendettas between clans that went back two, three, and even four generations.

Sampalis had bargained over bribes with the prisoners' relatives and on a designated night unlocked the men from their cells. With Sampalis leading them, they made their way to Patras where further bribery had prepared passports and tickets. With a considerable sum of money in hand from the prisoners' families, who had mortgaged their lands at usurious interest, Sampalis had a good start in America. He quickly saw that a *missitis,* a labor broker, made money easily without having to work for it. He never used a pick or shovel in America, never washed a dish, never sweated in the filth of slaughterhouses. As a benefactor to his family, he brought over several teenaged nephews who halfheartedly worked in Greek grocery stores where they cheated Greek labor gangs and boardinghouses under his direction. The nephews then advanced to becoming pimps, a satisfactory life for them and profitable, for Pocatello was a railroad terminal where thousands of Greeks worked on section gangs, in the rail yards, and throughout the sagebrush desert.

"Patrioti," Sampalis said, "the Corinthians are out to kill you. Let's take them on tonight. We can't let these threats against us Roumeliots go unchallenged. We've got to think of our filotimo. We'll go to their coffeehouse and if they want to start something, we'll give it to them."

That night they entered the Corinthians' coffeehouse and sat for almost an hour at a corner table, their backs to the wall. The Corinthians muttered among themselves but made no move. Sampalis and Yoryis left the coffeehouse; the feud was finished. The Corinthians had had their chance and they had not taken it. When word of the encounter came back to the gang, Stavros, a stocky, powerfully muscled Corinthian who had never lost a wrestling match, not even, so he said, to a famed Japanese in the Utah copper camps, admiringly called "The Beast," told Yoryis, "You showed *guts*," using the American word for courage that the Greeks had picked up. "Put that weakling brother of yours with me. He'll be all right."

The following spring Yoryis went to the Oregon Short Line offices in search of work and met a contractor who was putting in a branch line from Montpelier to Paris, Idaho. He asked Yoryis to bring twenty-four Greeks with him. Seeing no reason to have men paying the labor agents Raekos, Sampalis, and their partner William Karavelis, Yoryis merely stepped into a coffeehouse and returned with ten men to add to the Corinthians wanting to remain with him. The new laborers were all from his village, Klepá, among them Pericles Amarantos and Spyros Papachristos who had worked on railroad gangs from Wisconsin to Oregon since leaving Pueblo. Spyros became the courier for the gang, the *erminéas*. Among the men's orders were: hernia trusses, Cuticura salve, Doan's kidney pills, tobacco, matches, postage stamps, gloves, sweaters, pants, and shirts. Yoryis asked him to bring him a revolver when he went to town for supplies. Spyros brought back a four-dollar revolver, and Yoryis gave his cheap one away.

On the first payday, Sampalis drove out in a new, shiny black buggy to demand the padrone's share of wages. Yoryis refused. "This is my territory," Sampalis said angrily, the diamond in his gold tooth flashing, "and don't forget I went with you to stand up to the Corinthians."

"That's between you and me. These men don't owe you anything."

"No?" Sampalis said, smiling with a twist of his mouth and giving Yoryis the Greek salute.

Yoryis watched the buggy disappear in a cloud of dust, his hand on the pistol butt at his waist. Aaaa, what can he do to me, he thought, and went back to his gang.

On the day the men began laying tracks, a figure walked toward them, a slender Greek, his suit coat folded neatly over one arm. As he came closer, he pulled his loosened necktie in place and put on his coat. Yoryis went forward to meet him and at the touch of the man's palm knew he was not a laborer. A Roumeliot speaking school Greek, Yoryis Andoniou, George Anton in English, asked for two months' work until he could be hired as an interpreter in a Utah coal mine that was being opened.

"Can your hands take it?" Yoryis said.

"I need the work."

Yoryis took Pericles from Stavros and put the new Yoryis in his place. The new Yoryis smiled tentatively at the men, as if expecting them to make sport of him with that Greek relish of the wretched for the misfortune of the rich and the educated. George Anton hid his misery, tried to keep up with men who had worked with their hands all their lives, and at night wrote letters for them with blistered fingers.

Besides the arrival of George Anton, one other incident altered the sameness of sagebrush, work, food, and sleep. A bald, brown-bearded man drove out in a buggy and told Yoryis he was a Mormon bishop. "I had a revelation last night," he said. "God told me to come out here and take a look at you Greeks."

Yoryis shrugged his shoulders. "You look," he said. "We work."

When the Mormon left, the men hooted and slapped their thighs over the fool mortal thinking he had talked with God. "And what kind of bishop is he? Dressed like a farmer!" "Did God choose his wives for him? Does he keep a bell on his prick?"

A page from the account book of Spyros Papachristos, errand runner for a railroad gang, showing Yoryis owed him six dollars for a pistol. 1911.

At the end of August, George Anton rode back to Montpelier with the engineer. He shook hands with Yoryis. "I ask to be god-father to a child of yours," he said. "Go well!" the men called to him. For a few years he would be to Yoryis a true brother.

The skies changed and the fiery sunsets were tinged with deep reds that turned purplish black. The air crispened at night, reminding them of winter without work, two months or more in the smoke and noise of coffeehouses. They became surly.

The gang had come close to one of the farms in the sea of sage-brush. Yoryis asked two of the men to walk there, about two miles distance, to bring back chickens and fresh vegetables. The men looked across the sage to the narrow adobe house surrounded on three sides by rows of slender poplars. South of the house were fields of yellow wheat, light green timothy, dark green alfalfa, and two black fields lying fallow. Three figures, like sticks, moved at the edge of the wheat field. The men mumbled that they would rather eat slops than be turned away by the Americans. Cursing them, Yoryis went off, glimpsing Pericles looking on uncertainly.

He had taken several strides when Stavros caught up with him. They walked rapidly, winding their way through the sagebrush. Lizards darted across their path, and a gray, glistening snake disap-

189

peared into a hole. "In my part of the country," Stavros said, "a snake is a good omen," and waved his hands at the blue sky, the clear air, the pungent scent of sagebrush that reminded him, he said, of his Peloponnesian plain.

As they neared the house, two blue-eyed girls with long braids stood in the barren backyard between the house and a low-roofed root cellar and stared at them. Water lapped in the irrigation stream in front of the house; grass grew on the banks. When Yoryis stepped over the planks and entered the yard, one of the girls called, "Ma!"

A woman trudged up from the root cellar. Her skin had the paleness of Northern people, and her eyes, light blue like her daughters', were afraid. She gave a quick look to the distant fields where the figures were working. "Yes, what do you want?" Several children came from behind the barn and watched.

Yoryis pointed to the direction from where they had come. "We come from section gang. We want to buy chickens, eggs, and potatoes. You got to sell?" One of the smaller children giggled. Yoryis had said "putitoes," as his pocket dictionary instructed.

The woman spoke curtly to her daughters. One of them hurried down the cellar steps. The mother went into the chicken coop behind the root cellar, setting off a squawking and flurry of flapping wings. In a moment the girl climbed out of the cellar, dragging a gunnysack filled with potatoes, carrots, and cabbages, then returned and brought back a rag bundle of eggs. The mother appeared with six white chickens dangling from her hands, their legs tied, their wings open but immobilized, and gave them to Stavros.

Yoryis took out his leather purse and placed a silver dollar into the woman's palm, then another. "Enough," she said. Stavros with the chickens and Yoryis, the gunnysack over his shoulder, holding the eggs carefully in his other hand, turned to leave.

An old, white-bearded man came to the back door shouting, "Git those children away from them Greeks! Git off this property, you black Greeks!" The old man lashed on, shaking his fist.

As Yoryis and Stavros crossed the planks, they looked at the cool water flowing over pebbles. When the old voice faded, Stavros said sourly, "And not an offer of a glass of water for us. These

Amerikani! The most inhospitable people in the world! Even to a cursed Turk or Bulgarian passing through, we offered a cup of water. Our worst enemies we wouldn't let leave the village without water! Did you see that water, Yoryis? My mother never had a pot of basil in her house because she couldn't spare the water. Patridha, Patridha! Why do we pine for it when there's no water, no wood, no money for a bottle of quinine? Ach, my little mother. Manoula mou, Manoula mou, I'm coming back."

In autumn, just before finishing the branch line, their isolation was broken once more. Now the plain of sagebrush had become hilly and was disturbed here and there by small homesteads: fields of gold and green surrounding narrow frame and adobe houses, rows of yellow poplars, and great flocks of sheep down from the distant mountains for wintering, foraging for small green plants between the sagebrush.

A large band of Mexican sheepshearers camped a mile away from the railroad gang. They traveled from Mexico through the Southwest, northward into Colorado, Utah, Wyoming, Montana, Canada, and back down to Mexico shearing the sheep a second time. At intervals their voices came to the Greeks as clearly as if they were a few feet away. The Greeks talked little, not wanting to spoil the sound of other human voices. After the shouts and flurry of the shearing, dust rising to the sky, the large scissors flashing under the sun, the Mexicans sat around campfires, glowing yellow in the blackness, and sang. The melancholy singing filled with longing came with the fresh desert air, and the Greeks thought of their villages, their parents, and families. The day the sheepshearers moved on, Stavros came to Yoryis, shouting, "Get me my pay. Let me go! I can't bear xenetia. Let me go back *now*!"

When the railroad tracking was completed, the men still had to get through October and November before deep winter set in. Yoryis could not get work on either the Oregon Short Line or the Union Pacific. He had been blacklisted by Sampalis, and he had twenty-four unemployed men depending on him. Desperate, he telephoned Leonidas Skliris. The Czar of the Greeks sent Yoryis railroad passes to take his gang to Portola, in the Sierra Nevada of

California. Two other labor gangs worked ahead of them, one made up of a hundred twenty East Indians—three women among them, the paymaster told Yoryis. The three gangs worked on a stretch of rails fifty-eight miles long, digging out thirty-three tunnels.

Snow began falling. When it stayed on the ground, with more and more to come until it reached great heights, the men were laid off. Most of them went on to San Francisco. Yoryis asked the road-master for railroad passes to Chicago for him and Pericles.

16

Emilia dreaded the moment she would confront the *kyria* and *kyrios* with her decision. Even before she took off her coat, she lighted the vigil wick and prayed for strength. Then saying to herself, "They will not keep me here. I *will* go," she went into the living room where the *kyrios* was reading his newspaper and the *kyria* was telling Achilles one of the nice *hodtzas* stories. "I have something to tell you," she said. They looked up. "I have decided to go to Ameriki." They nodded sadly. "Yes," the *kyrios* said. "We expected something like this."

The *kyria* called in her dressmaker to sew a coat, suit, and two dresses for Emilia. All three spent hours in the dining room while Achilles drew pictures in a big book on the floor. The *kyria* bought fine cotton for underclothing; Emilia sewed the seams by hand because the now bent, gray little dressmaker was using the treadle machine; the *kyria* crocheted around the edges of the camisoles and pantaloons. She also bought Emilia a new dream book and a small straw sewing basket. In the evenings she talked with Emilia, as if they were sisters, equals, about her childhood, her schooling with the French nuns, and her dowry arrangements. At her icon Emilia asked forgiveness for all the times she had disliked the *kyria*.

The *kyrios* would not allow *Emilia* to go by steerage. He paid half of a third-class ticket for her and she the other half from her savings. Then Emilia, *Kyria* Namik, and the three little Namiks stood on the tier above the excited, shouting steerage passengers and waved to the *kyrios,* holding Achilles high above the screeching crowd, the weeping *kyria,* and their new servant girl, a ten-year-old from an eastern Thracian village. As the ship moved out of the clamoring bay, Emilia looked at the holy city, her heart beating unbearably.

Below, they could hardly turn around between the bunks in the stifling, airless room; the sharp, fresh smells of the children's vomit and urine overwhelmed entrenched stale odors. At first Emilia breathed through her mouth, then gave it up. She often took the oldest boy of seven out of the room, looking from side to side for stewards or men passengers who would block her way.

On deck, trying to keep the boy's unwilling hand in hers, Emilia watched a Greek woman come down from the upper-class quarters and talk with the Greeks sitting on the deck. Fearlessly the woman went about, speaking with this woman or that child, even to men! And she, Emilia, talked to no one that nothing would be known about her. One day the woman approached her and asked where she was going. "To New York, Kyria."

"Is someone meeting you or are you going on?"

Emilia thought she should lie so that the woman would not consider her immoral for traveling without a male relative, yet impelled to tell the truth, she answered, "I am with a Jewish family. The father will meet us."

The woman frowned. "But that won't do. You must be in the company of a Greek family. You'll be lost in New York. But I will see to it."

After several sleepless nights, Emilia told *Kyria* Namik about the fashionable woman. "I had better go with her, Kyria Namik. You are newcomers in Ameriki, and I will be a burden." *Kyria* Namik put her plump arms around Emilia and cried.

Three and a half weeks after leaving Constantinople, and after stopping in Piraeus to transfer to a larger ship and finding at customs that half their clothing had been stolen from their trunks, Emilia, the Namiks, and hundreds of immigrants pushed down the gangplank into the din of Ellis Island. The well-dressed woman left Emilia at a desk where a Greek-speaking Rumanian woman questioned her. *Kyria* Namik clutched Emilia to her before she and the children were lost in the crowd.

"We must have assurances," the Rumanian woman said, while Emilia struggled for breath. She sat stunned at the foolishness, the enormity of what she had done: she had left sweet, round-faced *Kyria* Namik, whom she had known for many years, to follow a strange woman, Greek though she was. Where would she take her? What would they do with her? Clutching her bag, she was shunted along to a line of women and children waiting for a doctor to place his stethoscope over their blouses and then to look into their eyes, mouths, and ears.

It was a Friday and evening was graying the room. Voices in many languages shouted directions: those who could not be processed before closing time would have to remain until Monday. Emilia and a group of women were led into a large room with a long row of cots on either side of the aisle. They lay down to sleep, some weeping, some praying, some laughing nervously. Emilia lay awake thinking of the Namiks and her horrible foolishness.

The reek of must, delousing spray, sweat, and cooking smells hovered in the air. In the great dining hall, Emilia ate only enough bread to keep the pangs of hunger from hurting. She gazed about at the shrunken people bent over and weeping while they ate, several to be sent back because of the doctor's denial, and at women with children whose husbands had not come for them. She was abandoned like them, without a family, a wandering derelict.

On Monday morning a woman attendant went down the row of beds and looked at the tags on the women's clothing. The woman beckoned Emilia to follow her. Carrying her suitcase with both hands, Emilia hurried. Again she was taken to the Rumanian woman. A Greek woman dressed in a brown, belted coat and a hat very like a man's stood at the side of the desk and welcomed Emilia to America in the speech of an educated person. Emilia could not speak from relief. "A good Fate," the Rumanian woman said, and turned her attention to another immigrant.

The well-dressed woman spoke pleasantly. "We're waiting for my sister and her husband. She was on the ship with you. They've

Maria Economidhou, Athenian journalist, traveling in the United States with a railroad gang, 1912. "Many young Greeks in the West wanted wives. I'll send you there." Maria S. Economidhou, *E Ellines tis Amerikis opous tous edha* ("The Greeks in America as I Saw Them," New York, 1916).

gone to see about your trunk." Although the woman was no older than Emilia, she appeared worldly to her, far more so than the *kyríes* of Constantinople. Emilia answered her questions about the journey with lowered eyes.

The sister and her stocky, mustached husband appeared, he wiping the perspiration from his fat cheeks. Emilia looked down at the floor: she knew she was an unwanted responsibility, but Greek *filotimo* demanded that they help her.

In the taxi, being driven through amazing streets of tall buildings, fast-walking people crowding the sidewalks, others in automobiles, Emilia was told that the woman in the belted coat was a journalist for her husband's publications in Athens. Her name was Maria Economidhou and she was traveling throughout the United States and writing about the loneliness of the immigrant men, their homesickness, the injuries and deaths in factories and mines, and the hate Americans had for them. The journalist burst out, "Ameriki swallows them! How many mothers wait in vain for them! Vanished! Dead, alive, no one knows!"

"Their mothers are to blame, too," her sister said. "Keeping after their sons to hurry with money for their sisters' dowries. Friki! Friki!"

"I'll be coming west," the journalist said to Emilia, "and I'll see you again."

Where is the West? Emilia wanted to ask, but wherever it was and whatever was there, it had all been decided for her. The journalist spoke of a banker, *Kyrios* Mathaios, who would meet her. She had sent him a telegram. He would find her a husband among the thousands of young Greeks working in the mines and on the railroads.

The following day Emilia followed the journalist's sister and her husband to a vast, teeming railway station where a new tag was tied to her coat lapel. She carried a large paper sack of bread, boiled eggs, cheese, apples, and oranges. While her host, carrying her suitcase, walked ahead, his wife spoke encouragingly to Emilia, but in the noise of the station her words were barely audible.

They boarded a coach, and at the first empty seat her perspiring host pushed Emilia's valise under it. He pointed to the seat and Emilia sat down. While his wife smiled above her, Emilia listened to the same message she had heard the night before and at breakfast from the woman's husband: she would be well taken care of; she should not worry; she would ride four days and five nights; she must not give any one an invitation to become friendly; all arrangements had been made with the railroad; the washroom was at the back end of the coach.

Two young men with black mourning bands on their suit sleeves took the seat opposite her; then a middle-aged man sat down next to her. The *kyria* whispered, "When a seat next to a woman becomes vacant, move there."

They were gone. Emilia looked through the windows for one more glance of them, but steam clouded the windows. Slowly, rows of tracks under steel girders went by the window. The smell of tobacco and a human sourness was in the moving coach. She covered her nose with a handkerchief to keep herself from becoming sick from the effluvia of human beings.

The train gathered speed, bumping gently, wheels clicking. With growing fear she looked through the soot-specked windows at passing smudged tenements and sprawling factories billowing out black smoke. She thought of how she had yearned for America, and now she was traveling deeper into the unknown, into that exile she and the servant girls had sighed over.

The factories and dingy streets of brick and frame houses gave way to hilly farmland—a good omen it seemed to her and her heart beat less hard. Yet it was odd. So vast were the farms and so far from hamlets that solitary farmhouses stood among the brown-stubbled fields far from each other. She dozed, awoke, and touched the tag tied to the lapel of her coat thinking it had disappeared and she would not be able to tell the uniformed official where she was going, who she was, or who was to meet her. She pressed her free hand against the hidden pocket of her skirt where she had sewn her money.

Several times during the day the three men, singly, made their way down the aisle to the washroom or to the smoker in the next car. Women and chattering children lurched to the washroom at the other end of the car. Emilia pulled her shoulders back to prepare herself for the perilous ordeal of walking the length of the car and entering a den occupied by strange women while her bag, without doubt, was being searched. The little room, jerking and rumbling loudly, was empty. The smell of soot and urine stung her nostrils. When she returned to her seat, her heart wild, she surreptitiously opened her bag to see if it had been touched.

At some stops vendors boarded and walked through the car with candy, apples, and sandwiches wrapped in white paper. Even from these men and boys Emilia averted her face to hide what surely could be seen—that she was traveling without the protection of a father or brother. Some passengers bought from the vendors; others undid newspaper-wrapped packets tied with string, opened paper bags or metal buckets. The odors of food and sweat were like that of greasy dishwater to Emilia. She recoiled from her paper sack of food.

By evening the car was half-empty—only two women remained. They smiled at her, but she could not bring herself to nod
to the forsaken women: the three of them were miserable human
beings. Pain grew in her head.

The cycle of dawn, morning, noon, dusk, and night repeated
itself. Her coat over one shoulder, she slept in bits of time, one
hand on the hidden pocket of her skirt, the other at times covering
her nose with a handkerchief. In the morning she made the dangerous journey to the lavatory, washed herself with breathless
speed, combed her hair and twisted it on top of her head, returned
and examined her bag. Her stomach resisted the cheese, hard-boiled
eggs, and fruit in the sack, but she was weak from hunger. She
nibbled on the bread, already stale, and the strong-smelling *kasseri*
cheese. She thought of buying whatever food was wrapped in white
paper, but she was afraid she would be stared at for pointing and
certain she would be cheated of the small cache of coins in the little
embroidered money purse that Hrisoula had given her when she left
Thessaloniki for Constantinople.

By the second night the air was gone from the dimly lighted
coach. The Rumanian woman at the desk in Ellis Island, the well-
dressed woman who had come for her, her husband with his naked,
untrustworthy face, the banker who would meet her were conspira-
tors, and Emilia knew she was trapped in the coach car as livestock
headed for slaughter were trapped in the cattle cars that flashed by.

At a long train stop the second evening a crowd of threadbare
blacks descended with pails and rags to wash the windows. Emilia
exchanged a fleeting, weary glance with one of them, pockmarked,
his eyeballs as yellow as those of malaria sufferers. She thought of
the *kyrios*, the *kyria*, frail little Achilles, the servant girls, and the
apprentices. It was strange to her that at the moment they were
going about their daily routine while she was on an American train
riding farther and farther from them. Hrisoula in Thessaloniki, her
faceless parents, brother, and sisters in the village were all living
that instant as they had always lived, while for her the unknown
awaited.

The train sped on. For an entire freezing night it did not stop.
The following day an endless plain of burnished grassland moved

past the window, flat, no hills or mountains in the distance. One long stretch was dotted with sod houses with thatched roofs. Smoke came from some of the chimneys, and figures plowing with a lone horse or two were breaking up the virgin grassland.

At noon the train stopped at a black water tower, a monster in the waving brown grass. At the side of the tracks stood a line of young men in old, heavy jackets, some with caps, some with gloves, some with bare dirty hands resting on sledges, shovels, or holding cross bars. Little clouds of steam came from their noses.

One of the men looked at Emilia. His eyes were dark brown; his mustache twisted upward into points. His lips moved. Then the men stared at her, and she shamelessly stared at them. The coach gave a great bound. Emilia looked frantically at the men while they stood riveted, straining forward, a look of wild recognition in their eyes. They were Greeks! Emilia turned her head, to raise her hand, to see their answering two-fingered Greek salute, but only the grassland was there. Turning back, she grieved that she had been too late and mourned for the young Greeks on the lonely prairie. If only she had been more alert!

She said the Lord's Prayer and the Nicene Creed, each three times, and asked the All—Holy and Christ to intercede with God that the young men would soon be with people and not like Sarakatsan nomads far from their hearths.

At intervals the train stopped, and Emilia was in agony that the conductor had forgotten her. He never looked her way when he walked through the car to punch the new passengers' tickets. Careful as she was, her clothes were wrinkling; her new coat was limp and covered with lint and dust; and the waist corset bound her tightly. Soot and grime had worked through her clothing and into her skin; her handkerchief was a moist wad in her sweaty hand. She no longer covered her nose.

Afraid she was improperly counting the four days and five nights, Emilia thought of Aristea's horrible eyes as she told of women and girls who had been fooled by lovers and disappeared into the winding, filthy alleys of Arab and Turkish quarters never to be seen again, forced to lose their honor to depraved men.

The prairie flowed into sagebrush plains. On the other side of barbed wire paralleling the tracks, herds of well-fleshed red and white cattle, their horns wide and gracefully curved, browsed between sagebrush clumps with no human beings about to keep them from being stolen. Magpies, red-winged black birds, and pale, mauve brown mourning doves perched on the barbed wire and flew off. All through the day birds swooped down to the arid earth and soared into the unbounded blue sky. Jackrabbits streaked away from the roar of the train. A coyote, tossed to the side by a passing train, lay swollen and stiff. Crows exploded from the carcass at the engine's noise, but greed brought them back, huge black maggots continuing their feast.

Somewhere she would be forced out of the car, Emilia knew. A man resembling the dark, mustached Anti–Christ on church icons would be waiting. Pain struggled in her skull. The people about her blurred. She leaned her head against a grayed napkin, and darkness fell before her.

A long time later, the conductor motioned her to come forward and picked up her bag. Her skirt hid her feet, so swollen that she had unlaced her ankle-top shoes and laced them up again with the heels under her instep. Teetering, she followed the conductor down the aisle and stood in the cold, rackety space near the door. People crowded behind her, talking happily in the bouncy American language. The train slowed evenly to a stop.

The conductor helped Emilia down and pointed to his side. She stood there on clubs of pain, her eyes flitting from one face to the other of the approaching, rushing, alien people. Not one Greek face! She was deserted!

"Dhespinis! Dhespinis!" an imperious male voice called. A short, thin man followed by a stout, breathless woman, a young man, and two boys came up to her. Twitching his mustache, the short man took out a telegram for the conductor's scrutiny. He shook hands with Emilia and spoke the traditional greetings. Tears of gratitude at hearing her own language after days of isolation fell from Emilia's eyes. The stout woman kissed her on both cheeks, and the young man and his brothers shook her hand. The father pointed to Emilia's suitcase, and his oldest son picked it up.

Perspiring and puffing, the woman took Emilia's arm as they

followed the mincing little man around a throng of people, up a concrete incline, through a crowded, high-ceilinged waiting room, and to an automobile. On directions from the stout woman, Emilia, amazed, got into the back seat of the canvas-topped automobile, the youngest son, between her and his mother. The father and oldest son returned to the station for Emilia's trunk. "Tripolis, Tripolis," the woman called, her plump hands held out, ready to receive the provincial town. "I left my Tripolis for this exile," she said in a thick Peloponnesian dialect. "My family, my country I left for this strange Ameriki!" For several minutes she cried copiously, sniffling into her handkerchief. The boy in the center of the front seat looked back at his mother with a smirk.

Quickly the mother dried her eyes at the approach of her husband, oldest son, and a black porter pulling a cart with Emilia's trunk on it. *Kyrios* Mathaios handed the porter a length of rope, stood by giving solemn instructions for tying the trunk on the back of the car, dropped a coin into the man's palm, and got behind the wheel. His son cranked the car, then bounded onto the front seat next to the window.

The car roared and bounced through macadamized streets and down the busy, spacious Main Street with its multistoried buildings, streetcars, horse-drawn carriages, wagons, and a few automobiles. The father talked about his automobile and its cost, mixing a few purist words with his dialect; everyone listened respectfully.

On through tree-lined streets almost as wide as town squares, the car puttered, passing other automobiles and a streetcar filled with people. Emilia glimpsed bright green lawns bordering the wide streets, mansions of rock and brick, and large wooden houses decorated with intricate carvings. The car stopped in front of a white brick house surrounded by a small area of grass and several trees.

Kyria Mathaios grandly opened the front door of her house to the odor of stale cooking and mothballs and led Emilia through six rooms. A glass chandelier hung in the living room over a wine-colored velvet sofa and chairs. The massive, carved dining room

furniture was resplendent yet dusty. Three bedrooms became pro-
gressively smaller and the furniture less ornate. A bathroom was almost as large as the smallest bedroom; its long porcelain bathtub set
on metal claws was ringed with several parallel black bands of dirt;
the big sink and toilet bowl were dingy with protracted, uncleaned
use. Behind the black, greasy kitchen stove, a marble slab was overlaid with soot and food splatterings. "Takis's room is upstairs,"
Kyria Mathaios said with finality, giving Emilia to understand that
she, an unmarried woman, would never be expected to enter her
oldest son's room. They returned to the smallest bedroom next to
the kitchen where Emilia's trunk and suitcase rested on a flowered
carpet.

Kyria Mathaios sat heavily on the bed. Wiping her moist face
and neck with a limp handkerchief, she said, "As you can see, I have
no servants. That's how life is in Ameriki. For us foreigners it's
hard. Oh yes, Kyrios Mathaios brought me twice Amerikanidhes.
Better, I told him, that I struggle myself! I couldn't talk to them
and give them orders. If they were proper servants, that wouldn't
have been necessary. They would have done the work without a
word from me. No, Ameriki isn't easy for me.

"So here I am with a houseful to cook for, wash, and clean up
after. Don't worry. You'll help me until we find you a good husband. Thousands of men here want wives. Women don't need dowries here.

"Life is different here. Plenty of money—yes, but what good is
it if you have to work like the hamalidhes on the docks.

"All right, now. Take a bath and we'll eat, then you'll want to
sleep. Tomorrow we'll talk."

Kyria Mathaios led the way to the bathroom. She opened the
sink tap and hot water streamed out. "That's right," she said, "in
Greece a servant heats the water and fills the tub, but then can
machines cook and wash dishes? No!"

Emilia scrubbed the tub using a rag under the sink, which she
first soaped and rinsed thoroughly. Then she filled the tub and
washed herself with her own soap. Her eyes were on the door. Although it was locked, she was afraid it would suddenly open and the

master or one of his sons would be there. Her swollen, throbbing feet flamed the color of boiled crayfish in the warm water.

After twisting her wet hair on top of her head and dressing in clean clothing from her trunk, Emilia hurried into the kitchen and asked for an apron. She wanted to hide the unpressed folds of her dress. "Ahh, now you look like a nice girl," *Kyria* Mathaios said.

Ashamed at how she had looked earlier, Emilia quickly wrapped about her an apron so large it almost went around her twice and took a platter of roast beef and macaroni from the plump hands. She looked at neither the father nor his sons as she walked into the dining room. Their talking stopped.

They ate the overcooked roast and macaroni under a circle of light from a dome-shaped blue, green, yellow, and red leaded-glass electric light fixture. *Kyria* Mathaios talked and ate. "Greek goat-herds in the mountains near here make feta, but who knows how clean they are. Necessity, necessity! 'In times of drought even hail is welcome' as we say in our unforgettable country."

Emilia ate carefully thinking all eyes were on her and tried not to think of men milking goats with dirty hands—only women milked goats in *patridha*.

"Beef! Beef!" Kyria Mathaios said, eating with great attention. "The Amerikani eat beef all the time. Lamb, young and tender, they turn up their noses." Not only that, she went on, they drank cow's milk and ate corn! Animal food!

The sons still had not spoken; the oldest who was called Takis, the diminutive of Petros, with small handsome features, ate in sulky silence. "And you lived in Thessaloniki and Constantinople? Fine cities," the father said in such a way that Emilia felt she was elevated in his eyes for having lived in them. "The few Greek women we have here came from villages, except for one. It's a good thing for the young men," he looked toward Takis, "to see a well-bred Greek girl."

In the silence, Emilia had to swallow again and again after each bit of food. Then *Kyria* Mathaios was off again, talking as she chewed about the horrible train journey she and her sons had made to be reunited with her husband: she would never forget Takis's diarrhea and vomiting. "Catastrophe! Catastrophe!" she cried, crossing herself, then suddenly shouted, "We'll take care of you like a daughter! The Greek customs and beliefs are the best in the world! We will never forget our Greek ways in this exile!"

"And what's this!" *Kyrios* Mathaios slammed a knife on his plate. Until then he had eaten with exaggerated dignity. He scowled at his younger sons. "You were in Greek Town today! At the Acropolis Candy Store instead of in school! Answer!"

The boys whined that the American children made fun of them when they tried to speak English. The mother demanded that the father go the very next morning to school and order the teacher to make the students stop it. The father vowed he would beat the boys until the priest looked like a donkey to them if they missed one more day of school. The boys whimpered that the father had told them that life would be better in America, yet he wouldn't even let them go to Greek Town to see a puppet show.

"Plug it! That's what I need—my schoolboy sons sitting in coffeehouses and watching those vulgar Karaghiozi puppets! You have time enough for those things when you grow up. And not another word that you were better off in the fatherland! Look at your clothes! Did you ever have good clothes like those in patridha? And money in your pockets for chocolates! Now shut your mouths!" He glared at them, then roared, "Get out of my sight!"

The boys ran outside. After a few moments of silence, *Kyria* Mathaios in subdued submissiveness said, "They have some justice for their complaints. They're little. It's hard to learn when others are laughing."

"What do you know? You never learned to write your name!"

Kyria Mathaios clapped her hands to her puff-pigeon chest and looked at the ceiling. "Do you hear! My sainted parents, do you hear!" Then, with haughty, narrowed eyes turned to her husband, she said, "If my brothers were here, you wouldn't dare talk to me like this!"

Emilia gathered the soiled plates and hurried into the kitchen. Closing the door, she began scraping the plates at the sink. She looked through the window at the two younger boys, each holding a paper sack, laughing, their mouths full, chocolate rimming their lips. As she watched them run off, Takis passed by the window, head down as if this would make him invisible. He glanced up at Emilia, startled, then with a sneer vanished.

Emilia washed the dishes while hissings and blurtings came through the dining room door. She went into her room and placed her icon of the All–Holy on the dresser behind an oil-smudged water glass used for the vigil light. She undressed, lit the vigil taper, and crossed herself. Then she looked at the All–Holy and said, "So, you sent me to this house of disorder."

Her eyes closed in fatigue, but suddenly *Kyria* Mathaios was slumped on her bed, crying, telling Emilia about her hard life in America. Children didn't listen to their parents in this exile. Takis had sneaked off to see a straw-haired waitress at the Acropolis Candy Store, not only a slut *Amerikanidha,* but a *Mormona.* The *Mormoni* once had even more wives than Turks. Their leader *Brigamo* had fifty! And her firstborn, her eyes, had gone crazy with love for that *Mormona!* And she had almost died giving birth to him. That donkey!

She wept on for a few moments, then sighing sorrowfully, said, "We'll be entertaining men who'll come asking for you." A profound grief came into her eyes.

Disorder, disorder, Emilia said to herself after *Kyria* Mathaios had gone. Calling her son that terrible epithet *donkey! Disorder, disorder.*

17

Young men off railroad gangs crowded into the Chicago coffeehouses, like Yoryis, looking for work. One night, discouraged, Yoryis was walking under the elevated tracks when he looked up to see a man approaching. Under a dim electric light, the gun in the man's hand shone. Yoryis grabbed for the revolver sticking out of his belt. Slowly the two men walked toward each other. A few feet away they stopped. The man was black; smiling at Yoryis's foreignness, he said, "You're one of us," and with a chortle waved him on. In a coffeehouse the next day, after Yoryis laughingly related his night's adventure, a Roumeliot told him there was an opening in the Gary, Indiana, steel mill.

The town of Gary, set on a dry plain, consisted of a few houses, saloons, stores, and the sprawling steel mill with tall stacks shooting up clouds of black smoke. Poles, Slavs, Greeks, and Italians worked on the railroad tracks and furnaces; the mill worked night and day. A labor gang of seventy Italians shoveled coal into ten mammoth, blazing furnaces. At all times eight furnaces were working and two were cooling. The heat was intense; sweat soaked the men's hair and plastered their shirts to their backs and chests.

One hundred sixty-five miles of railroad tracks in the mill yard transported coal to the furnaces and ashes from them. A steel gang laid new rails, an extra gang kept the tracks in condition, and two section gangs checked the road bed and did small jobs. Yoryis was put over the smaller section gang. One of its jobs was to spread the furnace ash over the earth and tamp it down to ready it for the steel gang to lay rails over it.

After four months Yoryis sent Pericles back to Greece: "You're too puny to be a laborer." Pericles eagerly packed his belongings. Yoryis gave him five hundred dollars for their sisters' dowries and sent him off with the order, "Don't get married." As soon as Pericles arrived in the village, he, the rich *Amerikanos,* was beseiged. Not long after, he married, using part of the dowry money for himself.

Yoryis was given the larger gang of one hundred men, all Greeks from various provinces in *patridha.* As the foreman he was supplied with a railroad sleeping car on the yards so that he would be available for emergencies. A telephone in the car was connected to the yardmaster's office. Late one night the yardmaster telephoned him to bring several men to extend the rails over a bed of ashes: the steel gang foreman and his men were sick, he said, "vomiting and shitting blood." Yoryis found only one of his men in the rail car living quarters. The others had gone into town.

Yoryis at one end and his *patriotis* at the other, the two lifted each five hundred fifty pound rail and laid it on the bed of ashes. The next morning the yardmaster telephoned Yoryis to come to his office. He handed him a box of high-grade Cuban cigars and shook his hand. "You saved me one hundred seventy-five dollars last night," he said. "I'll keep my eye on you."

One of Yoryis's men was a Peloponnesian who had had six years of schooling and who talked to no one. An hour before quitting time he would disappear into the privy to avoid more work. The men complained to Yoryis who warned the Peloponnesian. The following day he caught him as he was leaving the privy and bashed his fist into the man's face. The man fell, his head hitting a rail. When he did not move, Yoryis thought he had killed him. He hurried around the railroad cars and roundhouse wondering how he would get through the gates without his gang. He could be stopped and arrested for vagrancy, but the guard recognized him and he walked out.

He hid in Chicago, stayed away from coffeehouses where he was known, and bought cheese and bread to eat in a rented room. At night he lay awake for hours thinking he had killed a man, worthless though he was. He had left Gary without his pay; soon his money was almost gone and he had to venture into the streets. After pushing through crowds of unemployed at several agencies and being turned away when he gave his name, he called himself George Nelson and was made foreman of an extra gang west of Chicago.

Several weeks later he went into a Roumeliot coffeehouse on Chicago's Halsted Street. The *kafetzis* handed him a telegram from one of his Gary labor gang. The message read: "HE'S ALIVE." Yoryis was free, yet he could not forget the yardmaster's "I'll keep my eye on you." A well-dressed, handsome labor agent, also called Yoryis, was there taking on men for Wyoming and Idaho section gangs. Meintenes signed on Yoryis as George Nelson and sent him to Rock Springs, Wyoming, as a foreman.

One job as foreman followed another, several lasting a few weeks, some for months. He would remember their names until he died: Rawlins, Kemmerer, Converse, and Lyman, Wyoming; Elva, Meadows, Council, Evergreen, Payette, Rigby, and Lorenzo, Idaho. Other places lay on the sagebrush plain with no distinctive mark, water tank, or nearby hamlet that the men meeting each other years later could use to describe them. Of the nameless places where an accident or death had occurred, the men could only say, "You know, it was maybe two hundred miles north of Pocatello" or "about a hundred miles west of Cheyenne."

Many jobs would stand out vividly in the blur of sagebrush and toil. Near Rock Springs again, Yoryis's laborers were Cretans who had come directly from Crete wearing black pantaloons, vests, and fringed kerchiefs. They complained of the loneliness and at night sang doleful four-line *mantinadhes* about Crete ("that little piece of heaven"), love, and poverty. The next moment they were up dancing a frenzied *pentozali* to the music of a compatriot's *lyra*. With their first wages, they walked to Rock Springs to buy American clothes and visit a coffeehouse. Not all of them returned, and Yoryis forced those who came back to work two hours longer each day to finish the line on time.

In one of the nameless places they saw a family of Indians: a regal grandfather, a gray braid over each shoulder, a tall black fencepost hat on his head; a boy and girl; their fat mother in full cotton dress; and a wrinkled, toothless grandmother, the sun making a halo of her wispy white hair. Except for the grandfather, the Indians pulled tufts of wool caught on barbed wire when flocks were driven to the high country for summer range. They put the tufts into a gunnysack the mother dragged over the ground and guided about the sagebrush. Not once did the Indians look at the staring Greeks who were full of the sight. For a week they talked continually about the Indians and hoped they would see more of them.

In Alexander, Idaho, an isolated water stop, Yoryis needed more men than Meintenes had sent him and called Charlie Cayias, a labor agent in Salt Lake City, to send him forty laborers. An odd group arrived—new, young immigrants and older cardplayers rounded up in coffeehouses and looking for temporary work. Not realizing that Yoryis was Greek, they talked obscenely about him for working them hard. "When we're through," one of them said as Yoryis passed a group, "let's tie him up and shit on him."

Yoryis pummeled the cardplayer while the men looked on, startled. "You're Greek," they whispered. Yoryis discarded the name George Nelson. Some of the men went with him when Meintenes sent him to Bozeman, Montana, then to Rupert, Idaho, where they laid rails on five feet of snow, saw for the first time in their lives a man on skis, and then returned to Pocatello.

Yoryis rented the kitchen of a vacant restaurant in the winter of 1912 for three months at fifty dollars. In front of the building the owner sold liquor under the guise of soft drinks—Pocatello was a dry city. Yoryis and eleven men from his last steel gang used the giant, greasy coal stove to cook their beans, lentils, macaroni, and on Sundays a piece of meat. Each day they escaped from the blackened walls, the grease-soaked wooden floor, and the exposed rusted pipes to the barren but warm coffeehouses. At night they slept around the stove on the floor or on folding canvas cots while the coals crackled and burned to ash and the night wind howled.

Nick Zeese. At fourteen he climbed out of a window and escaped to America.

One freezing night the men huddled around the open oven door with blankets over their shoulders. Yoryis answered a knock on the door, his hand on his revolver butt. A young man stood there, a Greek, a slight figure in a gray coat with black fur collar. One hand was in his pants pocket pushing his coat back and revealing a well-pressed gray suit, a striped shirt, and a red crocheted silk tie ornamented with a green stone in a stick pin. Between small, even teeth he clenched a cigar; his brown eyes were mirthful, expectant; his eyebrows were peaked like Yoryis's.

Yoryis held out his hand. "Come in, patrioti. Who are you?"

"I'm your cousin Nikos Zisimopoulos from Nikolitsa." His palm was soft against Yoryis's work-scarred one. "Sampalis told me you were here."

Yoryis pointed to a wooden box. Nikos sat down and Yoryis looked closely at him. He had last seen him as a six-month-old baby when he and his father had gone to Lamia, and the judge had unsuccessfully defended Nikos's father for a vendetta murder. Under the dangling light globe, Nikos looked his age—sixteen. Yoryis gave his clothes a long look. "What kind of work have you been doing?" he asked.

"A little bit of everything," Nikos said and stopped smiling at the disapproving, patriarchal stare of his older cousin.

"With those clothes and those hands, you don't hold a pick and shovel, that's for sure."

"It's like this. I've got this knack for remembering figures. I can make more money playing cards than a laborer can earn in a week."

Yoryis reached over and struck Nikos on the ear. "You bastard! Blackening the family name! Move in here and in spring I'll take you with me on a labor gang."

"No! I almost went crazy in South Dakota as a water boy. I've worked! My first job was in a furniture factory in Grand Rapids. The noise made me jump out of my skin. I went into a mine in West Virginia, too. I couldn't breathe down there. I almost suffocated! I've got this knack with numbers—"

"I've got the knack too, you kerata! Now move in here and straighten yourself out!"

"I've got a room in a hotel."

"Why are you throwing your money away on hotels and fancy clothes? What about your sisters' dowries? Have you sent any of your shit money back for them?"

Nikos lowered his eyes in a false shame that inflamed Yoryis. He got up and grabbed Nikos by the lapels of his coat. "A cardplayer! Mixed up with street women too! Go get your clothes and move in here. You're not going to travel Ameriki and make trash out of our clan's name! I'll teach you filotimo if I have to kill you to do it!"

The men nodded soberly and admonished Nikos. "Listen to your elder. Yoryis is an honorable man. He has your interests at heart. Don't get mixed up with bad men and women. You'll get bad blood from those street women. Then you'll never be able to marry. Remember the proverb, 'He who pisses in the sea, eats its salt.'" Nikos looked doleful.

"Well, what brings you here?" Yoryis said, letting go of Nikos's lapels.

Nikos forgot that he was a shamed man and chuckled, the cigar still clenched between his teeth. "I cheated Skliris and thought I'd better not show my mug around Salt Lake City for a while."

The men leaned forward eagerly, "You got the better of the Czar of the Greeks?"

"I went to Bingham, Utah, to the open-pit copper mine, and I found one of Skliris's bootlickers. I told him I needed a job but I didn't have any money to pay him the fee for getting me work, but I'd pay it out of my first wages. He gave me Skliris's contract and I signed it.

"So then I told the bastard I needed work clothes and supplies and he gave me a note to the Panhellenic, you know, the company store. Skliris has an interest in it. And so," Nikos laughed, "I went to the Panhellenic and bought this *Stetson*." He tapped the brim of his hat with two yellowed fingers. "These *Florsheim* shoes." He lifted his feet off the floor and pulled up his pant legs at the knees. The shoes were a highly polished light brown with pearl buttons up the sides. "I got this silk shirt, a box of *Havana* cigars—and a pair of work gloves so the squashhead who waited on me wouldn't get wise." Nikos took a handful of thick, finely tapered cigars from his overcoat pocket and passed them around. The men laughed, jeering at Skliris:

"That's what he deserves. Shit to the shithead!"

"Eh, Niko, 'you're as happy as a wolf in a storm.'"

"'Forty for the horse! and sixty for the saddle!'"

"You gypsy," Yoryis said, but laughing. "They'll catch up with you. Your eyes four."

"Aaa," Nikos scoffed. "Skliris is in big trouble. He signed me up as a strikebreaker. Everything is salad at the mine. The Cretans joined the union just to get him fired as their labor agent. Those hot-headed Cretans have taken blankets and guns and have barricaded themselves on the mountainsides and shoot at anything that moves."

"Zito, the Cretans!"

The men talked for hours, wanting to know everything about the newcomer. His father, Nikos said, had died in prison. When he was fourteen, Lambros Zisimopoulos, a first cousin of his and second cousin to Yoryis, spirited Nikos at night through a window and brought him to America. Nikos's mother had refused to let him go, "so there was nothing else to do." Lambros and his brothers were working in the McGill, Nevada, copper mines. They had Americanized their names: Lambros Zisimopoulos to Louis Zeese; Demetrios to James, and Elias kept his name as it was. Nikos called himself Nick Zeese.

Late at night Yoryis reminded Nikos at the door, "Tomorrow, get your clothes from the hotel and come here."

Nikos did not return. The next day the coffeehouses were abuzz over him. He had lured a Japanese to his hotel room. The Japanese was on his way back to Japan with three thousand dollars in savings from fifteen years of section gang work in the West. With a magnet under the carpet, Nikos stripped the Japanese of his three thousand dollars using loaded dice.

"I'll slaughter him!" Yoryis fumed, but Nikos was already on a train bound for payday in the Butte, Montana, copper mines.

After another year as foreman on section gangs, Yoryis was hired by the Union Pacific as a detective for want of a better title: he routed Greeks out of freight cars and into railroad crews. He had been in America six years and had sent only one thousand six hundred dollars to his family. Each month he mailed a money order to his father, who could no longer work; and to keep Pericles's family from starving, Yoryis answered his pleading letters with money drafts and curses. Fearful that if she waited for more money from Yoryis for her dowry she would be stigmatized as an old maid, Maria married a man far older than herself, a widower with a halfgrown daughter. Yoryis was enraged at his lack of progress: he had two more sisters to dower, and he was nothing more than a wanderer.

A year later, Lambros Zisimopoulos—Louis Zeese—searched Yoryis out in Pocatello. Their fathers were first cousins, but the Xerovouni Mountain separated their villages and they had not met in *patridha*. Yoryis admonished Louis for bringing Nick Zeese to America without a goodbye to his mother. Louis was a slender, morose man, a few years older than Yoryis, and had a high school education. His Greek was sprinkled with American expressions he read in local and Greek newspapers: *sport, bill of fare, box, car—* pronounced *sportis, bill o fairy, boxa, carro*. He said he had been framed in the Greek army by two soldiers who accused him of stealing cheese from the commissary and selling it. Sent to prison for six months and knowing he could have no normal life afterwards, he came to America with his brothers, Elias and Demetrios, and his cousin Nick. His brothers were in McGill working in the copper mines in the day and spending their wages at night.

"I told them to go to the devil as long as they wouldn't save their money. I've got a thousand dollars with me. Let's go into business."

They walked through Greek Town, past grocery stores, coffee houses, restaurants, and small hotels. The labor agent Vasilis Karavelis and his partner, diamond-toothed Sampalis, contracted with railroads to provide laborers, stipulating that supplies would be bought at the grocery stores they controlled. The businesses were firmly established: five or six years was a long time in immigrant days. "We'd only make enough to keep our bellies from hurting," Yoryis said.

They went to Karavelis's office to get his advice. Karavelis was considered a good labor agent by the men. Even though he charged a fee for getting them a job and two dollars a month afterwards to keep it, he also went to court to represent them on disorderly conduct charges, usually for beating up Americans who called them "dirty Greeks." Most labor agents and interpreters charged for this service, but Karavelis often forgot to collect.

Karavelis did his best to settle feuds: vendettas gave Greeks a bad name in America. He was, though, a mystery to the Greeks. With his thick black mustache and heavy eyebrows, blue eyes perpetually alight with merriment, he was guilty of *paraxina pragmata*—strange things. He had married a "used" woman, an American at that, and even more astonishing, she already had a child. Because of Karavelis, the woman had divorced her husband, a section foreman. The foreman had let his wife and child go without taking his gun after Karavelis, without even beating him up. Such *paraxina pragmata* could only happen in America. The men commiserated with Karavelis's father, a priest, who came to Pocatello thinking he would remain near his son. He was appalled at what his son had done, and his redheaded wife was not properly respectful. "Him and his damn hat," she said about the tall black priest's hat that he wore everywhere. The priest soon returned to Greece.

Karavelis talked eagerly about a proposition. He had one hundred eighty acres and needed someone to clear the land and secure his claim. There was a new flurry of homesteading in the West. Wagons piled with belongings made deeper the ruts left by pioneers. Horses pulled dilapidated sheep wagons over Indian trails. Anyone who would live on one hundred eighty acres, clear it of sagebrush, plant it, and build a two-room cabin, each room with a window, could claim the land. Throughout Idaho patches of dry farms broke the expanse of sagebrush. Yellow wheat made triangles, oblongs, and irregular shapes in the sage; undulated over the hills; and replaced scrub oak, sagebrush, and wild currant bushes on the mountain slopes.

"All we know is growing corn in the rocks," Yoryis said, "but we're tired of wandering." They signed a lease with Karavelis for three years. He would provide a man to help them and after six months build them a house. When they learned how to grow wheat, Yoryis and Louis decided, they would file a claim for themselves.

Yoryis, Louis, and an older man of about forty-five, Sampalis's brother-in-law, would live in a tent. They got up at first light, drank coffee, and ate hunks of bread, which Louis had learned to

216

bake in the Greek army. He used a small stove set in the middle of the tent.

They hacked sagebrush until dark, stopping at midday for a lunch of bread, Kalamata olives, and feta, and drank from a canvas water bag. Yoryis and Louis talked about the earth, wondered if it were fertile. (The older man spoke little and was melancholy, pining for his wife and children in Greece.) They had seen sagebrush as tall as a man, but what they were hacking was no higher than two and three feet with roots gnarled and deep in the earth. They bought two horses to plow up the roots.

From an elderly couple homesteading a half mile away, they bought pieces of lamb and beef and potatoes. The spry old woman would not let them leave immediately, but insisted that they sit at the kitchen table and drink a glassful of a root drink she made. Yoryis and Louis disliked the taste but drank it dutifully.

Louis fried pieces of meat and slices of potatoes for their evening meals. One night, working nervously, swearing obscenely, he made a *pita*. He could have waited for Sunday, gone the six miles to Pocatello, and had one of the Greek women who ran boarding houses make it for him, but he wanted it right then. Louis rolled out the pastry leaves, layered each sheet with butter and eggs mixed with crumbled feta. The helper gazed with tearful eyes, Yoryis avidly. That night they fell on their cots, satisfied.

On the American celebration, Thanksgiving, the old couple invited the men to eat with them in their small, fragrantly hot kitchen. They were leaving: for five years they had lived on the farm to comply with the homestead laws for a son growing wheat on the adjacent one hundred eighty acres. At the door the old woman gave each of the men a gift wrapped in newspaper. "You must be her pet," Louis said, looking at the pink mustache cup she had given Yoryis. Under a raised gilt pansy with green leaves were the words: *Forget Me Not.*

When winter winds blew under the tent, they pulled their cots closer to the stove and fed it sagebrush roots during the night. The horses whinnied in a makeshift shelter of sagebrush tied to chicken wire. Snow piled high and winds blew it into drifts against the foothills. Again they were out hacking and pulling up roots. Their lungs hurt from the cold; their fingers were numb. In the dead of winter the ground froze and the plow could not pierce it. They hacked then with axes.

When the chinook winds came and softened the earth, they plowed, furrowed, and planted wheat. That autumn they threshed twenty-three hundred bushels, which they sold for a dollar thirty cents a bushel. Karavelis built them a frame house and brought a few pieces of second-hand furniture. One thing Yoryis knew: they could not live another winter without a woman to keep house for them.

18

The news of Emilia's arrival was out before she had cleaned the house to her satisfaction. Every evening, wearing her best mauve dress, her heart racing and her hands cold, she brought out the *dhiskos*, the hospitality tray, to groups of young men. *Kyria* Mathaios bustled about in a brown satin dress with wavery half circles of dried and fresh sweat under the arm holes. At the door, on leaving, friends and relatives of the young men made appointments with *Kyrios* Mathaios at his bank to speak for them.

Emilia carried tray after tray with glasses of cool water, liqueurs, sweets, and demitasses of turkish coffee and barely glanced at the young men or their representatives. Some were well dressed, smelling of the barber shop, diamond pins and rings flashing; others wore black Sunday suits, striped silk shirts, and shiny, buttoned shoes reeking of polish. Their hands were calloused, the fingernails black rimmed; the smell of their sweat came through their Sunday clothing.

Above the freshly barbered heads blue tobacco smoke floated, and a cigar stench hovered in the *sala*. The men hardly looked at Emilia in return, sitting either in deep silence or talking nervously in various dialects. On their first evening visit the workers, searching for a subject of conversation, pounced on their hated labor agent, Leonidas Skliris, the Czar of the Greeks.

"Why all the fuss?" Mathaios said in the conciliatory tones of a superior, his small palms held out to the men. "Didn't everyone

219

have to pay for work in our sweet country? Skliris could just as well give jobs to the Italians or Slavs, but he is a *patriotis*. He thinks first of his compatriots."

The well-dressed men smiled, nodded. The men with the black fingernails looked on stonily. One of them remonstrated, "To charge something, but not so much as he does. And then no one is sure he won't be fired and a new arrival put in his place."

A Cretan with a thick crown of black hair jumped up with clenched fists, shouted obscenities at Mathaios, and stalked out of the house. Emilia hurried into the kitchen at his first outburst, but even there she heard the words: *flesh peddler, whore licker, Virgin fucker.*

Kyria Mathaios came after Emilia, puffing, "Jealousy! That's what it is! Because my man has done well in Ameriki! Those! What were they in our country but shepherds and charcoal makers and barefoot farmers and now with a few dollars in their pockets! The effrontery of them!"

Emilia shook her head at each marriage proposal. Neither of the Mathaioses pressed her. The summer passed with young men still coming and *Kyria* Mathaios taking to her bed periodically over Takis's behavior or the boys' vagabonding. At least once a week Emilia and the *kyria* prepared dinners for visiting churchmen, reporters for Greek-language newspapers from the East and California, labor agents in partnership with Skliris, journalists from Greece, and Greek government representatives traveling throughout America to establish Pan–Hellenic organizations devoted to keeping Greek customs and language alive in exile and exhorting the men to return to Greece with their savings to help their country's economy. Maria Economidhou would call them all, and especially Spyros Matsoukas, jingoists who cared nothing about the poor living quarters and dangerous working conditions of the immigrants, whose only interest was fostering Greekism in America. Matsoukas, who also collected funds for the Greek armed forces, left with thousands of dollars after firing up the laborers with thundering predictions that Greek culture would die in America if he did not travel about and awaken his *patriotes* to the imminent tragedy.

Besides the surfeit of men visitors, several Greek women visited the Mathaios house in the afternoons. By 1912 only a few Greek women had come to Salt Lake City; one was the educated wife of a druggist, whose uncles had lost several buildings in the 1909 burning of South Omaha's Greek Town.

Kyria Mathaios beamed as the women exclaimed over Emilia's pastries. Her only complaint was that Emilia did not know how to read tea and coffee cups. "All I know, Kyria Efterpi," Emilia said, remembering sullen Aristea in Constantinople reading cups, "is that a smooth film means good fortune and clots mean trouble. In my house we did not make it a practice." She was careful never to say in the house of "my kyrios" or "my kyria." She feared each visit, apprehensive that she would say it without thinking and be thought a servant who had been used by her master. She saw herself being whispered about slyly by the women visitors, only two of whom could read and write, but who were well dressed in American clothes, wearing hats not village kerchiefs, plumpish, even stout with America's plentiful bread and meat. Emilia answered their questions with excessive politeness, hoping to dispel any suspicion that she had been brought to the house to be used by Takis to keep him away from prostitutes—as was common in the fatherland.

Kyria Mathaios pouted, "Say all you want. I've seen things come true that were shown in the cups."

In September the disorder of the house turned to pandemonium. The Western Federation of Labor called a strike at the copper mine in Bingham Canyon fifteen miles west of the city and *Kyrios* Mathaios was in and out of the house making telephone calls, waiting for telephone calls. Takis came in late at night more often now that his father's attention was consumed by the strike. "You filth! You donkey!" his mother screeched at him one night, her voice reverberating off the crystal chandelier in the living room. "Where were you? With that Mormona or with those filthy poutanes! You went to the poutanes! Good! Fine! Get skoulamentria and you'll see!"

"And if I do, I'll go to Doctor Hemenes for a needle of 606."

"Bravo! In our sweet country the sailors got those dirty diseases, but here in Ameriki, they're available to all!"

Emilia read the strike news in the *Evzone*, the Greek-language paper published in Salt Lake City, to *Kyria* Mathaios. *Kyrios* Mathaios would snap at his wife that the strike was not women's business, then proceed to roar at the ceiling to God, "It's those miserable Cretans, listening to those *egitators*, those *Wobblies!* They want Skliris fired! And if the Compania fires the strikers, they'll come to my bank and take out their money! And you worrying me all the time about your precious Takis!"

Kyria Mathaios wept over her beautiful Tripolis and her husband told her, "Plug it! If you had come from Tripolis, you'd at least know how to cook!"

While Emilia read from the *Evzone*, *Kyria* Mathaios sewed an amulet for Takis; inside a square of red silk she placed a blue bead to ward off the evil eye, a pinch of gunpowder from her grandfather's flask, a kernel of frankincense, and a minute corner of a page from a holy book. She told Emilia she would pin it under Takis's mattress, and perhaps its power would go through to him and quench his foolish desire for the *Mormona*.

The *Evzone* praised the Cretan leader, John Leventis. "That donkey," *Kyria* Mathaios said. "He'll eat it! But 'Does the deaf man hear the church bell?'"

At breakfast, dinner, and when he sometimes came home for lunch, *Kyrios* Mathaios read all three of the city's newspapers, the *Salt Lake Herald*, the *Salt Lake Tribune*, and the *Deseret News*. He read slowly, consulting a pocket dictionary frequently. Angrily pounding the table, he read aloud English words that were meaningless to his wife and Emilia: "'The better white element are leaving the copper camp.' What do they think we are? Chinese?"

One evening he spread the newspapers on the dining room table and smiled happily. "Look, Girl," he said, "they've got me in the papers." Pompously he read of the Cretan strikers taking blankets, guns, and food, barricading themselves on the mountainside, and shooting anyone who moved toward the mine. After the Greek priest convinced the men to come down to hear the governor speak to them, he, Mr. Mathaios, spoke to the Greeks urging them to be peaceful. He did not mention that the Cretans stormed out and up the mountain at his words.

The strike continued with Cretans slipping out of the canyon, catching freights to Salt Lake City where they bought ammunition, and returning to continue sniping at strikebreakers, guards, and sharpshooters sent from Fort Douglas.

Still, representatives for young men came with marriage proposals, and afterwards *Kyrios* Mathaios began his litany: what did she think of the cafe owner, the Nevada Greek from Lefkas? and Emilia shook her head.

Each month *Kyrios* Mathaios deposited a few dollars in his bank for Emilia. At her icon each night, she prayed to the All–Holy to send a man she would not be afraid of, a good man *because I have no brother or father to uphold me*. She ended her prayers by asking the All–Holy to give *Kyria* Mathaios light and lead her to Sunday liturgies and to repay visits so that women visitors would come again to the house. Her prayers went unanswered. Even when two Greeks were killed in a gun battle between strikers and mine guards and almost all of Greek Town attended the liturgies for the dead, *Kyria* Mathaios stayed at home. She talked constantly about her husband, how in 1907 when there was no work in the country, he had gathered the unemployed young men from the coffeehouses and with the priest held school for them in a lean-to where the clergy kept their vestments. "Several men," and she named them, "could not even write their names and my man taught them to write to their families in patridha. Every day the church paid for three meals a day for them and gave them ten cents for cigarettes."

Emilia remembered what her grandmother had said about a talkative neighbor, "She's talking to keep from thinking about something."

On Saint Luke's feast day in the middle of October, when the house was filled with men who had come to pay their respects to *Kyrios* Mathaios on his name day, the telephone rang. One of the boys answered and ran into the *sala* screaming, "Greece and Turkey are at war!" *Kyrios* Mathaios ran to the telephone. The men were on their feet cheering, "Zito, Ellas! Zito, the King!"

As with one voice they boomed out the Greek national anthem, tears streaming down their faces. A poignancy for her family and country clutched Emilia's throat, and she could not utter a word, could only listen.

> *I know you by the blade*
> *of your dread sword,*
> *I know you by your eye*
> *swiftly surveying the world*
>
> *Risen from the bones,*
> *a hallowed Greek trail,*
> *and valiant as of old,*
> *Hail, O Liberty, hail!*

Stanza after stanza they sang, the younger Mathaios boys standing straight, heads up. The men shouted that they would volunteer and in a body left the house for the Greek Town coffeehouses. That night Emilia dreamed of her dead grandmother.

Within days the men had bought American army uniforms from the Salt Lake Army and Navy store and in a field in Murray, a town a few miles south of the city, marched and trained under Greeks who had served their army duty before coming to America. In the Mathaios backyard the boys played at Greek soldiers fighting the Turks, hiding in bushes, climbing the frame garage. Periodically, Emilia was sent out by grieving *Kyria* Mathaios to force them down from the garage roof.

Takis was caught stealing and arrested. In his mother's wails the secret burst out. He had been stealing from his mother's purse and his father's bank from time to time. "From his own mother! To buy that Mormona poutana luxuries!"

His father and a Greek attorney asked the judge to suspend Takis's sentence to allow him to join the second contingent of volunteers who would leave for Greece after Palm Sunday services in the spring. The judge sentenced Takis to the state reform school in Ogden instead. "These Amerikani," *Kyria* Mathaios said, "they don't understand patriotism."

The strike in Bingham Canyon went on. Strikebreakers were mining less ore because they did not know the work and strikers were suffering from lack of food and coal. The Western Federation of Labor in Butte, Montana, sent seven thousand dollars for relief; single men were given three dollars a week and family men six dollars. Coyotes appeared on the mountain slopes in the moonlight and howled, a bad sign the American strikers said.

A Greek labor agent arrived from Pueblo to recruit strike-breakers for the southern Colorado mines. A Cretan, Louis Tikas, had become the leader of the Greek strikers and would be killed by the Colorado National Guard. Several Greek strikers left with the agent. "We've got to live," they said.

The strike was lost, but the Greeks won in their fight to have Skliris expelled as their labor agent. He fled the state: the Cretan strikers had vowed to kill him. (One of them had murdered a Skliris agent a few years earlier in a coal camp, and with the help of his compatriots had escaped.) Most of the Greeks returned to the mines, and the Mathaios's bank remained intact. More than two hundred Greeks went home to fight, this time the Bulgarians

Almost three years after Emilia had come to Salt Lake City, she asked *Kyrios* Mathaios if he would sponsor her sister Faní to come to America. He agreed. "But you both can't stay here. One of you will have to go to Nevada or Idaho. One of you can go to Karavelis in Pocatello, Idaho. There are thousands of Greeks up there. He's a good man even if he is married to an Amerikanidha."

"I'll go," Emilia said. She had turned away the young men who had come eagerly, hopefully, but as the months passed she had lost her status as guest and become a servant.

Two months later Faní arrived, short, eyes wild, and Emilia left for Pocatello, Idaho.

19

No matter how late it was when they came back from the fields, no matter how tired he was, Louis drove the wagon into Pocatello to play cards. If he could not take the wagon, he walked. He returned one midnight with a message from Karavelis. At the kerosene-lighted kitchen table Yoryis had finished recording expenses in a ledger and was writing a letter to his parents to send with a money order. Mathaios, the Greek banker in Salt Lake City, Louis said, had sent Karavelis an unmarried woman who had refused prospective grooms for more than two years.

The next day Yoryis drove the wagon to Pocatello to discuss the woman with Karavelis. "She wouldn't marry any of the patriotes who came to the Mathaios home. She has no male relatives. I'll act as her protector. Look her over and see what you think. She can read and write. And cooks!"

Yoryis laughed: it was a Greek Town joke that Karavelis ate in their restaurants in the daytime to withstand his wife's bland American cooking in the evening. "Who told you to marry a red-haired Amerikanidha?" Yoryis said, and Karavelis, blue eyes merry, smiled ruefully.

On Sunday, Yoryis and Louis drove to Pocatello. "Come and meet her," Yoryis said.

"Make up your own mind," Louis answered. "I don't want to be blamed for what happens."

"Cardplayer!" Yoryis shouted as Louis jumped off at a Roumeliot coffeehouse. Carrying a bundle of clean clothes and his suit draped over one elbow, Yoryis stopped at the YMCA, took a shower, dressed, replaced the gun in his belt, and went to Karavelis's house. In the musty, dim living room he shook hands with a slender woman of medium height, piercing brown eyes, and brown hair looped across her forehead and puffed about her ears.

"Sit down! Sit down!" Karavelis said, flinging out his arms toward big leather chairs and at the same time raising heavy eyebrows at his wife in signal. "Come on," he said impatiently in English to her. "Bring something for the people."

Still pretty, in her early thirties, Mrs. Karavelis stood where she was and made an outrageous suggestion. "No, they need to get acquainted. Take Emily to a picture show, George, and then have a dish of ice cream. Get acquainted!"

Karavelis frowned. Emilia Papachristou clasped her hands. "Oh, go on," Mrs. Karavelis said with a wave of dismissal. "You don't need to be married to go to a show. This is America for God's sake!"

"It's all right, Emilia," Karavelis said, now smiling. "Get ready and we'll be back in a little while."

"Well, what do you think?" Karavelis said as they walked uptown.

"I think she's all right."

"Mathaios said she grew up in Constantinople. Oh, yes, and Maria Economidhou, that Greek journalist who travels around, sent her to him."

They stopped at a flower shop where Yoryis bought a bouquet of spring flowers, and then they returned to Karavelis's house. Emilia looked up at him with alarm when he handed her the flowers. "Here, give them to me," Mrs. Karavelis said. "I'll put them in water." She jabbed her husband in the ribs with her elbow. "This-here Greek gave me a bouquet just like this once."

"Ready, Miss?" Yoryis asked Emilia, now wearing a mauve suit, white embroidered blouse, and gray straw hat.

Emilia glanced at Karavelis, who nodded reassuringly. "Have a swell time," Mrs. Karavelis said at the door and waved. Emilia walked quickly to keep up with Yoryis's long strides. The cool

Emilia and her sister Faní, Pocatello, Idaho, 1915.

spring air, heavy with the scent of lilacs, was chilly. She lowered her
eyes whenever someone approached, fearful that it was obvious to all
that she and the man a half step ahead of her were not married.
Avoiding Greek Town, Yoryis led the way to Main Street and
bought two tickets at a movie theater. A uniformed young man
pointed to the balcony. They climbed the stairs and sat in a humid

airlessness with other immigrants, mostly Japanese, and blacks. Down below the Americans sat. Yoryis ground his teeth and thought of leaving, but he didn't know what they would do to pass the afternoon.

Emilia also noticed that Americans sat on the main floor, the *xeni* in the balcony. She thought angrily of Sunday liturgy in the small, ugly Pocatello Greek church; the cloddish men who built it kept a peculiar old village custom: women and children looked on from the balcony.

The lights dimmed; a piano was being played below in choppy crescendos. The movie began. Actors chased each other, hid in closets and under beds. Titters came from the immigrants, hearty laughing from the Americans. For almost two hours Yoryis and Emilia watched wordlessly.

When the lights went on, they walked out and next door to a candy store. Yoryis ordered vanilla ice cream for them. He began with questions Greeks asked on first meeting: "Where were you born? What did your father do? Are your parents living? How many brothers and sisters have you?" Emilia answered in monosyllables. Yoryis gave her the same information about himself. When they finished the ice cream, he said, "Then, shall we get married?"

Emilia lifted her shoulders slightly and glanced at him: he was tall like her father; he had her father's name. "All right," she said, her heart beating as if to break.

Karavelis's wife took Emilia to a dressmaker who sewed her a beige silk dress with blue satin piping. Emilia wanted to protest the spending of her future husband's money on a dressmaker when she could sew the dress herself. She said nothing, thinking it was perhaps an American superstition that a bride did not make her own wedding dress.

No plans were made for the ceremonial wedding dinner. Yoryis told Emilia on his second visit that he had just sent a money draft to his parents and that they would need what money he had for furniture and living expenses until the wheat was harvested.

"I have a little more than three hundred dollars in Mathaios's bank," Emilia said, frightened that he would take it and she would have nothing left to dole out to her family. Yet, she knew that if she said nothing about the money, she could someday be justifiably called a devious woman.

"No. Why waste what little we have to feed gamblers and fools."

Karavelis spoke about having a small dinner at his house, but feared the uninvited would cause him trouble. "Just get the well dug on the farm," Yoryis said in a menacing tone that frightened Emilia. Every day Karavelis's troubles grew. He owed everyone, including laborers who gave him their money for safekeeping when they went out on railroad gangs. Although he was still the leading Greek labor agent in Pocatello, money was not flowing into his pockets as it once had. After the copper strike in Utah brought the padrone system into the open, many Greeks refused to pay him the monthly two dollars he charged, beyond the initial twenty to fifty dollars to get jobs on the Union Pacific and Oregon Short Line railroads. They had been in America long enough to learn that they could go directly to a foreman—unless the foreman was in league with Karavelis. The laborers brought the foremen bottles of whiskey, boxes of candy, five or ten dollars each payday and took care of their bribes directly. When the railroads needed large gangs, Karavelis still supplied them by signing on Greeks who had just arrived in the country. He was accused of peonage and taken to court by a Greek laborer while Emilia's dress was being sewed.

Mathaios was in even deeper trouble. Rumors had been circulating in the Salt Lake coffeehouses that his bank was a fraud; he was not affiliated with the Bank of Athens. Laborers daily drew out their savings, and suddenly he was without money, his only income from a hotel he leased in Greek Town. It was near the "stockade," where prostitutes were housed. Mathaios telephoned Karavelis that he could no longer keep Faní. He told her to work in the hotel, but she refused, and Mathaios was sending her to Pocatello. Several days after the telephone call, Mathaios was driving down Salt Lake's Main Street and collided with another automobile. He was unhurt, his wife was killed instantly.

Faní remained for over a week to cook the funeral dinner, sew black bands on coats, dye white shirts black, and drape black crepe over photographs and mirrors. Emilia wanted to attend the funeral for addled, illiterate *Kyria* Mathaios, but she could not go unchaperoned and risk being abandoned by the tall man she was to marry, now out in the cleared fields planting wheat. She thought of Faní with great apprehension. "You're going to rub your arm away, Emily," Mrs. Karavelis said at her anxious habit of stroking her right hand up and down her upper left arm.

Emilia attempted to tell Mrs. Karavelis that people would look down on Faní for remaining in a house with a womanless man. Emilia stopped at the puzzled look on Mrs. Karavelis's fair face. She knew that even if she spoke English well enough to make herself understood, Mrs. Karavelis was American and Greek ideas and customs were strange to her.

Soon after Faní arrived, Louis returned from his coffeehouse ritual early with the latest issue of the *Evzone* newspaper. On the front page the editor, Yoryis Fotopoulos, had exposed Mathaios. The rumors were true: Mathaios's Bank of Athens had no connection with Greece. Mathaios had collected the laborers' wages and each evening made a deposit at the First National Bank on Salt Lake City's Main Street. He had kept the interest on the laborers' savings for himself.

Yoryis drove the wagon to Pocatello and found Karavelis in the Corinthians' coffeehouse. The men were shouting over a telephone call from the Paradise Coffeehouse in Salt Lake City: Fotopoulos had just left his newspaper office; as he passed an alleyway three men dragged him into it and beat him unconscious.

Yoryis told Karavelis about Emilia's money. Together they went to the grocery store that Karavelis's nephews owned and telephoned Mathaios. "Send that money by tomorrow's mail," Yoryis told him. "I will. I will," Mathaios answered. "Be at rest. It will come."

Several days passed with no word from Mathaios. Karavelis said, "Write him that if the money doesn't come by return mail, you'll go to the immigration authorities and tell them he brought Faní here as a *white slaver*. He'll fill his pants over that!"

Yoryis wrote the letter as Karavelis suggested and added a line: *If the money isn't here by return mail, I'll come down and kill you.* A money order arrived two days after the letter was mailed. Mathaios bristled, searched for retribution, and circulated a lie that Yoryis had been fooled; Emilia was years older than he. The news spread from the Salt Lake to the Pocatello coffeehouses. "Is it true?" Yoryis asked. Sickened, Emilia shook her head. Every morning she looked in the mirror for the gray hair that would confirm the lie.

Yoryis told Emilia they would go to Salt Lake City the coming Sunday to be married. This would give them a few days respite from the farm, and they would not have to spend the little money they had on the obligatory wedding feast. Fani refused to go back to Salt Lake City.

When Yoryis arrived to take Emilia to the nearby train station, he told Karavelis, "The well better be dug by the time we return."

"Rest assured, rest assured," Karavelis said, smiling, lifting his cigar to emphasize the well was as good as dug.

Accompanying Yoryis and Emilia were one of Karavelis's nephews, who had asked to be the *koumbaros,* the best man, and a Roumeliot from the village of Sisnisis near Klepá. Louis had to stay on the farm. No one else was present for the marriage ceremony conducted by the priest on the mezzanine floor of the Peery Hotel. Afterward, the four of them ate in an American restaurant and Yoryis and Emilia went back to the hotel.

Emilia awoke before dawn and thought of the weddings in her village, in Thessaloniki, and in Constantinople. She remembered the week-long festivities, girls with flowers in their hair singing while bread was being kneaded and baked in the groom's and bride's houses, singing while the groom was being shaved and his hair cut, while the bride bathed, and while the dowry was delivered on belled and flower-ornamented mule or horse to her new home.

That day they ate three meals in restaurants, Emilia never raising her eyes. In the afternoon they attended a vaudeville at the Orpheum Theater and saw acrobats and dogs performing tricks, a man in blackface singing, and women with dresses above their knees kicking and singing in unison.

Yoryis and Emilia photographed after their wedding on the mezzanine of the Peery Hotel, Salt Lake City, May 15, 1915.

After breakfast the next day, Yoryis left Emilia in the hotel while he went to a Roumeliot coffeehouse and restaurant in Greek Town to learn if there was news of any of the men he had worked with on labor gangs. The proprietor had heard that morning of Yoryis's marriage. "Come tonight and I'll have a dinner for all the Roumeliots in your honor." Yoryis lied, said he was returning that night to Pocatello, and went back to the hotel, downcast that someone had offered to pay for his wedding feast because he could not.

Two days later they returned to the curtainless homestead house of bare floors and a few rickety pieces of furniture. The well had not been dug. "What about the well?" he shouted at Louis.

Louis shrugged. "I saw Karavelis every night in town and mentioned it each time."

"Mentioned it! Why didn't you tell him I would eat him alive if he didn't get the well dug?"

In the distance an automobile was coming up the dirt road with clouds of dust churning behind it. "Well," Lambros said, "here he comes. Tell him yourself."

Karavelis waved as the car noisily approached and came to an abrupt stop. He stepped out, a cigar under his thick mustache. "Welcome, the newlyweds!" he called and came forward with his hand out. Yoryis shook his hand with hard jerks. "Where's the well?"

"Eh, we'll get around to it in a day or two."

"You send someone today! Do you hear? Today!"

"Eh, be reasonable. Where am I going to find someone today?"

"You've had two months! Today!"

Emilia rushed to Karavelis's side. "Don't! He'll do it! Give him time!"

"Time! Who's going to go to the river for water? Are you? We lived like gypsies, Lambros and I. That well better be started today, Karavelis!" Yoryis raised his fist. "Or else!"

Karavelis took a step backward. "No!" Emilia screamed. "Don't touch him! He's a good man! He took me in!" She lunged to grab Yoryis's arm, and he swung her against the side of the house. She stood there in terror.

Karavelis got in his car and drove off. Later that day two men, one Greek, the other American, began digging the well. Faní came to live with them. Karavelis had not been able to find any man willing to marry a servant woman who could have been taken advantage of by Mathaios after his wife's death. "If only the church would allow Lambros to marry Faní," Emilia said. "What does it matter that he's your second cousin and Faní is my sister?"

"Lambros won't ever marry any woman," Yoryis said. "He's married to cards."

Louis and the helper set up cots in the empty living room, and Faní slept in their former bedroom. She and Emilia scrubbed, ironed, sewed curtains, and cooked for the three men. Louis taught them how to make *pita* by layering the cheese mixture between paper-thin sheets of dough rather than making cheese triangles that took much longer. When he came home from a coffeehouse late one night, a crushed sprig of basil over one ear, Emilia was mute with sadness: he loved Greece so much; yet, imprisoned by the army for supposedly stealing and selling cheese, he could never return. Who would trust him to do anything but make charcoal?

Yoryis wrote his family: "Two weeks ago I married." At the bottom of the letter Emilia added, "I too send you greetings." On reading the news, Yoryis's father cried out, "My wings are cut!" He would never again see his son alive. He would see him in the houses of David.

Several times during the summer, Yoryis, Emilia, and Faní drove in the wagon to Pocatello. The few Greek women in town were overjoyed to see others of their own, and immediately the kitchens were a flurry with rolling out of dough, roasting, basting, talk of pregnancies, births, folk cures, and condemnation of young Greek men who were forgetting their history, even marrying American women. None of the visits resulted in one marriage offer for Faní. Later, Emilia would hear that the journalist Maria Economidhou had been in Salt Lake City and the copper and coal camps of Utah, and she was in anguish that she had lost a chance to ask her help for Faní.

The journeys to Pocatello stopped in October when Emilia became pregnant and the jerking of the wagon increased the queasiness in her stomach. Louis continued his nightly visits to coffeehouses and returned one night with Nick Zeese who was more than willing to stay in the four-room house and not venture into town. "Hiding out from someone, you horned one!" Yoryis said.

One gray morning as Yoryis and Nick were driving to Pocatello for supplies, a flock of ducks flew over them and landed on a water hole. "Let's get them," Nick said, reaching for a shotgun and jumping down. Yoryis reined in the horse and taking his gun followed Nick into the cattails and reeds ringing the water hole. The ducks swam, their green blue wing feathers glistening. Suddenly they rose, fluttering their wings. The guns zinged; one duck dropped. As Nick got up to retrieve it, another flock in V formation flew over and down to the water. Nick crouched, getting ready to shoot again, but the sound of a rattling wagon sent them to hide in the reeds. The wagon stopped and footsteps scuffed over the road. A stocky man with a silver star on his coat came down the bank holding a rifle. "Come on up to the wagon. I'm taking you in for shooting ducks out of season."

Yoryis and Nick walked toward the wagon. "Put your guns in the back," the game warden said, "and sit up next to me."

The wagon bumped on with the men silent. "Greeks are you?" the warden said, after a mile or more. "Yes," Yoryis answered, and the conversation ended.

As the wagon neared a hill about which the road wound, Nick said in Greek, "When he turns at the hill, let's jump out and run to the irrigation creek and hide in the bushes."

"Stay where you are!" Yoryis hissed.

The warden looked at them from the corner of his eye and pulled the reins slightly to the left. Nick jumped out. The warden reined in the horse, but Nick was lost from sight in the clumps of sage and reeds. "You kerata, I'll slaughter you!" Yoryis shouted.

The warden looked across the expanse of brush and reeds and flipped the reins. Standing before the justice of the peace in town, Yoryis paid a fine of ten dollars. He walked back to get his wagon and horse, went on to Pocatello, bought the supplies, and arrived at his house late at night. Emilia met him at the door, her face white. "I thought you'd been killed," she said. "What foolishness," Yoryis answered.

Louis smiled sardonically at Yoryis's gnashing his teeth over Nick's escape. "That whoremaster! What did he think I was going to do with my farm, my wife, my sister-in-law by hiding in the bushes! I'll fuck his Virgin!"

Her face white, Emilia hurried into her bedroom. Fani followed. "Our father never used such words," she said coldly. They sat on the skimpy mattress and listened to the men's voices.

"You know why he was hiding out?" Louis said. "He didn't want me to tell you because he knew he'd get it from you. He's got this trick when he's out of money in a strange town. He goes to a jeweler and offers to sell his platinum watch chain. The jeweler examines it and offers him about half of what it's worth.

"Nikos puts the chain in his pocket and pretends to walk out. Then at the door he stops and says he'll take the money. He goes back and he reaches into his other pocket, pulls out a *silver* watch chain, takes the jeweler's money, and gets out of town. Only he made the mistake of going to a jeweler in Pocatello who recognized him from before. That's why he zipped straight as a bullet out here to hide." About a week later Louis drove the wagon to the railroad station. In the back, under rags and straw, was Nick's expensive leather suitcase. Nick had left word at the Roumeliot coffeehouse that Louis was to send the suitcase on to Great Falls, Montana.

When winter set in, the morose, older man who worked with them moved back to Pocatello, and Yoryis, Louis, Emilia, and Fani were isolated on the hilly plain of drifting snow. Fani railed at Emilia for bringing her to America. "We'll send you back tomorrow!" Yoryis shot at her, and she did not again speak her misery when he was around.

In spring Louis brought back the coffeehouse news: Karavelis, who had not been able to pay his debts, was being threatened by three brothers to whom he owed twenty thousand dollars. To keep them quiet for the time being he was going to give them the wheat farm. Yoryis put on his coat and hat, lighted the kerosene lamp that hung at the side of the door, and went out. "Where are you going! Where?" Emilia screamed. "It's night! Someone will kill you! Come back!" She followed him into the cold, stinging wind. "Get back in there!" Yoryis ordered as he hitched the horse to the wagon. He drove off. Her voice trailed, "Come back! Come back!"

It was midnight when Yoryis arrived in Pocatello. He went from one coffeehouse to another until he found Karavelis in a Greek poolhall. "I'm desperate," Karavelis said. "I'm afraid for my life."

"You'd better live up to your contract with me. Lambros and I put in everything we had and worked like mules on top of it. We lived in a tent like Vlachs. Give them the farm and you'll be afraid for your life from two sides."

Three nights later Louis returned from a coffeehouse and told Yoryis that Karavelis had given the farm to the three brothers. Yoryis again put on his hat and coat. "I'll get our money or go to jail," he said.

Emilia stood in the doorway screaming, "Don't hurt him!"

"Him! What about me? What about my money and killing myself to make a farm out of this desert! What about what he did to Lambros and me!" He pushed her out of the doorway while she screamed, "You have no heart! You're a cold man!"

The road to Pocatello was lighted palely by the moon. In his fury Yoryis had forgotten the kerosene lamp. He thought of his wife screaming: he had married an unreasonable woman. He found Karavelis in the Corinthian coffeehouse. "Get up and walk into the back room," Yoryis said, knowing anyone in the coffeehouse could point a gun at his back: though Karavelis was a labor agent and owed everybody, he was liked; he was a "good" padrone.

They entered the small dark room. Shaking, Karavelis faced Yoryis. Yoryis closed the door. "I came to kill you," Yoryis said. "I'm no longer single. I put everything I had into the farm and I just as well go to jail as be left without a dollar to support my wife."

"Yoryi, give me more time. Please, a little more time."

"Twenty-four hours."

Just before the time was up, Karavelis came to the farm and said no one would lend him the two thousand dollars. "I have a third interest in my nephews' grocery store," he said. "I'll give it to you to take care of the two thousand."

Yoryis moved Emilia and Faní to a small frame house in town and began working in the grocery store. Louis took a room in a hotel near the rail yards and every day came to Yoryis for an allotment of money. The new partners, Karavelis's two nephews, were Yoryis's best man at his wedding and his brother, called *Katirghatis* or Crook in English, an American word the Greeks quickly added to their vocabulary.

Yoryis looked in the store's ledger daily and at the book of receipts. When he went to his house for lunch, he ate quickly, wondering if Crook were taking cans and sacks through the back doors to restaurants and boardinghouses. "I've got to be my own boss," he told Emilia.

In late June Emilia awoke with pains. Yoryis hurried to the Roumeliot coffeehouse, awakened the owner who slept in the back room, and returned with him in his second-hand touring car to take Emilia to the hospital. Faní made the sign of the cross over and over again. "I'll stay with Lambros until Emilia comes home," Yoryis said.

He sat in a small foyer outside the delivery room. All through the day he waited there, sometimes alone. At times several men and women came in for a short time. Nurses went through swinging doors that opened and shut on a tiled room and a white-draped figure on the delivery table. Emilia's moans came to him with the talk of nurses and occasional orders from the doctor Karavelis had sent them to. By night the moans became shrieks, and Yoryis remembered the young mother whose screams had charged the village air, whose child had been pulled out in pieces, and still she had died. He remembered his mother, held under her arms by Konstandinos, giving birth to Sophia. He jumped up and rushed through the doors. "Get out of here!" the doctor shouted. "Go get a cup of coffee. It's going to be a long time."

Yoryis went out into the cool night; he was sweating profusely. He walked to the Bannock Hotel restaurant, sat at the counter, and ordered coffee. He tried to sit there for at least a half hour. He glanced at the clock ticking in the quiet above the mirror. Ten minutes later he hurried back to the hospital.

The next morning a baby girl was born, its head elongated from the long struggle to get through the birth canal. Forty days later, Emilia, white and weak, Yoryis, Faní, Louis, the Karavelises, and a few Roumeliots looked on while the baby's godfather, Karavelis's nephew, laved consecrated oil over the squirming, screaming child. Following ancient custom, the *koumbaros* who had exchanged the wedding crowns for Yoryis and Emilia became the godfather of their first child. Emilia hoped their *koumbaros* would allow them to choose the baby's name, but he carried out his prerogative and gave the baby his mother's name, Pangahiota, after Panaghia—the All-Holy.

The baby cried continuously, and Louis made only short, perfunctory visits to the house. Nick came with him one evening. Yoryis cursed and threatened Nick; Faní hurried to set the table; and the baby cried while Emilia held it and stirred a pot of stew at the same time. "Quiet that baby or I'll throw it out the window," Yoryis shouted.

When the baby was a few months old and Emilia was pregnant again, Yoryis accosted an extra gang foreman who owed the store one hundred seventy-three dollars. "I paid it," the foreman said, and showed Yoryis the receipt signed by Crook. Yoryis went over the books and found that Crook had not recorded the money.

"Oh, I used it, George," Crook said offhandedly—he called all Greeks by their American equivalent to show his urbanity. "Here's fifteen dollars. Go buy yourself a new pair of shoes."

"I don't want fifteen dollars! I want one hundred seventy-three dollars put down in this book! And I'll be watching for it."

The next time Yoryis went into the back room to look at the books, they were gone. Crook had locked them in the safe, and only he knew the combination. Yoryis and his *koumbaros* were alone in the store. "Yes," his *koumbaros* said, "he knew you were watching him and he locked up the books."

Yoryis was always the first to leave for lunch, but that day he said, "You go ahead and eat. I'm not hungry yet."

Crook came in soon after and went directly to the office. Yoryis locked the front door and walked back to Crook sitting at the desk and looking through a ledger. "You son of a bitch," he said, "why did you lock the safe?"

Crook stood up irritably. "That's my responsibility."

"I'm a partner! It's my responsibility too! Open up the safe or I'll blow your brains out!" Yoryis took the gun from his belt and pointed it. Crook opened the safe.

"Now, you're going to pay me off or you're going to die!"

Crook stared, eyes popped, at the gun. From the front door came a jiggling of the doorknob. Greeks in the adjoining poolhall had heard the commotion and run to the store. Crook's brother pushed them aside to unlock the door. While he was at home eating, the thought had come to him that Yoryis planned to kill his brother. "Yoryi!" he called, running through the store, "don't be a killer for a thief!"

Crook blurted, "I can get you fifteen hundred tomorrow."

"Two thousand!"

"Listen," Crook's brother pleaded, "if he can't get the whole two thousand, I'll put in the five hundred. Don't ruin your life for five hundred! If he can't get it, I'll put in the five hundred!"

The next morning, a Sunday, Yoryis and his *koumbaros* waited in a nearby coffeehouse. Crook came in and paid Yoryis the two thousand in paper and gold pieces. Yoryis put the money into his pocket and shook hands with his *koumbaros* who said bitterly, with a nod to his brother, "It's the first time he tried to cheat you, but he's been cheating me a long time."

Yoryis walked down the street to a Roumeliot coffeehouse, hoping he could get information on work from the off-shift rail yard workers or gamblers. The coffeehouse was noisy, festive over Yoryis's encounter with Crook. He was congratulated, toasted with ouzo, and offered suggestions.

A gambler who had just returned from the eastern Utah coal fields where a new mine had begun operations said, "They scratch the ground and find coal. Patriotes are coming in on every train. They need a coffeehouse." The men showed him the latest issue of the *Evzone:* thousands of unmarried Greeks, especially from Crete, were living in shacks and tents because only a few boardinghouses had been built; mines were opening constantly. The gambler had talked with the owner of the new mine about renting space for a coffeehouse, but then, he wondered, "Why should I tie myself down serving coffee to a bunch of villagers?" Yoryis wrote the owner's name and Salt Lake City address in his small black book.

He hurried to the rented house and told Emilia and Faní to begin packing. "But what if we go to this mine and the owner doesn't want a coffeehouse or he's given it to someone else?" Emilia asked.

"Then I'll work in the mine until I find some kind of business." He was eager to see George Anton, who had blistered his palms working on Yoryis's Idaho steel gang.

Emilia, frightened, continued rocking the baby. Often on Sunday in Salt Lake City, funerals were held for young men killed in the mines, mills, and smelters. The unmarried were given *thanatoghami*—death weddings—with a wedding crown on their heads, gold bands on their ring fingers, a sprig of white in the lapels of their black Sunday suits. She had read about them in the *Evzone.*

Faní rushed about hurrying, smiling. Emilia lighted the vigil light and prayed to the All−Holy for their safety, good fortune, and a husband for Faní.

20

$\mathcal{T}wo$ *days later, their furniture tied together* with ropes in the mail car, the family and Louis rode in a Union Pacific coach to Salt Lake City. The furniture was sent on to the new coal camp, Cameron.

When the train stopped in the Salt Lake City rail yards, Louis sprinted off to nearby Greek Town. "I'll stay with a patriotis," he called back. Yoryis had doled out ten of Louis's dwindling one thousand dollars and knew he would gamble it away by evening. Yoryis signaled for a taxicab to take them to the Moxum Hotel downtown, rather than a hotel or rooming house in Greek Town: he did not want Greeks to see his family traveling like homeless refugees. As soon as they entered the cheapest rooms on the third floor, Yoryis left the women and baby and walked to Mr. Cameron's office.

A hearty, silver-haired man, Cameron agreed to rent space in a small building under construction in the mining town for an advance deposit of a thousand dollars. He would also rent Yoryis a four-room house that he said would be ready in two weeks.

They shook hands. At the door Cameron said, "Say, George, do you know how to butcher meat? A lot of the Greek boys are batching it in company houses and you know how they like lamb."

"Yes," Yoryis said, although he had only helped his uncle Konstandinos with butchering, never done it alone.

For two weeks the family lived in the hotel, going out to eat

245

frugal American food: pancakes, mashed potatoes, canned green beans, stringy roast beef. Emilia and Faní took turns holding the baby to keep it from crying and feeding it bottles of half canned milk and half lukewarm water from the bathroom tap. On top of the dresser they set a drawer and lined it with blankets for a crib. Emilia continually washed the baby's few diapers and draped them over radiators to dry. She and Faní spent the rest of each day ripping off Yoryis's frayed shirt collars and cuffs, turning and sewing them back on. They darned underclothing and stockings, took apart Faní's faded navy blue skirt and turning the fabric, remade it.

At night Emilia lay awake long after the streetcars stopped running, unable to find comfort for her pregnant body, her head hurting from some kind of fear. She could hear Faní in the adjoining room walking about.

Each day Yoryis made purchases. At the Vasilakopulos importing store he bought fifty pounds of Turkish coffee and several boxes of *loukoum* and *baklava*. He wrote to a Greek company in Chicago, which advertised in the *Atlantis* newspaper, for two dozen thick white demitasse cups and four brass *briks* for brewing coffee. Emilia told Yoryis she and Faní would hem two dozen muslin dish towels when they reached the coal camp. At a second-hand restaurant supply store Yoryis found five round tables and twenty chairs, the backs and legs made from twisted rods. "Ice cream" and "candy store" tables and chairs, the salesmen called them. For brewing Turkish coffee, he bought a small, table-top kerosene stove in which a lighted wick on the bottom was topped with a sheet of metal layered with sand to increase the heat. After each purchase Yoryis returned to the hotel, added up his expenses, and, scowling, counted his vanishing money. He paced the floor, kicked the furniture, cursed. Emilia and Faní sat quietly, not speaking or looking at each other until he left the room.

"Our father was not like him," Faní said spitefully one day, and their anxiety burst out into bitter quarreling. They sewed in cold silence until they heard Yoryis's quick, heavy tread coming down the hall. "He's come!" Emilia said. Hastily they made themselves and the baby ready for the walk to the restaurant.

When Yoryis was away, Emilia was afraid that something had happened to him; when he was with them, she wished he were in Greek Town, but he seldom went there. He stopped in the *Evzone* offices and subscribed to the newspaper, to be sent to George Zeese, Coffeehouse, Cameron, Utah. Yoryis Fotopoulos, the editor, and short, blue-eyed Stylianos Stagopoulos, a reporter who made regular visits to the coal fields for subscriptions and news, gave him the names of several Roumeliots there. George Anton, they told him, was in Denver on business. Stagopoulos, who called himself Stylian Staes in English, said the Roumeliots were either sheepmen or in business. The first to arrive, about forty of them, had been brought by the padrone Skliris directly from the villages around Lamia in central Greece to break the Italian-led strikes in the early 1900s. Whenever possible, Skliris used men beyond his province for the dangerous job of strikebreaking. As soon as the men had saved a few dollars, they got out of the coal.

"Their villages are just over the mountains from my own village," Yoryis said. He walked back to the hotel, eager at the thought of meeting men from his own province.

As he passed the Open Heart Coffeehouse, Louis ran out to ask him for ten dollars. "Here," Yoryis said. "And don't ask me for another dollar until we get down to the mine."

"It's my money," Louis said.

"You devil! Shiftless cardplayer! If I didn't watch your money, you'd be on the street!"

Yoryis avoided Greek Town the rest of their stay. He had been in America almost ten years, had had fifteen jobs, but had not remained in one place long enough for the three years required before applying for American citizenship. In the hotel room he took out three books, which had arrived from the *Atlantis* company just before they left Pocatello, to begin his studies.

The grammar book was described as a "method of teaching the English language in 50 lessons." Yoryis went through the pages.

May I sing a beautiful Greek song? You may if you can, but I think you can not sing tonight.

You are the printer's son, I think. Will you come here? I want to speak to you.

Excuse me, sir, I am not the printer's son. I am the baker's cousin.

Was your uncle a musician or a schoolmaster? I am not quite sure, but I think he was either a surgeon or a sculptor.

You do not love your brothers and sisters? Yes, I do love them; but I know they do not love me because I am sometimes sulky, often idle and always dirty.

Yoryis threw the book into the wastebasket and returned to reading American newspapers with a thick new Greek—American dictionary open and ready. The third book was a history of the United States in Greek. He was surprised at the British whom the Greeks had loved since Lord Byron had gone to Messolonghi during the Revolution: the English had not been honorable to the American colonists.

At the end of the two weeks, Yoryis returned to Cameron's office to ask if the house and coffeehouse were ready. His secretary said they were. With Louis they took the next Denver and Rio Grande Western train for the one-hundred-fifteen-mile journey southeast. Soon after the train left the city, it clipped through Mormon farmland, mountains on both sides. Fields in neat squares of dark green, light green, blue green spread out from lone adobe houses, a few with newer frame or brick houses nearby and all with a row of poplars as windbreakers growing at one side.

The farms thinned out until only an occasional homestead cut into a valley of sagebrush, and the rugged, granite-tipped mountains converged to form a narrow canyon. Side by side a dirt road, a river, and the railroad tracks curved between mountain slopes covered with brilliant red and orange maples and scrub oak; in draws where two mountain slopes dipped, white-barked quaking aspen were a stunning bright yellow against dark pines. Emilia and Faní took turns rocking the baby and gazing. Emilia's fears of the new venture left: they were going to a beautiful country.

The train moved slowly as it climbed to a plateau. On both

sides great flocks of sheep were being driven to winter range on the desert. Men on horseback rode slowly behind the sheep while dogs sped around and around them, racing with incredible speed, jumping on the backs of the animals, and resuming their swift race. The family watched in awe. "In all Greece," Louis said, "in all Anatolia there couldn't be flocks this large."

The train stopped at a town near the summit, a cluster of yellow and brown frame railroad houses, a few boardinghouses, and poolhalls. A helper engine was hooked on to pull the train over the summit and down the winding canyon. Slowly the two engines, regular and helper, chugged up an ascent to a tabletop summit. The train then clipped along for ten or fifteen miles. In the distance other great flocks of sheep moved like gray clouds toward the tracks. The train gathered speed as it descended into the narrow canyon. When it reached the river below, the family looked up barren, juniper-dotted slopes to dun-colored rock on the crests of the mountains.

The train stopped at the Castle Gate mining town, a mile away from Cameron. Leaving the women and baby in a small, cold waiting room, Yoryis and Louis walked to Cameron. When they returned, mud and coal dust thick on their shoes, Yoryis's eyes were wild: neither the house nor the coffeehouse was ready, and the town had no hotels or restaurants. Hungry, the baby drinking cold milk and water, they waited for the next train and went on to Helper four miles away.

The town that took its name from the helper engines was divided by a muddy street; yellow and brown frame Denver and Rio Grande Western railroad houses lined the east side, a two-story rock building and one-story frame, brick, and cement block stores the west. Beautiful country, Emilia said to herself with a shake of her head.

Yoryis led the way to the first restaurant they came to, a small room with wooden booths. Louis immediately went off in search of Nick Zeese's friend Karakostas, whom he had heard was in Helper. After a meal of greasy fried meat and mashed potatoes, Yoryis walked back to the depot with the women and then looked for the

Roumeliot coffeehouse. It was almost deserted in the daytime. He introduced himself to the proprietor and asked about the men whose names were given to him. "There's one of them over there," the proprietor said, and led Yoryis to a corner table where a man was reading a Greek newspaper. The man stood up and shook hands with Yoryis. The two were about the same age, thirty. The other Roumeliot was not so tall as Yoryis; a fleshy, handsome man, he wore a plaid wool shirt, breeches, high-top shoes, and a stockman's Stetson, the fashion of Americans who raised cattle and sheep. The man walked to the back corner of the coffeehouse in the serious manner of someone used to being asked favors. He put his palms into his back pockets and rocked on his heels.

"I have a contract with Cameron to run the coffeehouse at the mine. Could you lend me five hundred dollars?"

The man lifted his eyebrows in the feigned surprise used by old-country moneylenders. "So you have a contract with Cameron and you want *me* to lend you five hundred dollars?"

"Yes."

The Roumeliot smiled sardonically. "What money are you talking about? There is no money," and he left the rest of the sentence unsaid: *for you. There is no money for you.*

Yoryis lifted two fingers in salute and walked toward the door. "Sit down," the proprietor said. "Sit down, patrioti, I have a coffee brewing for you. Tell us the news from the city."

"Some other time," Yoryis said and hurried into the brisk air that cooled the humiliation on his face. Then rage took hold of him at being treated with contempt, just as he had been in the fatherland. He went into the Chinese–American Cafe and asked the smiling, bright-eyed Chinese standing behind an ornate cash register where the bank was. He knew he could not risk asking one more Greek for money or he would become the butt of coffeehouse quips. The bank was a cement block building with an iron-barred tellers' counter on one side and three desks across from it. Immediately on entering, Yoryis was approached by a big man in his early forties with bushy eyebrows, thick mustache, and wavy hair parted in the middle. Yoryis recognized him as a *xeno* like himself.

"I'm Joe Barboglio," the man said. "I'm president of the bank. Sit down."

Yoryis told him he had a contract with Cameron and needed five hundred dollars. "You bet your boots," Barboglio said and turned to a young Italian at the next desk. "Make out papers for a five-hundred-dollar loan."

"This is a good place for Greeks and Italians," the banker said, "if you keep your eyes open." He was, he said, one of the first Italians to come to the coal fields and one of the miners who went on strike in the early 1900s trying to get the United Mine Workers recognized. Mine guards had rounded up the strikers and put them in corrals near the rail yards in the county seat, seven miles away. The strikers cooked spaghetti in coffee cans and danced around bonfires at night while guards sat on sheds and pointed cocked guns at them. Barboglio had escaped and for several years ran a saloon in Missouri where he married an English immigrant, then he returned to become the town banker.

Yoryis told him about his predicament: no house for his wife, baby, and his sister-in-law. Barboglio immediately telephoned the town marshal in Castle Gate who kept a boardinghouse. They shook hands and Yoryis walked quickly back to the depot to wait for the next train. By evening they were again in Castle Gate in the marshal's boardinghouse built against a rocky, rearing slope, the odor of fresh coal, mud, and junipers sharply in the air, and from everywhere the hum of machinery, raucous shouts, and barking dogs. In the night, the baby asleep at last, Emilia in exhaustion heard the shuffling of footsteps. Quietly she went to the window. An uneven line of yellow lights moved in the blackness, rose, then suddenly one after another disappeared—miners entering the mine.

The next morning the family ate with American miners and railroad men in silence while boisterous talk shook the room. After breakfast Yoryis walked the mile to Cameron to hurry the carpenters. The unplastered walls infuriated him. He was disgusted with himself for having to resort to public quarters for his family, ashamed that they were dependent on strangers instead of Greeks. He walked back to Castle Gate and to the small depot where he

251

talked with an elderly woman dispatcher about his furniture. From there he went to the two-story company offices and store, built of pinkish dun rock quarried from the upright mountains by Italian immigrant masons. The store was crammed with barrels, harnesses, canned goods, kerosene lanterns, miners' carbide lamps, picks, shovels, blasting powder, overalls, rounds of cheese, bolts of cloth. He opened an account.

After lunch he brought Emilia with the baby and Faní to the store. The manager got up from a rolltop desk, put his pen behind the top of his ear, and came toward them wearing a green visor and black shirt protectors over his sleeves. Yoryis thought of his father; how often he had seen him similarly at work. "I want this," Emilia said and pointed to a bolt of heavy muslin. Faní looked on with respect for Emilia's ability to speak English. The manager began unrolling the muslin. "How much do you want?" he asked. Emilia held down the end of the cloth and drew a length to her nose; she did this three times. The manager cut the cloth, measured it with a yardstick, and wrote up the cost.

In the boarding house, Emilia took out her sewing box and she and Faní cut and hemmed dish towels. Yoryis went back to the coffeehouse, now locked, walked around it, and looked into the windows. The walls were still unplastered. Then a great rolling whistle boomed out, followed by several others shrilling farther away.

Within a few moments men walked down the dusty road, smudged, their miners' caps askew, empty lard pails swinging from one hand, a pick or shovel in the other. Even before their talk and laughing reached him, he knew they were Greeks, and almost all of them Cretans. Instinctively, they knew he was one of them and rushed toward him, shaking his hand, welcoming him, asking him the old questions. One of them pushed through the crowd. "Zisimópoule!" he shouted, his eyes joyous, and shaking Yoryis's hand with vigor, looked around at the men: "We've eaten bread and salt together!" He was one of the Cretans sent to Yoryis's Idaho railroad gang wearing the black pantaloons, embroidered vest, and fringed kerchief of Crete. The miner laughingly told Yoryis he had not forgotten how hard he had worked the gang.

Yoryis assured the men that he and his cousin Lambros would soon have the coffeehouse open for them. "Where are you staying? We'll find space for you, Tall One."

"I'm staying at the marshal's boardinghouse with my wife, baby, and my wife's sister."

The men lifted their shoulders, aghast at his strange situation. "Patrioti," his Idaho friend said, "forgive us. We have no houses to invite you to stay with us. Some of us live in a *compania boardinghowz* with Italians and Serbs. And there's a Cretan bekiariko by the river. Every bed is used twice in twenty-four hours. One man gets out, another gets in. The rest of us live on porches and washhouses with a few patriotes who are married. Forgive us."

Relieved over meeting the Greeks, Yoryis returned to the boardinghouse. He thought that someone among the hundreds of unmarried Greek men in the Castle Gate and Cameron camps would take Faní for a wife, perhaps even a Cretan, although they seldom married women beyond their island.

When they moved into the four-room house of cement blocks cast to resemble rock, the walls cool from the still wet calcimine, Greeks off shift with festive calls and snatches of song helped Yoryis and Louis carry the furniture over the muddy roads and into the house. Yoryis poured ouzo into glasses and coffee cups and toasted the men, "To your wedding crowns," he said in the traditional greeting. "Whatever you desire," they answered.

Emilia stood in the clutter, holding the baby, miserable because she could not properly offer hospitality to the young men. Faní dusted the few chairs and retreated.

Louis returned from Helper and asked Yoryis for more of his money. "You've lost all you had on cards," Yoryis said and cursed him. With a look of contrition, Louis helped the carpenters finish the coffeehouse: he had been apprenticed for a short time to a carpenter when he was a boy. Unpainted, the coffeehouse was deemed ready by the company. Yoryis and Louis cleaned it, set up tables, chairs, and the stove, and tacked up a calendar of a garlanded blonde woman sent by the Vasilakopulos importing store, newspaper pictures of King Constantine and Premier Venizelos, and a poster of President Wilson. Above the pictures, Louis crossed small

Greek and American flags. In the back room he set up a cot so that gossip would not arise at his staying in a house where an unattached woman lived.

Louis was well liked by the men; he was better educated than any of them and often wrote letters for the illiterate and the barely literate to their families without charging them as interpreters did. At times he and Yoryis had to talk with the marshal to explain their countrymen's assaulting Americans who derided their Greekness. Both also went with certain fearful miners to the company store on paydays; they had been cheated, the men said, or were sure to be cheated. One of them, a short, square Cretan, bought the largest pair of overalls in the store, cut off the bottoms, and sewed clumsy gloves from the remnant to save money. Mostly the men liked Louis because they had all won from him in *barbout,* their favorite card game.

Louis let it be known that he would have married Faní if he and Yoryis were not second cousins, which the men knew would have meant the mixing of two families' bloods and would have been incestuous. "She is well mannered and chaste," he said and added pointedly, "She stayed with the Mathaioses a very short time."

Until midnight the coffeehouse rocked with the exhilaration of men released from black tunnels where they had swung picks and shoveled coal into cars, eaten bread, onions, hard-boiled eggs, and Greek olives in damp darkness. Avidly they read the Greek newspapers, the Salt Lake *Evzone,* the New York *Atlantis* and *Ethinikos Kyrix*—the *National Herald.* With Greece vacillating over entering the war—King Constantine favoring neutrality, Premier Venizelos the Allies—Yoryis and Louis had to clamp down their own volatility for survival. Royalists, they cajoled the Cretans who taunted the few mainlanders in the camp for favoring the king. A *Karaghiozis* puppet show and musicians playing for a fat singer, *Kyria* Sophia, took the men's minds off politics for a short time. Accompanied by violin and *laouto, Kyria* Sophia sang, as Maria Economidhou, the Greek journalist who had sent Emilia to the Mathaioses, would write of her performance elsewhere, "with the grace of an elephant and the voice of a wolf."

Through the doors and windows of the rock house the shouting and laughing in the coffeehouse penetrated. "I can't hold up my head!" Emilia whispered sharply behind the closed door of their bedroom late at night. "I'm ashamed of this bad business you're mixed up with! I can't look my neighbor in the eye!"

"I'm not ashamed of running a coffeehouse to support my family!"

"You haven't tried hard enough to marry off Fani!"

Yoryis threw a shoe against the wall and silence followed. In the gray ledger where he kept his account of expenses and the day's receipts was a letter from his father. Yoryis's sister Vasiliki, for whom he had sent money to buy linens and household furnishings, had married a man thirty years older than she. An enclosed picture showed a man no more than five feet tall, who had gone to Rumania years previously, returned with a hoarded sum, and never worked again. Vasiliki had agreed to marry him because "she was getting of an age when men would be looking at younger girls." "Well off," the letter said. "Well off," Yoryis repeated sardonically. "One sheep more than we have."

He thought of his mother and father: for the second time he had failed his parents. His sister Marigho had married a much older widower because she too had become of an age and could wait no longer. Now his second sister Vasiliki—if his family had waited nine months, he could have sent them enough money to increase her dowry because the coffeehouse was doing well enough to leave a little left over after expenses. He cursed the poverty of his country that left women unmarried or to become the wives of old men. He cursed the customs of *patridha* that kept men from marrying a servant woman. He said nothing to Emilia, snapped and snarled at her attempts to speak to him. When she received a letter from her *kyria* and *kyrios* in Constantinople that little Achilles had died, she grieved alone.

21

Yoryis and Louis had their coffee-making interrupted throughout the day by owners of boardinghouses and other Greeks who lived in bachelor houses, the *bekiarika,* and took turns cooking. They preferred buying meat from their unskilled countrymen butchers than from skilled Americans at the company store. Besides yearling lambs sold by Greek sheepmen, Yoryis bought an occasional piglet from Serbian and Slovenian miners who raised pigs in their backyards, a calf and chickens from Italians who had turned to farming on the banks of the Price River after being blackballed during the strike of 1903, and deer from Americans during the hunting season.

One of the Greek boardinghouse owners banged a dishpan with a poker whenever he had cooked a special dish: rabbit stew, deer meat with wine, cloves, and bay leaf, or pork with celery in lemon sauce. At the ring of the poker in the narrow valley, men slapped down their cards, Louis among them, and hurried toward the riverside boardinghouse conjecturing on what delicacy awaited them.

Several months after the coffeehouse opened, a Cretan on his way to San Francisco stopped to see a fellow villager and showed Yoryis how to butcher meat properly.

Only for about an hour in the early morning was the coffeehouse quiet. Sometimes a Cretan miner would come in to have Louis write a letter to his family. With enthusiastic care, like a dedicated schoolteacher, Louis changed village speech to formal epistle style.

If the miner ended his dictation with the usual "Long live Ven- izelos!" Louis was tempted to substitute an innocuous declaration, but his honesty would not allow it. When he and Yoryis were alone, he swore obscenely at the premier and begged the All–Holy to strike him dead. "For the good of Greece, strike him dead!" "Pat- ridha, patridha," he mumbled tearfully while sweeping and wiping tables.

"Why are you sniveling for patridha?" Yoryis said scathingly. "Its poverty chased us away."

"No! If I hadn't been framed in the army and sent to prison, I'd have had a good life."

"Good life! Your father had five sheep to his name."

"How can you talk against our holy country?"

"I'm talking about its poverty and as long as you can never go back, forget it!"

Every Saturday evening Yoryis walked the four miles to Helper, carrying the week's money in a small canvas bag, his gun pushed behind his belt. After putting the bag in the brass night depository, he went to the Grill Cafe whose manager, Vasilis Ghiourghiotis, had recently changed his name to Bill White. George Anton waited at the counter for him. They sat in a leather upholstered booth, ate a piece of American pie, drank a cup of American coffee, and talked.

The blisters and thickened palms George Anton had developed while working on Yoryis's Idaho railroad gang were gone. Besides interpreting in a Spring Canyon coal mine, he made the rounds of Greek boardinghouses and *bekiarika* in the evening as a representa- tive of a Greek tailor in Salt Lake City. The miners carefully went through his large, green catalogue, examining illustrations of fas- tidious men underneath which were small squares of fabric. Because it was a big expenditure, some miners spent the entire evening discussing styles and fabric before George took out a tape measure. Others asked him to choose because "You're an educated man."

For over an hour the two Yoryises talked about business oppor- tunities in America, responsibilities to their families, politics in the fatherland, and immigrant happenings reported in Greek news- papers published in the United States.

One evening they were joined by Stylian Staes, whom Yoryis had met in the *Evzone* office in Salt Lake City. Staes had not dared to be seen in Helper for over a year because of a ruse connected with choosing the site for the Greek church. The Helper Greeks expected the church to be built in their town: more Greeks lived there and in the surrounding coal camps than in Price. The Greeks of Price contended that the church should be built in the county seat. A meeting was set in Helper to vote on the site.

As the Greek vice-consul for Utah, Wyoming, and Nevada, a respected interpreter in courts and before justices of the peace, and a correspondent for the *Evzone* newspaper in Salt Lake City, Staes opened the meeting. For almost an hour he told *paramithia*, fables, and anecdotes. Suddenly two Price Cretans burst into the room shouting, "A big card game is going on in the Lendaris coffee-house!" The Helper and mining town Greeks ran out. While they were gone, a vote was taken and Price won.

To celebrate Staes's reappearance in Helper, Bill White brought them whiskey in coffee cups—he did not have a saloon license. "If anyone comes in to grab me," Staes said, "Tall—One here will protect me." The men laughed, and Staes tapped the side of his nose with a tobacco-browned index finger.

In good weather, the sky still light around nine o'clock and the road dry, the eight-mile round trip walk was routine for Yoryis. When winds blew cold, when the road turned to mud, when snow piled in drifts, he left Emilia and Faní shriveled in unspoken fear and cursed Louis who could not be trusted with money.

One night after a late August rainstorm, the dirt and coal dust had become a muddy ooze and Yoryis's shoes made a sucking noise as he trudged. When he neared the bridge the loud rush of the river become a roar. He grabbed the butt of his gun: bridges were dangerous places, often inhabited by Nereids, beautiful women who lured men to their death or took away their senses.

He could see the bridge dimly, the wooden beams in geometric designs. He stepped on it. Planks moved under his feet. With great leaps he jumped to the other side as a horrendous creak of ripping wood shot into the blackness. He looked back to see the beams collapse and disappear. Making the sign of the cross, he plodded through the mud as fast as he could.

Exhausted, sitting across from George Anton in the Grill Cafe, he began to laugh at himself—grabbing his gun to shoot Nereids! He telephoned Louis to tell Emilia what had happened and that he could not return until the next day. In a room in the Carbon Hotel he made a decision: he would give Louis his money and be rid of him and his gambling. "Go to the devil because that's how you want it," he told him on his return to Cameron.

Louis stood in the busy coffeehouse, carrying a worn black bag, not much larger than a doctor's satchel, that held all his belongings. With him were Nick Zeese and his gambler friend, Karakostas, both immaculately dressed in sharply pressed gray suits, gray fedoras, striped silk shirts, and diamonds in their silk ties. "Did you bring Karakostas to protect you?" Yoryis asked Nick.

Karakostas strutted from table to table, one hand in his pocket to reveal a platinum watch chain across his vest; the other hand, the fingers, like Nick's, brown from tobacco, cupped a burning cigarette. With condescending heartiness, Karakostas talked with the men drinking coffee in their off-shift clothes, dark pants and cotton shirts. The name Karakostas—Black Kostas—had been given to his grandfather after he led several men of his clan to capture three Englishmen traveling through the mountains of central Greece; when ransom was not paid, they killed the Englishmen and considered themselves *palikaria*—manly, daring. *Palikaradhes,* Yoryis's father had called them, a derisive twist of the word—thinking themselves *palikaria* when they were not.

Karakostas and Nick each had a one-fourth interest in four brothels in Utah, Idaho, and Arizona. Only foolish gamblers like Louis would play cards with Karakostas who spent most of his time making a circuit of mining towns on paydays looking for games with American, Japanese, and other immigrant miners. Yoryis eyed Nick from his gray fedora to his polished shoes, then looked at Louis in his old black suit and yellowed shirt. "In this company, Lambros, your thousand dollars isn't going to last long." Louis reddened and Nick laughed. "Worthless!" Yoryis took a step toward Nick. "Blotch on the Zisimopoulos clan! Bastard!"

"Karakostas!" Nick laughed nervously as he hurried out the door. "I'm leaving!"

In June, almost a year to the date of their first child's birth, a second daughter was born. Each day a German neighbor came to supervise Faní and give advice. While Emilia was still in bed for the regular two-week recuperation doctors advised in America, a Greek woman appeared at the house. She was a blue-eyed blonde with a three-month-old baby in her arms and a small girl clutching her skirt. They had walked most of the four miles from Helper. "I heard," Eleni Jouflas said in the Roumeliot dialect, "that there was a Greek woman here. I couldn't come earlier because I was pregnant myself."

Although Emilia was supposedly in bed, she was fully dressed, ready at any moment to heat a bottle of milk for the baby or to pick up the older child who was learning to walk and falling constantly. Faní boiled coffee in the *brik*, and the three women sat in the sparse living room sipping it and eating *koulourakia*. They talked about the fatherland, Faní speaking only when the visitor questioned her. While she was in the kitchen feeding the little girls milk and cookies, Emilia asked quietly, "Is there any chance my sister can find a husband here? No one has come to ask for her."

Eleni Jouflas shook her head and said tersely, "I was a servant girl myself. Yes, I know about your sister. News flies. I was sent to Athens by my family. But I was one of the lucky ones. A man took me. We had a farm between here and Helper, by the river. There was a flood and he tried to save a cow. He got pneumonia and died. A widower with a little boy married me. I was one of the lucky ones. A man won't take a servant for his woman here."

Yoryis sold the coffeehouse and moved the family to a white frame double house on the dirt road leading to Helper's main street. The house had three rooms, a dark, crowded kitchen, a middle bedroom for Yoryis and Emilia with the two children in small cribs, and a living room where Faní slept on a pull-down, second-hand leather sofa. On the other side of the wall a plump, pretty Italian woman, her scrawny husband, and two little daughters lived.

For a few months Yoryis and a man he had met on a railroad gang in Iowa—Nasopoulos, who had changed his name to Nass—

operated a coffeehouse in a frame building on a corner of Main Street. The coffeehouse was filled continually with men off their morning, afternoon, and graveyard shifts. Sheepmen in town for the winter spent long hours reading in Greek newspapers about the war in Europe and political battles in the fatherland and reminiscing about their village Marvrolithari—Black Rock—on a chain of mountains parallel to those of Klepá. They regaled each other with the same priest and nomad stories that Yoryis had heard from the time he was a child.

Again, no man sent a friend or relative to ask for Faní. George Anton, who intended to return to Greece within a few months, and Staes, who asked every peripatetic Greek newsman to find Faní a husband, had been unsuccessful in their efforts. Each morning when Yoryis left for work, he felt the women's reproachful eyes. "It's no use," he told Faní. "Either you go back to your village or become resigned to live with us."

"I will never go back! And I can't stay in this house!"

A few days after her outburst Yoryis read an advertisement in the *Atlantis* newspaper placed by a Roumeliot from the town of Karpenisi, a long day's walk from Klepá. The Karpenisiot was searching for a woman to help his sick wife. "I'll go," Faní said.

Yoryis wrote to the Karpenisiot, and within a month Faní crossed the continent to Washington, D.C. A few months later she married a restaurant cook, a man many years older than she. Her letters came with regular lament: none of the Greek women visited her, thinking her beneath them.

Emilia was again pregnant. Several times a day the room reeled and she looked into blackness. Philomena Bonacci, the Italian landlord's wife, came every day to see her. Sarah "Kilarney" Reynolds, the wife of an Irish railroader, brought soup and fed Panaghiota and Eleni. George Anton had asked Emilia for the name she would like him to give her second daughter. Gratefully she had answered "Eleni," her mother's name. When the Reynolds's daughter, Florence, returned from school, she often took the children to her house.

Each night in the middle room of the house where the children slept, Emilia lighted the vigil light before the icon of the All—

Holy. From the dresser the glow spread over the two cribs into the living room where she and Yoryis slept on the pull-down sofa and into the kitchen where the coal stove murmured, clinked, and thumped. Emilia prayed for her family's survival. She prayed for courage for the Papadimitrious who had written that the Turks were making life harder for the Greeks and could Emilia's husband help them come to America. She asked the All–Holy to see that they stayed close to little Achilles's grave. For what could an educated man do in America but turn to using his wits to live, becoming a hated labor agent or a threadbare Greek newspaper correspondent?

Emilia thought of her failure to her family: Faní whom she had hoped to have near her was across the continent, married to an unknown man, good or bad no one knew; her brother Yiannis, whom she had hoped to bring to America after he had served his army duty, had been sent to the border when Greece joined the Allies and had been taken prisoner immediately. Emilia's sister Anna had written: "Yiannis sent us a letter from a German prisoner-of-war camp. It came through the Red Cross. 'Send me a sweater,' he said. 'I'm cold.'" She prayed to the All–Holy for her people and for a son.

Yoryis sold his partnership in the coffeehouse to Nass and took in a new partner, a Lebanese named N. S. Malouf, a dark, big-nosed, handsome man who was an occasional labor agent. His first name was unknown; he called himself N. S. Malouf at all times. In the front of a store they sold cigars, cigarettes, and soft drinks—although Malouf always carried a handy silver flask of bootleg whiskey. Since the first of August 1917 a dry law was in effect. In the center and back of the store were ten pool tables and an ornate player piano that had cost three thousand dollars. A door in the back led to a small room where mine managers played cards without fear of being caught. "I will never be able to hold up my head," Emilia shrieked.

The poolhall was a busy meeting place. Men gave up their jobs to play pool while waiting for their draft call or came in to celebrate before enlisting. Jim Galanis and Tom Avgikos who owned the Golden Rule Store, George Anton, and a few other Greeks enlisted immediately, but most immigrants not only did not enlist but refused to report for induction after being drafted. "We're not citizens. We're going back to our own country," they told Yoryis, "and that fool," they said of Stylian Staes, the Greek vice-consul, who had told the men they could ask for exemptions because they were aliens, but it would be to their credit to enlist, "that fool wants us to go sleep and eat with the Amerikani, die with them when we can't even understand them when they talk!"

Brawls erupted on the boardwalk outside the poolhall. The weekly Helper and Price newspapers called the immigrants "un-American," "whelps who think nothing of getting American dollars under the American flag but who would not turn a hand over to save that flag from being dragged in the dirt by the Kaiser's dirty cutthroats." The "low-down grafters" were promised some "early day western treatment." With Greeks continuing to enlist and the Mahoutas brothers taking their prostitutes near army camps, Yoryis and other Greek businessmen thought the uproar would subside.

Instead, Americans pounced on unmarried Greek coal miners and their compatriot gamblers and procurers alike. From behind boulders boys and young men called out to the Greeks as they left mine portals, "White slavers! Scum! Gamblers! Go back where you come from!" Emilia spent the long nights rocking the children, using the remedies Kilarney Reynolds advised for their teething and illnesses, going constantly to the icon of the All—Holy, terrified when she found the vigil light had unaccountably gone out. Every few minutes she pulled back the living room curtain to look out; frenzy mounted and abated only when she saw Yoryis's big silhouette, hand on the gun at his belt, come down the street.

"It's the men, the men," Emilia and her diminutive landlady Philomena Bonacci said to each other, speaking in Italian, angry at both Americans and immigrants. North Italian and South Italian miners fought each other over whether to call a strike. Centuries-old South Slav hate sprang up, refreshed: Croats and Slovenes were exempt from induction because they could well be fighting their kinsmen in the Austro—Hungarian army; the Serbs could not ask for exemption because Serbia had sided with the Allies. In coffeehouses, tables and chairs crashed as royalists defended King Constantine's thwarted wish for a neutral Greece and Venizelists upheld the premier's leadership in bringing the homeland to join the Allies.

When America first entered the war, Yoryis's mother took the old Grivas icon of Saints George and Demetrios to the church of Saint George as a *tama,* an offering to ward off her son's going to war. The icon of Saint George on his white horse and Saint Demetrios on his brown horse was framed with intricately carved wood overlaid with gold leaf. The whole was encased in a glass box. Yoryis had never looked at the icon closely, nor did he know of his mother's sacrifice.

Women came hurriedly to Emilia's kitchen to have her read in her dark red dream book: Italian, Cretan Greek, Roumeliot Greek, French, and even the lank-haired American woman next door who was married to a morose Greek barber. When meat and sugar became scarce, the women came more often: hunger and war went together. Although the women knew the village interpretations of dreams, a book had authority. The dreams often had to do with the color black, a black bird, a man dressed in black waiting, watching, a procession of black-dressed women. These visits made Emilia's fatigue worse: the three rooms had to be spotless, the children always clean, coffee and sweets ready. With her third pregnancy the early-morning sickness went on beyond the first three months. The exhaustion she felt before falling asleep was still in her when she awoke; she put aside for a later time her anger at Yoryis, at first patient, then angry at her questions about his business partnerships: "It's not a woman's affair!"

Emilia often awoke in panic at a recurring dream of herself and the children alone in a silent house. Married men with children were being drafted. She thought of Yoryis already gone, never to return, and she left to feed and clothe her children with the few gold coins and silver dollars in a cloth sack in the bottom of her trunk. Kilarney Reynolds said no, the war would be over in a few weeks.

It went on, and although the Greeks held "Get out the Coal" rallies in every mine, led the Americans and all immigrants in tonnage, bought war bonds in large numbers—the miners in the Winter Quarters mine nine thousand dollars worth in one day—people congregated on the boardwalks and complained loudly that soon there would be no red-blooded American boys left in the country and the Greeks and Italians would take over. Several young Greek men married American women, and the shrilling of "Greeks marrying white girls!" came throughout the day to Yoryis behind the cash register. One of the Greeks walked into the poolhall with several friends as his protectors against ambush. Yoryis said, "A man's beard was on fire, and someone said, 'Don't douse it until I light my pipe.' " The men smiled sheepishly at the old proverb.

As days passed, demands and shouts grew to near hysteria outside the poolhall. On a May night at the Saltair depot in Salt Lake City where excursion trains took people to the Great Salt Lake for bathing and dancing in a pavilion, a group of Americans taunted several Greeks and a fight broke out. One of the Greeks shot and killed Bruce Dempsey, the seventeen-year-old brother of Jack Dempsey, the boxer. The Greeks liked the boxer; he had swept floors in Salt Lake's Greek Town restaurants at the beginning of his career. Yoryis read about the fight in the Salt Lake newspapers; the victim was called "the lad," "a boy," "little Bruce Dempsey" who sold newspapers in the true American tradition of helping his family. A reporter for *To Fos—The Light*—in town to write an account of a baptismal festivity, said the Greek Town merchants called him a *mortis,* tramp, and *ghourouni,* pig. With a gang of other newsboys, he regularly had run down Greek Town sidewalks holding out sticks that hit displays of fruits and vegetables and scattered them into the street.

The murderer was known to the Greeks for his unusual red hair. A posse under a Greek detective traced him to a farmhouse and brought him to the city jail. When one of the Salt Lake newspapers reported a vigilance committee was meeting outside the jail the following night, a crowd gathered. At shouts for a lynching, Greeks in the crowd stole away to the coffeehouses and returned with armed countrymen. Deputies talked soothingly to the mob, but not until the Greeks were noticed did the crowd disperse.

Near the time Yoryis expected he would be drafted, a Cretan cardplayer was almost lynched in Price for giving an American girl a ride in his new yellow Buick. A posse gathered and stopped the Buick as it was coming down a mining camp road into Price. The girl jumped out of the car and ran. The posse took the Cretan to the courthouse jail where a crowd rushed to lynch him. The sheriff and two deputies stood on the top step of the courthouse. Greeks ran to the two Price coffeehouses and telephoned coffeehouses and boardinghouses in the coal camps. An Italian businessman rallied the Italians: "If they hang a Greek today, they'll hang an Italian tomorrow!" Armed Greeks swarmed into town; Italians arrived with knives and pitchforks. The crowd, muttering, slowly fanned out, stood in small groups at a distance, and looked on stonily.

Nick Zeese had almost been lynched himself in an Idaho hamlet. He had been on his way to Boise, Idaho, driving a dark red Buick coupe. Buicks were symbols to Greek gamblers of having reached the top. Then twenty-one years old, he had become as finicky about his car as he was about his clothes and had the Buick polished twice a week. He decided to remain that night in the Idaho town because he could not reach Boise before dark. Not finding a poolhall or candy store in the quiet Mormon town and no one on the street likely gamblers, only farmers in overalls, he walked to a store that had been converted into a movie theater.

Inside, he sat among farmers and their wives, older ones wearing sunbonnets. With his Stetson fedora on his lap, he smoked a cigar while waiting for the theater to darken. Heads turned in his direction; eyes looked at him from the corners of hooded eyelids. He shifted in his seat while whisperings filled the room. To placate the Mormons whose Word of Wisdom prohibited their using tobacco, he put his cigar under the seat.

The lights went out and a player piano tinkled as the Pathe News flashed on the screen. Wounded American soldiers lay on hospital cots; captions told of the Hun's atrocities. In mud, in doorways of bombed French farmhouses, American dead were sprawled. Rumblings rose, more sinister with each picture of suffering soldiers, refugees, destruction. A peacetime Kaiser reviewed his troops, a small animal skull embedded in his tall fur hat. With a rush and frenzy of obscenities, men dragged Nick screaming outside and down the dirt street to the hanging tree. "Look in my pocket! I'm an American citizen!" he yelled his lie. "I buy bonds! Look in my pocket!"

While a man went off for a rope, another looked into Nick's vest pocket and brought out five hundred dollars worth of bonds. The crowd reluctantly let him go. "Get out of town, you foreigner!" they shouted, pushing him along. Someone kicked him. Nick hurried to his Buick and drove onto a dirt road that cut into the sagebrush, his expensive valise filled with silk shirts, another custom-made suit, and a pair of Florsheim shoes left behind.

Later, safely back in Helper, he laughed about it. Like all Greeks who traveled, he carried war bonds for just such an emergency—it was recommended by *To Fos,* the new Greek newspaper in Salt Lake City. It was not that Nick read Greek newspapers; he had heard the advice from others.

Both Greek and American newspapers told of a new horror: throughout the world millions of people were dying from a terrible kind of influenza. In army and refugee camps the dead were buried in mass graves. Newspapers printed the advice of doctors: boil drinking water, stay at home, wear masks when outside. Wagons and sometimes a truck passed by the Bonacci house with plain wooden caskets on their beds. People wearing masks rode behind in buckboards and cars to the small graveyard on a rise of sagebrush and rocks.

The patriarch of Greek Town, John Diamanti, still sporting the long mustaches of the old country, came to compatriot houses with a doctor who gave influenza injections at a dollar each. Emilia dug into her trunk for four dollars. When she told Kilarney Reynolds, the Irish neighbor shook her head. "I think the man wasn't a doctor at all. The shots were probably plain water."

Emilia knew that stocky, kindly John Diamanti or Barba Yiannis, Uncle John, as the Greeks called him, had thought he was helping his people. He and his wife had come to Helper in the early 1900s, the first Greek couple in the coal fields. Barba Yiannis was a folk healer; he foretold the sex of an unborn child, looking away from each pregnant woman in shame. He read the shoulder blade of the Easter lamb and divined what the coming year would bring. A sheepman, he had delivered all eight of his children himself; his wife, Yiannina—villagers called women by the genitive of their husbands' names—was ashamed to have a man, the company doctor, attend her. "It's no different from a ewe and a lamb," Barba Yiannis said. When Americans mentioned Uncle John, though, they praised him as the best bootlegger in the state.

Troop trains stopped at the depot on the way east. In dark blue uniforms trimmed with gold braid, the Italian band stood on the wooden platform and played marching tunes. People gathered to cheer the town's draftees, some with immigrant faces. "They're showing their countrymen what their duty is," the *Helper Times* said. One of Nick Zeese's gambler friends wrote him from Fort Douglas on the outskirts of Salt Lake City: "If they snatch you, act dumb. Pretend you don't understand a word of English. That's what I did and they put me to taking care of the horses."

Letters came from Faní pleading to let her family come west. "No Greek woman will have anything to do with me because I worked in the Karpenisiot's house," she wrote.

The new baby, Demerra, Demetroula, cried incessantly and sometimes went limp. While Yoryis slept soundly, a gun under his pillow, Emilia jumped up at every cry and wet the baby's face with damp towels. One morning Emilia fainted. Kilarney Reynolds called the Castle Gate mine company doctor who said she had the influenza and prescribed a bitter tonic. While Emilia burned with fever, Greek women came to the back door and handed bowls of food to Kilarney Reynolds or to a woman who worked as a practical nurse.

Yoryis met Nick on Main Street. Nick was shivering, his breath reeking of whiskey and garlic. "Go to your hotel and get in bed," Yoryis ordered. "I'll send a doctor."

"No. If I go to bed, I'll die. With whiskey and garlic I'll make it."

More whites than foreigners were getting the flu, Americans

said, because of the garlic the foreigners ate; nobody would get near enough to give them the germs.

The Armistice was signed. Yoryis stood in the doorway of his store and smiled at the laughing, cheering, crying people on Main Street passing bottles of bootleg whiskey around. Jim Galanis and Tom Avgikos returned to their Golden Rule Store, Gus Tsangaras to open a men's store, The Toggery, and Jim Papacostas, the Palace Candy Store. Bill White again managed the Grill Cafe. Jim Papoulas and Ted Jouflas went back to their sheep camps, and former miners rode miles into coal tunnels again. Others returned sick or maimed: George Anton with the dread mastoid infection that would kill him; two soldiers each with a leg missing, another with an arm gone; several veterans acting strangely. A young Italian strode down Main Street singing arias at the top of his voice. "Shell shocked," Kilarney Reynolds told Emilia. Other soldiers had been killed or sent directly to hospitals, and those who had left neither widows nor children to remind people of them were quickly forgotten.

In all, the newspaper said, eight and a half million men had been killed, over twenty-one million wounded. In the United States alone over a half million had died of influenza. Several Americans and the Mahoutas brothers returned with their American prostitutes. To protect themselves from white slavery laws, they had married the women and continued to pimp for them. Sugar, meat, and butter were no longer rationed, and immigrant veterans were given citizenship.

22

Yoryis bid to provide the labor on a water line over the summit twenty-five miles away and into Helper and Price. The water they were drinking at present, the Americans said, required a spoon. Needing money for tools and provisions, Yoryis took in as partners the Greek vice-consul, Stylian Staes, and Angelo "Liar" Raekos who had helped him in Denver when he was penniless. Their low bid of two hundred thirty-five thousand was accepted.

Leaving N. S. Malouf to run the poolhall, Yoryis and Liar—as Raekos was called because of his fantasies—drove up the narrow, dangerously curved road to Colton. The small truck was pocked from flying rock and its paint flaked off from wind and snow. The automobile dealer who rented it to Yoryis had given him a lesson while they were parked on Main Street, then had him drive around town for fifteen or twenty minutes. When Liar settled himself into the truck for the journey, he immediately launched into his stories, but as the road climbed and Yoryis stripped the gears and cursed, he became silent, staring at the river so far below it looked like a small stream. When they reached the summit, Liar jumped out and began singing in a raucous, joyful voice.

The Denver and Rio Grande Western train stopped before noon, bringing tents, equipment, and a gang of Mexican laborers Raekos had contracted for. The men had fled the Mexican Revolution in 1910, worked as strikebreakers in the copper mines west of

Salt Lake City in 1912, and later as muckers in metal and coal mines when work was available. "My name is George Zeese," Yoryis told them, and they nodded, caps off in the old-country manner of respect.

George returned from his first visit to Helper with a brown mongrel dog given to him by an Italian farmer. It was still a pup, and Louis on one of his sojourns from Nevada had cut off its tail. George named the dog *Leon,* Lion. Leon followed George everywhere and slept at the side of his cot. When George shouted at his men, Leon barked alongside him.

Six weeks into digging the trenches for the water pipes, George caught Liar taking money and whiskey from the men in return for lighter work or for sitting, supposedly sick, in the tents during bad weather. Americans and Irish had begun the practice when Japanese and Mediterranean immigrants arrived. Greeks and Italians were perpetuating it with the newer immigrants. "You've got to go," George told Liar. Raekos left, flushed but laughing, smoothing his graying mustache. "Let me be godfather to your next child," he said, and they shook hands.

While George carried out the engineer's orders, Stylian Staes sat in a small office in Price next to a coffeehouse wearing a green eyeshade on his bald head. Around him was a disorder of old and new Greek newspapers, mail, and all manner of containers overflowing with cigarette butts: metal and pottery ashtrays, water glasses, restaurant dishes, tin cans. Through a blue haze of tobacco smoke he typed on a Greek-alphabet typewriter using his index fingers. He wrote letters to Greek newspapers published in America on immigration problems, to the Greek consul in Washington, D.C., for documents, to families in Greece for illiterate compatriots. He typed business agreements between Greeks and stamped them with a notary public seal retrieved from the clutter on his desk.

Staes also wrote letters of protest to the local newspapers about the American Legion campaign against the immigrants, "foreigners" as they called them. In the Helper Liberty Hall the American Legion national commander shouted to a gathering of Legionnaires wearing dark blue uniforms and overseas caps, "The foreigners and Americans are like oil and water, they don't mix! If they don't attend the compulsory education classes and learn English, they should be deported! Sent back where they came from!" Murmurings of assent and clappings cut into the speech every few seconds. The Greek, Italian, and Serb volunteers looked at each other questioningly, then angrily. They began shouting, "We fought for this country! We're American citizens!"

The commander stopped, puzzled at the waving fists. The local commander stood up and whispered to him. The national commander raised his arms, smiled, and waited for the men to quiet down. "Don't get hot under the collar," he said smoothly. "It's not you fine, patriotic men I'm talking about, it's the kind that bite the hand that feeds them."

All Japanese dutifully attended the compulsory education classes. A few Greeks, Italians, and Slavs went to the night schools, carrying tablets and exercise books like schoolboys. Most of the Greeks walked straight to the coffeehouses after work and, when Staes admonished them, said they were too tired shoveling coal all day to go to school. "They're afraid they can't do it," Staes told George. "They can hardly read and write Greek let alone English. Some are just lazy."

"And they think it's a waste because they'll be going back to patridha next year or the next."

"How many years have you been here?"

"Almost twelve."

"How many years did you tell your parents you'd be away?"

"Five."

About citizenship papers, though, the men listened to Staes when he told them, "Even if you someday go back to patridha, Amerikaniko citizenship gives you freedom. People can't treat you any way they want if you're an Amerikanos citizen." "Become Amerikani citizens," the Salt Lake City *To Fos* said, "and you will feel free to travel anywhere in the country."

Staes and George Anton tutored the men in the questions that could be expected. Usually the judge asked applicants a few general questions: "Who are the president and vice-president of the United

States? Have you ever been a Communist? Have you ever belonged to the I.W.W.? Are you a polygamist? Can you say the pledge of allegiance?"

Most often the men passed without difficulty. If the judge had been hearing a rash of assault cases or was testy, the men had to return. One Greek was forced to come back again and again; he fidgeted, forgot, stood mute. "Forget it," Staes told him and gave the judge a gallon of John Diamanti's bootleg whiskey to get the man his citizenship papers. Not long afterwards, while sitting at the counter in the American Candy Store, a woman took a seat next to the new citizen. Her hair was cut short and her skirts came to her knees. He could hardly understand English, but suddenly he was married to her. Six months later he boasted in coffeehouses, "It takes other women nine months to make a baby. My woman did it in six months!"

George gave Staes an ultimatum: either come to the camp to keep books or get out at a loss. Sighing, Staes arrived at the small colony of tents with his green visor and a supply of cigarettes. The Mexicans had become sullen after Liar left. George slept with his gun under his pillow and Leon on the floor near his cot. Late on Saturdays George got into the driver's seat of the small, muddy truck he had rented and with Staes beside him drove down the sharply winding road to Helper. From there Staes took a stage to Price where he spent Sunday catching up on correspondence and tutoring.

Emilia feared the night alone with the children. Each creak of the floor or shifting of coal in the kitchen stove and she stared into the icon-hazed darkness expecting to see a black, hulking shape in the doorway. One night, in listening dread, she knew the fire had gone out in the stove. The house grew cold, yet she could not move. She thought of herself getting up from the pull-down sofa, walking through the middle room between the cribs and into the kitchen, lifting the stove lid, pushing the grate in and out, seeing no embers, making a new fire with paper, sticks, a few pieces of coal, and returning to bed. Then knowing she had done none of it, she tried to force herself up and into the kitchen. When dawn filtered into the house, she hurried to start a fire and saw as she stepped into the middle room that her youngest child, Demetroula, was uncovered; her legs and hands were cold. With anguish she covered her and quickly built a fire in the kitchen and *sala* stoves.

A few days later George was at home. The baby's face had turned red with fever, and phlegm rattled in her chest with each breath. Kilarney Reynolds telephoned lanky Doctor McDermid, the Castle Gate company doctor, who put a stethoscope to the baby's chest and said, "Double pneumonia."

The two women bathed the baby in cool water, kept wet cloths on her head, fed her broth and camomile tea. When Florence Reynolds came from grade school, she watched over the older children, now called Josephine and Helen in English.

Demetra grew worse. Her godmother left her younger children with the oldest, a nine-year-old girl, on their sheep farm five miles away and came to stay with Emilia. The nights of little sleep, she lay on the floor at the side of the crib. During the day, she and Emilia put mustard plasters on the baby's chest and back. Three days later the fever left and the godmother returned home. The baby, a year old, still cried out at night. "Whatever it is," Doctor McDermid said, "she'll outgrow it."

Emilia gave birth to another daughter, stillborn.

By autumn twenty-five miles of ditches over the summit plain, gouged out of the canyon walls, and into Helper had been dug, but because of war-produced shortages, the pipes did not arrive. When winter came rain and snow pushed mud into the ditches; and in spring the men had to begin digging again. George and Staes had expected to make a twenty-five thousand dollar profit, but after the water line was completed, their earnings came to half that amount.

While George and his men were working in mud, the poolhall burned down. The insurance barely covered the ornate piano, a mass of twisted, blackened wires. N. S. Malouf left, as he said, "to look around in California." Emilia thanked the All—Holy for the fire. It was a sign that Yoryis must find respectable work. George cursed her All—Holy. "I didn't steal! I didn't kill! I'm not ashamed of any work I do to raise my family!"

Taking in two Cretans, Theros Sargetis and George Gigounas, as partners and using a portion of the money from the water-line contract, George bought the frame store on Main Street that he had rented for his first poolhall, razed it, and built a two-story building. The first floor was occupied by a Rexall drugstore and a restaurant, George's new venture, and the top floor by a hotel. George called the building the New House after an imposing structure in Salt Lake City. Because Faní's husband was a cook, he gave in to Emilia's pleadings to bring her family west.

They came immediately with their furniture following by freight. The *sala* was made into a bedroom for them until their furniture arrived and they could rent a house. In the middle room George and Emilia slept on a heavy mattress set on a metal frame; the baby's basket and two small cribs were jammed about it. In the daytime half of the mattress was pushed up against the wall and half the frame was folded downward. The kitchen was a busy prison of mothers, babies, children, pots steaming on the coal stove, the gray, square electric washing machine chugging most of the day.

The restaurant opened with Faní's husband as cook and two young Greeks as waiters. George hurried from the cash register to the kitchen, helping to serve the unmarried Greek miners and roamers. He saw that Faní's husband could never run the kitchen; he could only doggedly keep at one pot at a time. When George told this to Emilia in the cramped bedroom, she whispered, "It's you! You want everything done before you finish talking! You brought us to this wild place from Pocatello when the house wasn't ready! The minute you think of something, it has to be done!"

"You want me to sit around until the opportunity is gone! This is Ameriki, not that wretched Turkish country you came from!"

From the *sala* harsh whisperings came. In the daytime Faní began long, dark silences, then ragings at Emilia for being brought to America, for being a servant, for marrying an old man, for coming west again. Before their furniture arrived, she and her family rode back across the continent.

When the furniture came, George paid the freight, saw what miserable pieces of wood, springs, and cloth they were and sold the lot to a Greek family for twenty-five dollars. He sent a money order for the amount to Faní's husband. *I never want to hear from you again,* Faní wrote Emilia. Pregnant again, Emilia cared for her three daughters in blunted silence. From time to time, Faní's husband wrote Yoryis for money, the letters sent from the restaurant where he worked so that his wife would not know.

Emilia's damaged heart nearly failed when her fourth daughter was born. Each morning Kilarney Reynolds took the baby, christened Sophia by Liar, and kept her until night. A midwife-nurse, who had recently moved into town from Oklahoma, came in the morning, and Florence Reynolds helped with the three little girls after school.

The doctor instructed Emilia on preventing pregnancies. Emilia burst out, "Now we won't have a son to carry on the name," and George said, "Kyria, we could also have another four girls." As he spoke, Emilia thought he gave the icon of the All-Holy a reproachful look.

George leased the restaurant and opened another business he called the Bank Cigar Store because it was near Barboglio's bank. He often ate lunch with the banker in the Grill Cafe. The building was of brick and in good condition; again he installed pool tables and sold soft drinks and tobacco. Coffeehouse habitués seldom came into the store. Store managers, doctors, attorneys, and city officials were frequent customers. Trusted patrons were allowed in the back room to play cards; the owner of one of the Spring Canyon mines was a regular loser. These select few brought hip flasks of bootleg whiskey; others preferred, temporarily, Hires root beer, the franchise of which George had won.

George told Emilia that as soon as he had accumulated enough money for his youngest sister Sophia's dowry, he would establish a business dependent on trade; but she would not be satisfied, and he no longer listened to her complaints.

"The world has become ruined," Emilia told Philomena Bonacci. Speaking Italian, the women blamed the foolish new American law that prohibited making and selling whiskey and wine.

Mrs. Bonacci said scornfully, "The Amerikani aren't like us—a glass of wine with dinner. They get drunk."

While Kilarney Reynolds taught Emilia American cooking, she

spoke of bad times, but Emilia could not see that the recession had any influence on bootlegging, or the jumpy music coming from candy stores, or women driving sedans or coupes with rumble seats that opened up on the outside back of the cars. That these women smoked openly and were not ostracized by all was an enigma to her: smoking was a man's prerogative.

Sheepmen were affected by the recession more than other businessmen. Many of them, Greek, Basque, French, and Mormon, lost their savings and had to begin over again. The Roumeliot who had refused to lend George money when he arrived in the coal camps was suddenly without his fortune.

Mine managers lowered wages. Two miners entered the office of the Kenilworth company manager and demanded to know why wages were cut when the price of coal remained the same. They left the office and called a strike.

The most numerous miners, the Cretan Greeks, became leaders of the 1922 strike. They had been only mildly interested in unionization attempts because they kept expecting to return to Crete, but years of being short-weighed on the coal scales, of paying bribes to get a car for their coal, of being given the worst places to work with their feet in ice-crusted water, and they exploded.

The American Legion revived its tirades against the immigrants who were so un-American, they said, as to want to belong to unions. Although a number of Legionnaires were members of the American Federation of Labor as carpenters and joiners, they thought themselves craftsmen, above the unskilled miners whose unions were merely industrial.

Americans congregated in the Bank Cigar Store. "We haven't anything against the Greeks, George. It's the unions. They're no good for the country."

Strikers were forced out of the company houses and set up tent towns; the one in Helper was south of town. Families moved in with each other, their furniture, other than cots and stoves, piled outside. Babies cried throughout the day and night. Women scrubbed their wash in tubs of cold river water and hung it on makeshift clotheslines anchored to bushes and poles.

Strikebreakers came in on every train, and detective agencies sent in the usual street men to act as mine guards. The Cretans chafed in the tent towns. After several strikers accosted a deputy on Main Street, a Cretan runner—no different from those who had covered the valleys and mountains of Crete to bring news of Turks—burst into the tent town. The deputy's car, he said, had broken down on the road to Spring Canyon. Yiannis Htenakis and another Cretan pushed their guns behind their belts and ran at the side of the river to an Italian orchard where they saw the deputy working under the hood of his car. Shots rang out and Htenakis fell dead.

Emilia stood at the living room window and watched the hearse go by, followed by a long line of cars with Greek flags tied to the radiator caps. Black-dressed Cretans sat inside them.

Two Greek Legionnaires holding American and Greek flags led the funeral procession down Price Main Street to the church. The Italian band marched behind them playing a dirge, and farther back came a throng of eight hundred Greeks, many of them carrying small blue and white Greek flags.

The two Price newspapers reported that during the procession the American flag had been set on fire. The Greeks denied it. They would continue to deny that Tenas, Htenakis's American name, had carried a gun and that the Greek school teacher had tried to burn the flag. The teacher had suddenly bolted from the procession and screaming, "They slaughtered our lad!" attempted to hold a lighted match to the flag before other Greeks grappled him to the ground and forced him out of town.

"Don't say anything to anybody!" Emilia demanded when George left the house. "Don't say anything to make them angry!"

"Who can talk to you?" George flung at her and stalked out of the house. To the Cretans, few of whom had families, he said accusingly, "You don't have children. That's why you can be hotheaded."

On the day the Utah National Guard came into town, strikers hidden behind boulders and sagebrush waited for a trainload of scabs for the Spring Canyon mines; "scum picked up on Salt Lake

279

City's Second South Street," the men said of guards and strike-breakers. Cretans riddled the train with bullets; the scabs and guards fired back. One of the Cretans was hit in the arm, shattering his bone. Several strikers carried him to a town doctor and with guns drawn watched him sew the torn flesh. They then placed the wounded man on the back floor of a car and drove him to a hamlet in the Uinta Basin where they hid him with a fellow Greek.

Mostly farm boys, the National Guard marched down the dusty road and through town. When they passed the house, Emilia was again at the window. People lined both sides of the road, cheering, hissing. Their commander, Major Elmer Johnson, chose the Bank Cigar Store for his headquarters. "That horned one!" George ranted to Emilia. "He knows I'm Greek! And he chooses my store!"

Major Johnson had brought his wife with him, and a Cretan was told to give up his hotel room for them. "He wouldn't leave her home where she belongs," the Cretan whispered angrily to George, "and I have to sneak on a train to meet my bride in Salt Lake." When he returned he told George, "She'd been on the train for four days. Until she got cleaned up, I didn't think it was worth it."

The major had an orderly put two tables together at the front of the store and fashioned a desk for himself. Soldiers came in and out bringing messages from mine managers and deputies. Leaning over to pick up a cigarette wrapper, George dropped his gun. Major Johnson took the gun, telephoned the sheriff, and George was fined. By evening he had another gun.

The major told George he could not understand how guns were being smuggled into Helper. He kept patrols on Helper's streets and back roads and at the railroad station. His soldiers searched all cars, and only American citizens were allowed to leave town. "Where are they getting their guns?" he demanded.

George shrugged as if the question had no answer. All Greeks knew that Cretans in other coal camps were crossing the mountains at night and bringing guns and ammunition. Major Johnson ordered his troops to go through every poolhall and coffeehouse to look for guns; they found none. He then sent his men to the tent colony with orders to march the strikers to the Helper grade school.

There the strikers were lined up, and the general manager of the Standard Coal Company, who had been injured when miners had tried to stop the train on its way to Spring Canyon and had killed a deputy sheriff, went up and down the lines and pointed out fourteen Greeks and one Italian as the killers.

Seeing people hurrying down Main Street, George went to the doorway of his store. "Something's going on at the school," a man answered him. A short time later men, a few women, and a crowd of children drifted back, talking excitedly. A Cretan stopped to talk with George. "Some of our men were picked out who weren't there that day and some who were there weren't."

Emilia had seen the people passing the house. She heard the neighbors in the backyard talking, but she could not drag herself out to join them. She would learn what was happening when George came home after midnight.

The trials began. Sam King of Salt Lake City, called Sam King-adakis because he regularly represented Greeks, especially Cretans, came to defend the men. The county attorney based his prosecution on the men's being undesirable aliens who did not serve in the war and who were involved in the un-American activity of joining strikes. One after the other the men were sentenced from ten years to life imprisonment, and the trials went on. The Price newspaper, the *Sun*, said the "Greeks were unfit for citizenship . . . must America be a haven for the foreign born, criminally inclined persons?"

Stylian Staes rushed to the mining camps to talk with the strikers and was arrested, the *Sun* reported, "for going to Kenilworth with W. H. Bennet, well known throughout local coal camps as an agitator. . . . Efforts to secure his release on the ground of the privileges of his position as Greek consul availed Staes little as far as the arresting guardsmen were concerned."

The rival *News Advocate* blamed the United States citizens for not demanding immigration laws to keep out undesirables, laws that would "place the burden of proof on the alien who is a menace so that he can be deported easily and quickly," and for not demanding Americanization schools where aliens would be compelled to learn the language of the country.

Of the 3,000 Greeks in the country, only 100 of them are married.
. . . . The aliens claim they are too tired to go to school in the
evening. They should have thought of that before coming over. . . .
The local Greek priest has been in America twelve years and can
not speak or understand a word of English. . . . If he doesn't want
to learn the American language so that he can converse with local
people, he should go back to where Greek is the national language.

Humiliated, Father Yiannis left town immediately without finding out where he was to go. A copper baptismal font George had ordered for the church came at this time. On presenting it to the church board, he, as the new president-elect, said the newspaper was justified in condemning Father Yiannis for not learning to speak English; the next priest had to be someone other than an almost illiterate village priest.

The new priest wore American clerical dress on the streets. His curly hair was short and parted in the center; he wore metal-rimmed eyeglasses and sported a Charlie Chaplin mustache. Immediately, all mothers with whiny babies, Emilia included, took their children to have him read the baptismal service over again: Father Yiannis, so good with the evil eye, could have left out a word and the holy oil not taken.

The priest was quoted in the local newspapers. He wrote a long letter to *To Fos* in Salt Lake City and was praised by the newspaper as the "flower of the Greek clergy in America." Greeks were suspicious of a well-educated priest's being sent to Carbon County, Utah, "the Siberia for Greek Orthodox priests in America," as they called their parish.

They nodded knowingly when, two weeks after his arrival, the priest showed himself for what he was. As he was walking on the sidewalk toward church, he passed under a tree being trimmed by a Greek sitting in its limbs. A branch fell, barely missing the priest. Glaring up at the man, the priest said, "May you be like this branch." With a thump the man was on the ground holding his broken arm. Later that day he went to the coffeehouses and showed his arm encased in a plaster cast. "It was the priest," he said. "He gave me the evil eye."

23

When the room darkened before her,
Emilia quickly sat down, broom in hand or the baby Sophie in her
arms, and waited patiently until she saw clearly again. Her oldest
daughter, Jo, a second-grader, played with Helen and Demetra—
Lula she was usually called—Jo the prim, exacting teacher, they the
docile students. Jo taught them American ditties, to play hopscotch
in the cramped space between the sink and door and jacks on the
worn linoleum. She built houses out of playing cards for them.

In the town of Helper, desolate mountains rearing up, people,
Emilia thought, lost their senses. Soldiers and strikers were shooting at each other; in a coffeehouse a Roumeliot and a Cretan quarreled over King Constantine and Premier Venizelos. The Cretan
pulled out a pistol and killed the royalist.

A Cretan woman arrived with her mother to marry one of the
Gigounas brothers. Angry that his objections to his goddaughter's
marrying a man he did not like were ignored, a miner hid behind
the American Candy Store and shot the future groom when he came
out to empty a pan of dishwater. "Bring him to me!" the woman
screamed, "and I'll strangle him with my two hands!" Many men
asked to marry her, but she refused and returned to Crete.

George Zoumadakis had to take his pregnant wife to live in the
isolated Uinta Basin or else kill or be killed by a fellow villager with
whom he had feuded since they were boys. The Zoumadakis house
had been on the road to the Spring Canyon mine, and miners had

passed it going to and from work. While hanging up the wash at the end of a day shift, Zoumadakis's wife saw a group of miners approaching, one of them her husband's enemy. She hurried into the house but not soon enough. "Kyria," the miner called, "what do you want with that husband of yours? You need a real man like me!" The miners laughed.

At first she was afraid to tell her husband because someone would be killed. Then, if she did not, he would hear gossip, might suspect her, and also be enraged that his *filotimo* had been tarnished, unavenged. She begged her husband to think first of her. He told George in the Bank Cigar Store that he had to control his boiling Cretan blood and leave town or his bride would be either a widow or a prisoner's wife.

Emilia and other Greek women mourned the family's leaving: "Monaxia, monaxia"—loneliness, loneliness—almost as horrible as hunger to them.

And a Xenakis daughter! Three days before her Sunday wedding to a staid Cretan, she eloped with John Michelogiannis who had nearly been lynched during the war for taking an American girl for a ride in his yellow Buick. "Mother," she telephoned from a mining town, "we're coming home."

"Dead you will come," the mother answered, "alive, never."

The couple went on to Illinois, following the American custom of a honeymoon. In a rowboat the bride reached to pick a water lily. The boat overturned and both drowned. The mother's curse, the worst of all curses, had been fulfilled.

After the year of mourning ended, the two Michelogiannis sisters visited Emilia. They were soft spoken, inordinately polite, spoke no word of gossip. They sighed over their spinsterhood, and Emilia said, "There is still hope," yet knew sadly that there was none: the younger sister walked with a limp, one leg much shorter than the other; on his deathbed their father had made the family take an oath that the older would not marry until a husband was found for the younger.

Greek women often spoke of life in America as *salata*—salad, mixed up. In Constantinople with the Papadimitriou family, it now

Emilia's brother Yiannis in Smyrna, 1921, during the disastrous invasion of the Greek army to regain its lost lands.

appeared to Emilia, everything had been orderly, day after day passing peacefully. The *kyria*'s pretensions and hysterias, little Achilles's illnesses, her fatigue, Turkish reprisals, the bombings by the Bulgarian Komitajis who wanted Macedonia to be a nation, the gossip and intrigue in the gray store apartment were forgotten.

Emilia's brother had survived the Asia Minor campaign: the Greek army had failed in its invasion to reclaim the land that had been theirs since antiquity until the Turks had overrun it in the fifteenth century. He had sent a picture of himself in soldier's uniform, dark mustache, strong jaw, handsome. He was seated with his sturdy, khaki-wrapped legs crossed against a backdrop of painted flowers and vines and a banner at the top with the words Greetings from Smyrna.

She wanted to cry for people: her mother who had died after being bedfast for months, Anna with four children and her silk dresses covered with a bed sheet, the Papadimitrious who had left Constantinople for Smyrna in time for the Turks to herd Armenians from the interior to be raped and beaten, to die of thirst and hunger on the way. The remnants rushed into the sea along with the other Christians, the Greeks, while Smyrna burned behind them. Of the ships flying the flags of many nations, only the Greek and British would take aboard the thousands of people floundering in the water among burning oil pools. Foreign sailors hacked off the hands of people who would not let go of lowered boats; they were under orders not to anger the Turks.

Emilia was desolate when she thought of Faní: it would have been different if *he* had not been so impatient, so exacting. When she thought of her brother her head was in turmoil with anger, and she had to ask forgiveness time and time again at the icon of the All–Holy. Yoryis was at last able to send him passage to America. He had finished paying for his sister Sophia's dowry, money sent twice. The first time, Pericles had taken it for his own family's dire needs. But Emilia's brother had been flattered, had his head turned by the village priest's offering his daughter to him. What dowry the bride brought to the marriage, Anna's letter did not say. They lived in the family's ancestral house and he worked his father's land. "Don't ask me to send another penny to the fool!" Yoryis shouted.

George sold the cigar store and with a younger Greek, John Gerendas, bought the Independent Meat and Grocery Store from Pete Jouflas and Jim Koulouris. John Gerendas had come to America at the age of thirteen and had graduated from a business school in Salt Lake City. They changed the store's name to Success Market.

The family moved into one of the four-room, frame Bonacci houses across the tracks. The extra room had space for a sewing machine, a round oak table on which Emilia put her best cloth, a dark linen with crocheted grape clusters bordering it, a glass-fronted china closet, and a buffet. Emilia was now able to serve her children's godparents properly. In the living room on a narrow table, the legs ornately carved, was the treasure of the house, a tall lamp with a yellow glass, domed shade.

The house had no bathroom, and George continued to go to the YMCA for weekly showers. People laughed at them, Emilia said, for his using the public baths. Along with the store's aprons and towels, he sent his shirts to *Koumbara* Jouflas to wash and iron—she had begun a home laundry after her husband became sick. "You wear special shirts," Emilia said, "and go to a public place to wash." But he would not use a tub in the precarious privacy of the kitchen.

The new neighbors complained about the dog Leon. He jumped on anything that moved in the dark, and they and their children were afraid to go to the privies at night. George gave Leon to the Reynolds family who had moved east of the rail yards to a row of yellow and brown railroad houses moved down from Soldier Summit. A week later Leon streaked back to the Bonacci house, running wildly in circles. George threw rocks at him, trying to force him back to the Reynoldses. Jumping on George and then running in larger circles, Leon fell, gasping, looking at George through closing eyelids, and died, poisoned.

Emilia tried but could not sleep getting up every few minutes to look for Yoryis, silhouetted on clear nights, his elbow crooked, his hand on his revolver butt. Often she hurried to the window expecting to see him being attacked by another black figure, struggling, falling to the tracks. Then it began to seem to her that he was not in his store at all. There were those brazen American women who called him "George." Let him say that American women called men by their first names. Men had to be watched. Those Mahoutas brothers, living off prostitutes, no shame, even bringing them to celebrations in the church basement, to picnics, lipsticked women who smacked their mouths over Greek food, who used toothpicks.

Two years after the strike of 1922, while the trials of the strikers arrested for killing a deputy sheriff were still going on, now in Salt Lake City, the earth shook once, twice. Emilia ran outside to look for her daughters. Women and children were rushing to the railroad crossing at the side of Emilia's house. Boys were running toward town, shouting, screaming at each other. Whistles were blowing, far, near.

The obese neighbor who lived next door to Emilia puffed and waddled out of her house. "The Castle Gate Number Two has exploded," she called. "I just spoke to Central."

Cars roared up Main Street, a short distance west of the tracks, toward Castle Gate. Women drew closer, talking above the scream and roll of the whistles. "My brother works at Number Two," one of the women who lived in the row of railroad houses said and began walking quickly over the railroad ties. Another woman and several excited boys followed. The whistles stopped. A breeze swept over the tracks. Where the rails curved around Steamboat Mountain, junipers were on fire, and the breeze carried a strange, far-off sound, sustained, blurred. They would hear that it came from the widows and children weeping in the debris of the mine.

Holding Sophie, Emilia went inside with frantic thoughts: she should go there to the Greek mothers; she should feed their children; she should stay with the families, but how could she take her children? Would Yoryis leave work to drive her in the new car? The house rapidly grew dark. She slumped to the floor feeling Sophie slide from her. When she opened her eyes, she looked for Sophie, pulled herself up, and hurried outside. Neighborhood children were sitting on the small square of lawn in the front yard talking about the explosion, and Sophie was on Jo's lap watching them.

Emilia saw efficient, worthy women like Kilarney Reynolds passing the house, being driven to Castle Gate where they would man respirators, cook over open fires, cover the waiting women and children, cradle crying babies. Women brought their canaries to the rescue teams. As soon as the birds flew into the rubble of tunnels and survived, the rescue team knew the danger of gas was gone and they could dig deeper for bodies.

Black-dressed widows keened the ancient Greek lamentations, the *mirologhia,* at the side of their husbands' open caskets, flanked by Greek and American flags; final photographs were taken for remembrance—unless the bodies were mangled. Two men, unrecognizable pulps, were put in one casket. Most of the fifty dead Greeks were brought to a hall for the death liturgy because the church was too small to hold the caskets.

Emilia began a frenetic cooking and baking; that the children of the dead miners were hungry was so vivid to her that she saw their howling faces. She forced the food on Yoryis who took it angrily. "They're not hungry. We've brought sacks of flour and left them on their porches."

On a Sunday six weeks later, George drove his family to the Castle Gate company houses. The girls remained in the car under Jo's care while the forty-day condolence calls were made. The widows cried, they and their children in black, reeking of acrid dye. The relief committee wanted to pay their passage back to Crete; several widows who had agreed to return were reconsidering: "You know what a widow's life is like in patridha. And how will we educate our sons? We'll be paupers." One widow returning to Crete was trying to sell her embroidered dowry articles. Emilia bought a cutwork scarf for ten dollars but didn't want to take it. The young widow curtly insisted that Emilia take the scarf. In a third house, the mother sat bedraggled, her hair lank, the unwashed children whining, and the odor of urine and excrement strong in the room. George and Stylian Staes had asked the committee to send her back to her family. While the mother stared, an Italian neighbor set bowls of soup on the table. She looked at George and Emilia and twirled her forefinger at her temple with a meaningful look at the widow. Two months after her return to Crete the widow was dead.

A month later a town doctor told George to take Emilia to California for a rest because she was dangerously anemic. Leaving

Kilarney Reynolds with the girls, they took a train to Los Angeles and a taxi to a hotel Nick Zeese recommended. "That's where I met Nick the Greek," Nick said.

"With the praise of two big-shot cardplayers," George said, "it must be class A."

Three times a day they ate in the hotel's dining room. In the afternoon they attended a movie; the rest of the day Emilia lay on the bed in misery at having left the children, wondering if they thought they had been deserted, if they would eat Mrs. Reynolds's food, if they were afraid of the night. Impatient, thinking about his new store and that he should be there, George went to restaurants, shoeshine stands, and grocery stores to find men with whom he had "eaten bread and salt" on labor gangs.

Most of the men were prospering. They sat with George in booths, in back rooms talking about their first years in America, reminding each other of incidents, tragic and comic, when they knew little of the English language, when they had to resort to cunning to survive. He asked about Karavelis, the Pocatello labor agent, who, he had heard, had been in Los Angeles several years and had money troubles. With directions to the Farmers' Market, he found a Greek grocery wholesaler, a Peloponnesian, behind the cash register and introduced himself. "He's in the back room. That's him singing. Go on back."

George walked between crates and lugs of fruits and vegetables into a dim room. Under a dangling electric light globe Karavelis sat on a stool hacking off the outer leaves of a head of lettuce. Not seeing George he kept on with an Italianate song about a Russian woman:

> In the Zappeion one day
> As I was walking
> I chanced to see a Roussa,
> Red-haired—

"Yoryi!" He bounded from the stool, shook George's hand vigorously, and upended two orange crates for them to sit on. He poured coffee into tin cups, and they talked about "the days," Karavelis said, "when I strutted around like a cock, a diamond on my finger and another in my tie."

"Remember when you were ready to kill me over not digging the well! And about the farm? Those were the days." Karavelis smiled, eyes crinkling, mustache gone. "They didn't last too long and the money came easy." In English he said, ruefully, "Easy come, easy goes."

Karavelis walked to the door with George. They shook hands. As George walked down the street, Karavelis's joyous song burst out. When George returned to the hotel and told Emilia about seeing Karavelis, he was aware she was not listening.

"Are you ready to go home?"

"If you are."

The vacation had lasted five days.

Night. Holding Sophie, Emilia with her older daughters stood at the kitchen window and looked at a cross burning on the mountainside. The last coal lump of the day clinked as it burned itself out. Emilia's face, tongue, mouth were numb. She led the children to make their cross at the icon, pulled blankets over them, and went into the kitchen. She opened her green book, *Robinson Crusoe* in Greek, but read the words without remembering them. She stiffened at every creak of the house and sweep of wind rattling papers against the railroad tracks.

The Catholics answered the Ku Klux Klan with a circle of fire on the opposite slope, for the word *nought:* The Klan was nothing, would come to nothing. George and Joe Barboglio found notes in their post office box. In capital letters written in pencil were the words: TAKE THE GREEKS AND ITALIANS AND GET OUT OF TOWN. Men stormed through Greek candy stores and restaurants, forced American waitresses out, and warned them not to work for Greeks.

A huge cross burned in the rail yards a hundred-fifty feet down from the house. Railroaders were divided; Irish and a few Mormons against the rest of the Mormons and Protestant Ku Kluxers. Kilarney Reynolds's husband led Irish and Italian Catholics to Salt Lake City and returned with Knights of Pythias members and a charter.

Their women cooked a banquet for them and served it in the Liberty Hall. On Main Street people clustered, talking about it, curious about the meaning of the new chapter, and knew the Catholics had given a message: they would not be intimidated by the Klan.

The Klan went out at night and painted large white KKK letters on cement railroad abutments, on store buildings belonging to immigrants, on an Italian farmer's barn. Chasing them with a rake, the Italian fell dead of a heart attack.

Whisperings, telephone calls, and the names of the Klan members became known. "Why you do this to us?" Emilia asked the husband of their obese neighbor, a railroad brakeman. "It's not you Greeks we're after, Mrs. Zeese," he said. "It's the niggers."

That night Emilia dreamed she was sleeping. In her dream she opened her eyes. The brakeman was at the open window. "We are all Ku Klux Klan," he said. She awoke, her skin clammy.

Louis and Nick Zeese came to town and walked behind the children on their way to school. In Nick's Buick they followed George's car and waited until he parked it and entered the house. "Go on!" he called. "I've got my six brothers here," and he patted the gun behind his belt.

A professional boxer who wandered over the West, up and back from Alaska, told George, "You Greeks and Italians should stop buying new cars and building houses and stores for a while. That's what's bothering them. Jealousy. They don't like foreigners getting ahead."

George was building a large new house, with six rooms, a tiled bathroom, and a walk-in basement that included a garage. It was north of town at the base of Steamboat Mountain where doctors, attorneys, and businessmen lived.

The boxer often came into the grocery store to talk with George. He was the black sheep of a wealthy Boston family. "He speaks good English," John Gerendas, George's partner with the American education, said. Businessmen and railroaders were staying away from Klan meetings, the boxer reported; only loafers and stragglers were still attending them.

George asked the old Ku Kluxer, the brakeman next door, to

tell him when the president of the Denver and Rio Grande Western was on board his special car: he wanted to get on while it was stopped at the depot to propose leasing the east side of Main Street, moving the company houses, and building a row of stores.

The president of the railroad offered George a cigar—George smoked fifteen a day—leaned back against a luxurious green-tufted, brass-trimmed chair, and listened. He was skeptical, he said, but would think about it if George could get the financial backing. George asked Joe Barboglio for it, but he demurred. The Carbon-Emery Bank of Price agreed, contingent on the railroad's terms. George took a train to Denver; the president vacillated; he returned twice more to the railroad offices and on the third day left with the promise of a lease.

The plans were drawn up and George was made a director of the Price bank. One of the directors invited him to attend the Republican convention in Ogden, forty miles north of Salt Lake City. George was surprised at the bootleg whiskey in the open. He told Emilia, "It flowed like water in the convention hall." "I hope you didn't drink too much," she said testily to him who had never been tipsy in his life. He exploded with curses.

The nearly completed house burned and had to be rebuilt on the inside; the scorched brick was painted red and the once-white mortar with strips of black. Children were blamed—roasting potatoes in the basement. Emilia said to herself: the Klan.

On the day of the fire George found a black-edged letter in his post office box. His uncle, the priest Papa–Christos, had died. He had been buried sitting up as befitted a priest, and his grave had been covered with gray slabs of rock from the top of the Xerovouni mountain.

Soon after, he received another black-edged letter. His father had worked all day on legal papers for a merchant in nearby Arahova. In the evening he put down his pen, finished, and quietly died in his chair. That night his daughter Sophia dreamed of him. "Sophia," he said, "take the papers to Arahova. I've already been paid for them."

"Father, how did you leave this earth? What did you see?"

"A woman in white, glowing with light, came for me."

Seven years later, in 1931, George's mother would die. On a cold, sunny February day, the villagers took advantage of a lull in the wintry blasting of wind to scurry through snow banks on errands. Pericles had taken his horse north to Krikellon for supplies, and Zaferia made her way to Upper Klepá to visit her daughter Sophia. She was sixty-three or -four years old and had been blind since her late fifties, yet she walked everywhere in the village unaided. In her honor Sophia killed a chicken and invited a few of her mother's old friends to celebrate with them. They toasted each other to long lives and a good old age.

Late in the afternoon a villager came to the house. A storm, he said, was raging in the mountains around Krikellon, and Periklina was summoning men to go with her in search of Pericles. Distraught that her four grandchilden had been left alone, Zaferia set out for her house: Pericles and his family lived with her. As she stepped into the iced ruts of the Great Torrent, a stroke sent her toppling head first. Villagers carried her to her house where she lay unconscious a month and died.

George and Emily moved to the new house. When the draperies were up, the carpets down, the new furniture in place, Emilia went from room to room. The house was still; the children were across the dirt road talking to schoolmates. The smell of new varnish, the sharpness of fresh paint, the piquancy of cut wood came to her as she stood in the spacious living room. Tears fell down her face. She hurried into the tiled bathroom and sat on the edge of the tub, afraid the children might see her. She sat for many minutes overwhelmed with relief: they were now proper people; her husband no longer had to take a bundle of clothes under his arm to shower in the YMCA public bathroom. At last she had her own home. She had come to America for it and now she had it.

Epilogue

Emilia sometimes talked about this Helper house in the ever-closing circle of aging: "It was big and airy; a good kitchen with plenty of space." "The floors had a gold color. Don't they make wood floors like that anymore?" "We could push the bookcases against the walls and put leaves in the dining room table, and it would reach all the way into the living room. Twenty people could sit down with room left over."

Those few years in the new house could have been the best for her, no longer debilitated by yearly pregnancies and the anemia that had been the then little-known thalassemia; her children still young enough not to rebel strenuously against her Greekness; her own home open to all, the table crowded with Greek and American delicacies, great glass bowls of fruit, imported liqueurs.

I drove her into the countryside. In her late eighties, incredibly wrinkled, she sat in a deep silence, always a prelude to a long-held thought that would at last be spoken. "I was so happy when you children were little and going to school. I only went two years and then my father taught me at home."

We passed through a valley of subdivisions that twenty years ago had been an expanse of sagebrush. In an occasional empty lot a few vestiges plumed, graceful, silver green, but the sun was not hot enough to bring out their acrid scent. "Is that our Prophet Elias Church?" my mother asked as we neared a red-brick, white-spired church and crossed herself.

"It's a Mormon church," I said and felt guilty at the annoyance in my voice. Couldn't she see? Couldn't she use her head? White steeple! New England architecture!

"There was a Prophet Elias chapel in the mountains beyond my village. I started out for it one day when I was very small because my father had a plot of land up there. Then I remembered stories of klefts in the mountains and ran back." In a clear, high voice she began to sing softly:

> There in those mountains
> is a wilderness church.
> Its bell does not ring.
> Neither chanter nor priest does it have.
> Only one candle dim
> and a cross of stone,
> the only ornaments of
> the poor little church.

I drove on, sad, silent, then said, "That's the first time I've heard you sing, Mama. You have a beautiful voice."

"Anna, my sister Annoula, had the beautiful voice, like Demetra's. My father had a good voice too. He sang and played the tamboura."

In the balm of autumn we swept on, past more subdivisions and regional shopping centers. I turned into a somnolent string of shops to buy ice cream cones, strawberry her favorite. This was how old age should be, quiet, with small pleasures. A few miles away, beyond the maze of parked cars, Mount Olympus rose, green, granite-tipped, a faint brush of orange and yellow sweeping under dark green pines. Leaves were turning. I started the car; I would prolong the day for her who loved color, nature.

"Where are we going?"

"Into the mountains for a short ride."

"I think we better go back. Your father's all alone."

"He doesn't mind being alone."

"We should have brought him."

"He doesn't want to come. The jarring hurts him and he can't see anything. It only makes him miserable."

In the nearby canyon the sun shining through pink, red, and orange maple leaves and farther up through the yellow of quaking aspen gave them an airy transparency.

"We should go back. He doesn't like to be alone." She was looking straight ahead.

"It's your idea that he doesn't like to be alone. Look at the beautiful colors."

"Women come and visit him when I'm gone."

"No one wants your ninety-some-year-old husband."

She had had a small stroke at seventy, the first of many. My father had telephoned me to hurry. She sat at the dining room table and fingered a cheap, machine-embroidered tablecloth—she no longer used her exquisite linens—and half crying, her eyes frightened, said, "Has Zeese come home from school yet? He shouldn't come home to an empty house."

"Zeese is away at college, Mama."

"College! Isn't he in grade school? Oh, what's happening to me?"

A few days later she remembered my son was away at school. She went back to gardening, interminable cooking, bossing and lecturing my father with growing irritability.

Our everyday ritual began with my taking my father's blood pressure, then giving them vitamin B injections. After a lifetime of jumping up the moment his eyes opened in the morning, my father could not remember to get up slowly to prevent his blood pressure from plummeting. He fell several times during the night and early morning on his way to the bathroom. My mother could not lift him. He would wait until he had the strength to pull himself up, but sometimes he could not manage. "Come and help us," my mother would telephone me. Then the two of us would struggle with his big, weighty body. Once my mother asked their long-time postman to lift him.

She balked at the vitamin injections. "No," she said with a helpless look, "don't give me anymore. I've lived long enough."

"They don't prolong your life. They make you feel better."

She had become extremely thin. "Your mother isn't eating," my father said angrily. "She's starving herself. I have to die first."

She peered at the food I brought, picked at it. At times she left pans burning on the stove while she was out searching for stray weeds to pull, berating her husband for being too lazy to help. Her face white with pain, I took her to the doctor who put her right arm in a sling to ease tendonitis of the elbow.

With numbed mouth, I stopped by after a dentist's appointment. "Eat something. Eat. Eat," she kept telling me, oblivious to my litany of explanations. Despairing, I spooned a little sauce from a meat and zucchini stew simmering on the splattered stove and dipped bread into it. When I washed the dishes, I noticed three curled green zucchini worms that she had fished out of the stew and put on a plate next to the pan.

Every day there were scenes, my father exasperated, my mother distracted, not knowing what she had said or done to provoke his outbursts. "Why shouldn't he raise his voice? You accuse him of taking your Social Security money, and I spend hours looking for bits of it you've hidden all over the house!"

"Put in a new light globe," my father said, "above the stove. Use a one-hundred watt."

"Better a small globe," my mother said, "so it will last longer." (Angry snorts from my father.) "And give me the old globe and I'll try it in another socket. Maybe it will work in another one."

My father, furious, "If it won't work in one, it won't work anywhere! Don't you understand? It's electricity!"

I hurried into the kitchen to change the globe before she came in. I had just climbed on top of a four-step ladder and was unscrewing the globe when she walked in and clutched my ankles. "Mama!"

"Don't worry. I'm holding you so you won't fall."

"I'll fall for sure if you don't let go!"

The moments when her thoughts were clear were becoming rare. "Why don't men give their wives any consideration?" she asked sadly. "Women wash their clothes, cook for them, sleep in the same bed, but they give them no consideration."

"Your father is afraid to die," she said after he had had a kidney stone attack. "We shouldn't be afraid to die. What is it anyway? We close our eyes."

In the kitchen beyond his hearing, my mother smiled, eyes merry. "And what? Do angels come down with a basket and put the dead in them and fly up to Heaven?" She wiped her eyes, laughed quietly. Then her ruined face became sober and she repeated what she had said years earlier, "There might be a Heaven, so I guess we had better believe."

How could I ever know this woman who had been strict with the Holy Weeks of our childhood, who had cooked Lenten foods while admonishing us if we tripped about, who had reminded us constantly of Christ's Passion? She believed in Christ but not in Heaven.

Before my father went to the hospital for the kidney surgery, I tried to talk with conviction about God's knowing human beings were not saints and that it was repentance that would judge us. In answer he quoted biblical Greek passages, but by his silence, his filmed eyes turned away from me, I knew he was afraid. I telephoned Father George Stephanopoulos to speak with him. Father George was one of the Greek priests who had come from Greece in the thirties at the urgent call of the Patriarch in Constantinople to minister to the small, far-flung communities in the American West. With a railroad pass he had traveled from Great Falls, Montana, throughout the state, into Canada as far as Edmonton, and circled back, marrying, baptizing, and burying on the way. Father George, slender, blue-eyed, graying hair, clean shaven (his son Elias and all younger priests were now bearded) spoke earnestly while my father nodded politely.

He was not afraid of the actual dying: "But I don't want to suffer like Nick Zeese." He was afraid of meeting God. He dreaded, too, the moment of death when the soul flies swiftly everywhere the body has been: "I never want to see some of those places again!"

What sins had he committed? He had never been "mixed up with white slavery," the worst of sins to him. He had "never looked at another woman," one more on his list of unforgivable sins. He had always been rigidly honest, business associates said. He was afraid to meet God. Perhaps in the eight years of wanderings before his marriage he had known many women. What dark fears of Hell had seeped into him, swinging the smoking censer while his priest-uncle, gaunt Papa–Christos, intoned the Scriptures?

The icon of the All–Holy and Christ, the water glass with burning vigil taper, and a bouquet of fresh flowers from my mother's garden were set on a small table in the back bedroom where my father kept his desk. Whenever he entered the room he crossed himself and on leaving crossed himself again. Before I drove him to the hospital he stood at the icon and prayed.

The surgery left him gray, eyes sunken, face skeletal. I thought this was the end of him, but he survived to suffer the martyrdom of constant pain, internal bleeding, gout, arthritis, and high blood pressure. "The Greeks have a saying," he said. "'Whom God loves He tyrannizes.' Can't He love someone else for a while?" After a silence he added, "If it weren't for my religion, I'd take all my pills at once."

Like most immigrants, they had left their parents still young; they had been spared seeing them age, sicken, and die. Without such memories they were intimately experiencing for the first time the misery and inevitability of their last days.

I wished him free of my mother's tyranny. Hardly had I left with him for doctors' appointments when she began calling my sisters at work. "They're late! Something's happened to them! Find out what happened!" At night she would come into his bedroom every little while to see if he were breathing, alive.

While she and I sat in her kitchen drinking tea and eating a sweet I had baked, she spoke in whispers, her head cocked toward the door beyond which my father sat on a sofa trying to catch what the television newscaster was saying or listening to records I had brought from the library for the blind.

". . . and I invited these two American women for lunch in our new house in Helper. After we had eaten, I peeled an apple, quartered it, and handed each one a piece on the end of the knife. The one woman looked at the other and said, 'Would you do that?'"

"They weren't insulting you. They were trying to say you were giving them extra attention. Would they talk in your presence and say you didn't have good manners?"

Perplexed frowns. "I don't know. I never talked to them again."

She retreated into the over fifty-year-old memory as if thinking it over again, mulling it for the hundredth time or so. Her eyes were still sharp behind the film of age, that same sharpness, that same silence in the houses of my childhood.

She burst out, "Your father says he can't see to drive, but it's just that he doesn't want to go anywhere. He never did. I told him Mrs. Souvall came home from the hospital and we should go see her—after all we're koumbari—but he says he can't see."

"He can't see!"

Petulantly, "Maybe so, but still. . . ."

"He's an old, old man. He has kidney problems. He's had three operations. He has holes in his intestines. He hurts all over. He can't see. He doesn't hear well. Why don't you leave him alone?"

"Who says he has holes in his intestines?"

"The doctor says so, and I've told you a hundred times."

"He just likes to howl."

"You said that to Mrs. Siouris on the telephone the other day and that was shameful."

My father came to the door. "You can't be logical with her," he said, "so don't try." Yet he kept trying as if by saying it one more time, she would understand. "'I blow on it and it doesn't cool,'" he said, an old proverb on futility.

Bringing food now was no longer an occasional stew or extra portion of dinner for them. It loomed, a twice a day necessity. "Let's try that service that brings food to the house," my father said, but Meals on Wheels was not for people like them who had eaten Greek food for nine decades. The cottage cheese and gelatine squares went into the garbage. "Why do Americans call Jell-O a salad?" my mother said wonderingly. They probed the creamed dishes and left them uneaten.

I bought aluminum freezer trays and made halibut, chicken, and roast beef dinners. "Put two in the oven at four hundred degrees," I said, but found her dividing one tray between them.

"You're starving Papa. You're not saving me work. You're giving me headaches."

I resumed taking food at noon, enough for two meals. "In the evening, heat what's left." She could not bear to throw anything away and saved dabs of mashed potatoes, meat, vegetables, mixed them together and served it to my father, either cold or scorched.

"She didn't eat all day! She's starving herself! I have to die first!"

Often the food disappeared. Where? Vague replies: "We ate it I guess." I looked into the garbage pail: a small salmon barely touched, pieces of intact chicken, and my father always hungry. "What did you bring?" he would say as I came into the house with a bulging sack.

She lost weight. Although she walked carefully in fear of falling, she fell, hitting her head on a rough cement corner of the front porch steps. She often walked to the 7-11 store down the street to get out of the house, to see people. ("I'm locked in this house like a wild animal, caged! Yes, you girls come, but—") Often she would forget to bring money or could not remember what she wanted and walked past the shelves until something caught her eye. I brought her home many times, had her sit in the car while I bought groceries and did their errands, but the excursions blunted her restlessness only a little.

About twice a week I brought them to my house for lunch or dinner. My father came, even though he was in pain, because "pretty soon I won't be able to." I often took them to a restaurant for late breakfast. A far cry from the hunk of coarse corn bread and cup of barley coffee in his village, the American breakfasts he had eaten in Helper's Grill Cafe and in Salt Lake City's Alex Pistolas's Grill, Castle's Cafe, and Latsis's Grill—later Lamb's Grill—had been his welcome herald of mornings. My mother exclaimed and tsk-tsked over the bill. "She thinks she's back in the Depression," my father remarked sourly.

One icy day I found her gone. My father did not know she was not in the house. She was walking toward the house of her long-dead friend, Mrs. Diamant, whom the grandchildren of the family had called "the little black yiayia"—grandmother—because of her black mourning dresses and stockings. I brought her back, lecturing her about falling and breaking a bone. "No. Don't worry. See how I go. Small, small steps and I slide. I won't fall."

I continued admonishing her. "I can't sew," she said with that uncharacteristic helpless look that now often came into her eyes and dispelled some of their sharpness. "I get tired of television. I get tired of sleeping. I can't read anymore." The green book she had read many times over, annoying my father, lay untouched on the small table next to her rose-brocaded chair. I picked it up one day with a prick of guilt: I had never cared enough to ask what she was reading. It was a Greek translation of *Robinson Crusoe*.

What was to be done with them? She could not cook or take care of her house. She found fault with the cleaning women we sent her, and we sisters scrubbed her bathroom, washed her windows and woodwork, shampooed her rugs while putting off our own housecleaning. Her solution was simple: one of us should move in with them. She would never leave her house.

While taking the Italian–American chiropractor next door some Greek pastries Jo had baked, she fell and lay in the snow in excruciating pain. A college student walking by carried her into the house. My father asked him to call me because he could not see to dial. I followed the ambulance to the hospital where she lay unattended for half an hour in horrible pain. She hallucinated, screamed, thought she was standing up and could not be convinced she was lying on a hospital bed. Immobile with drugs, she lay with blood and glucose dripping into her veins.

She was taken to Jo's house in senile agitation. Every few minutes day and night, without the necessary cane or walker, she looked for my father, afraid he had disappeared, and finding him, ranted for her lost home, raved that she had to go back there immediately. Tranquilizers passed through her brain without a trace.

I dreaded facing her each day. "What is this foolishness—us living in a strange house?"

"It's not a strange house. It's your daughter's. You're not in your own house because you broke your hip. You left pans burning on the stove. You couldn't take care of yourself."

"Buh. Buh. What talk is this? When did I break my hip? Why are you telling lies?"

She got up from bed one morning, took one step, and broke her upper thigh. After her hospital stay, she came to my house to recuperate, but she insisted after a week that she had to return to Jo's. "Your father is lonesome," she said, rubbing her right palm up and down her left upper arm, that old habit of agitation. Once at Jo's house, she berated her husband for taking her from her home. For almost five months no one slept through the night; two house-keepers fled. "I'll die if this goes on," my father said, and moved up the street to Demetra's house where he was well fed, listened to Greek music, and slept in exhausted relief.

For a short time she was in a Mormon nursing home until the Catholic Saint Joseph Villa had space for her. Between bouts of heavy sedation she packed her bag, tried to use the telephone which she could no longer manage, and raged to go to her house. My father moved to an adjoining room. "Our religion says a couple must stay together until they die," he said.

He was ninety-two then. We went down the long hall, past open doors where women sat, some tied to chairs, wispy white hair, staring eyes; in the hall a man in a wheelchair looked at us sadly. A small, thin woman walked toward us holding a securely wrapped doll with hair sticking out wildly. "My Johnny needs some milk," she told me. An emaciated woman, speaking rapidly in a Germanic language, skittered past leaving a stream of urine seeping down her legs to the highly polished asphalt tile floor. A nurse's aide hurried after her.

The Irish nurse-nun smiled as she showed us the two rooms with connecting bath. My mother sat in her rose wing chair and gazed at us, baffled, not knowing where she was or why. My father's dimmed eyes tried to see his room. "How big is the room? As big as mine at home?"

"A little smaller. We'll bring your big chair and desk."

She wept for her lost house, now owned by a grandson and his wife, packed her bags continually, spewed invectives at us, her daughters, for bringing her there, fell trying to get out of bed, fell in the bathroom, fell because she would forget to use the walker. She was caught on the third-floor stairway attempting to escape to her house. "My home, my home," she lamented. Once she suc-ceeded in reaching the parking lot and got into an empty taxicab, but then she could not tell the returning driver the address of her house. "I'm nothing, nothing. I have no home. I'm nothing."

For days, for weeks we explained why she had to be there. "You're making it all up," she said. Sister Columba told us it was no use talking. "They get something into their heads and all the talking in the world won't get it out," she said, still retaining, after years in America, an Irish inflection.

She thought the fires and car accidents on her color television were happening that very moment outside the nursing home. The murders, deaths, hospital scenes on soap operas were real events to her. Shrunken, the brown splotches becoming darker on her face—she had tried to rub them away—she dozed with Mellaril, was quiet during cyclic rampages with Thorazine (the rampages had to do with a full moon, Sister Columba said), ate whatever was placed before her, and slept.

"Why is that child crying? Go help it."

"It's not a child. It's a poor old woman who has lost her mind."

"Have you got food for Nick?"

"Yes, a stew."

"Now whenever you don't have food ready, take a few chops, brown them quickly, cut up lettuce for salad, add some Kalamata olives and a piece of feta cheese, and you'll have his dinner in no time. Don't worry so much about food as I did."

"All right."

"Now, let's see. How many children do you have?"

"Two. Zeese and Thalia."

"Do they still live together?"

"They haven't lived together since they left home over twenty-two years ago."

"Do they have children?"

"Zeese has three, Demetrios, Cleo, and Eleni. Thalia has two boys, Nick and Luke."

A short silence. My mother looked at her thin, veined, brown-splotched hands. Even in extreme old age, the little fingers turned in gracefully. "Now, let's see. How many children do you have?"

Old guilts would emerge. "I hated the brown spots on my

grandmother's hands. I wouldn't let her touch me." "One night when your father was putting in the water line, the fire went out and I was afraid to get up and light it. The house got cold. As soon as dawn came, I hurried to start the fire. Demetra was uncovered, ice cold. She got double pneumonia."

My little granddaughter Eleni and her mother walked ahead of us to the solarium. Eleni's little fingers turned in at the tips like my mother's. Already forgetting who they were, my mother said, "Look at that mother holding her little girl's hand. I didn't know how to take care of you children and you were always crying."

"Now how many children do you have?"

I dreamed one night that I looked down into the grassy, tree-shaded hollow at the side of my house. My mother was there, eating some kind of fruit. She was straight, slender, her hair white, yet full, drawn into a bun at the nape of her neck, her skin pleasantly wrinkled. She walked a few steps toward a tree, lifted a hand, and pulled an apricot from it. The sun was bright on her hair. The pure peace of Indian summer was in the hollow. When I awoke I knew the dream was how I wished her in her old age.

The smells of most nursing homes were absent from Saint Joseph Villa. Urine and fecal odors were quickly taken care of, except once when the entire third floor was overwhelmed by them. One Christmas energetic Sister Columba, whom my father quickly came to admire, put a small glass of wine on each patient's tray. All except my parents, who were used to wine, developed sudden, violent diarrhea.

Life at Saint Joseph's had its institutional routine: blood-pressure readings, early breakfast, medications, twice-a-week showers ("Once a week is enough," my father said, but, no, rules had to be followed), lunch, nap, medications, blood-pressure readings, solarium visit where old women sat in wheelchairs and stared at each other or at Sesame Street and old situation comedies, fruit juice drink, supper, medications, bed.

Yet the minutia of their everyday living loomed large for my father in his helplessness: whether the empty roll of toilet tissue had been replaced; that the rubber tip of his cane had worn out; if the bottle of Metaxas was nearly empty; had we placed his pajamas and robe at the foot of the bed, his clothing for the following day on the bed stand in the order he would put them on—he could only distinguish shapes by then.

No matter his pain, he wanted to know the state of his rental properties, their taxes and other expenses, what checks I had written, the bank balance, and the interest on his bank certificates. While I added and subtracted with a pen, he asked the numbers and told me the final figures before I had finished.

He was always angry at my mother: "She won't tell them when she needs something or when she hurts. I keep telling her we pay, but she doesn't want to bother them. What's going to happen to her when I'm not here to send them in to take care of her?"

I mused on them as they drank Turkish coffee I brought in a thermos, regretting that the brown foam, the *kaimaki*, had vanished by the time I poured it. As they ate a sweet or a piece of *kasseri* cheese in a roll, I thought about the people they had come from, about the incidents and events that had made them who they were, and the accidents of life that had brought them together, a quick, honorable man from the wild mountains the Turks had feared and a slow-moving woman, often illogical, always realistic, from a wide plain the Turks called theirs, the only one of her family who dared to look beyond the village, her entire life revolving around her children, grandchildren, and great-grandchildren.

I recalled words they had said, proverbs spoken that acknowledged people's humanity. I contemplated mysteries about them: how was it that he, with his phenomenal memory, could not remember his younger sister Olga who had died early? His father's worn, cardboard-covered law book that I found while cleaning out a basement storage room—had he intended to study it during his first few years in America, then enter law school on his return to Greece? What kept me from asking him? Had my mother tried to starve herself when she realized she could no longer control what was going on in her head?

As I prepared to leave, I became apprehensive if she mentioned her house, the sign that she would be going into my father's room at

Christmas 1950. Three generations in America. George and Emily, their daugh-
ters, husbands, and grandchildren. Back row left to right: George Georgeson,
Ted Heleotes and son Evan, Nick Papanikolas, Basil Theodore, Sophie Heleotes
and daughter Teddy; center: Helen Papanikolas, Josephine Theodore holding son
George, Emily, Amy Theodore, George, Demetra Georgeson holding daughter
Niki; seated foreground: Thalia Papanikolas and Mark Theodore; behind them,
Zeese Papanikolas, Kimon Georgeson, and Aglaia Georgeson.

night to revile him. Any more medication would kill her, the
nurses said. "I feel cut up," my father would say after such nights
and for days would not be able to take his ten-lap walk around the
solarium; he thought it kept him from becoming bedfast, his constant horror. Yet a morning never went by that he did not use his
electric razor and want the *Salt Lake Tribune,* the *Greek Star,* and
the *Greek Press* read to him.

Still, "I feel closer to her now," he said, "even though her
mind's gone, than ever before," and brokenly, "I have to die first. I
don't want to be alive and her dead."

I gathered my sack, kissed them on the cheek; my father had

begun the ritual when he arrived at Saint Joseph's, thinking that any night he might die and not have given the final kiss. I walked down the three flights of stairs taking melancholy breaths whenever my last task was to walk through the kitchen to the dietitian's office and complain again that cottage cheese, Jell-O, and vienna sausage had been served to my parents.

"They probably won't last more than two months," Sister Columba had said when we had brought my parents to the Villa. The two months became many months, then one, two, three, five years. My father sat in his big chair and looked sightlessly at the wall. For ten years he had been unable to see well enough to read and watch television; he no longer listened to his portable radio because he could hardly hear. Sometimes he turned on a tape recorder and listened to Greek *kleft* songs my son Zeese sent him. He had long since told me to bring no more records for the blind. He had listened to all the Zane Grey books many times over, to mysteries, to Walter Lippmann's history, and to John Kennedy's war experiences. He had become nauseated at the sound of recorded voices.

When Darvon kept his pain bearable, he thought of his life and the mistakes he had made. "I forced my family to leave Mitikas for the village, the worst mistake I ever made." He mused over other failings in family affairs. He became obsessed with the humiliation his parents had suffered when his money draft for one of his sisters' dowries had been delayed in reaching them. "If the money isn't here by Friday, the wedding is off," the groom had said. His sister would then remain unmarried, stigmatized, because an engagement was as binding as marriage. His parents would lose their self-respect, their *filotimo*. His brother Pericles's wife "went on her hands and knees to her parents and begged them for a loan" until the money arrived from America. "My poor parents to be treated so, to be humiliated so."

"When I turned eighty, I wrote all of them back in the old country. I told them I was eighty years old and not to write me for money anymore."

He talked about going with my mother to Greece after the Second World War and the ensuing Greek Civil War. They expected to stay four months; in a few weeks they were back. It was no longer the country they had left. They found faults, compared it to America and found it lacking. It would always be their mother country, but they preferred America.

"Do you remember my dog Leon?" my father asked. "We gave him to the Reynolds family because the neighbors complained he jumped on them. He ran back one day, clawing the door, running in circles, and I threw rocks at him to force him away. I didn't know he had been poisoned." His voice cracked. "He came to me for help and I threw rocks at him."

He remembered a fishing trip he had taken with my husband to Fish Lake high in the central Utah mountains. They went on, higher, to a plateau, and he smiled as he said, "We stood there and looked. As far as we could see flowers of every color spread, thick, beautiful, a panorama." I glanced at my mother, hoping that she heard and understood, but she was gazing off. In the past she had said, "Your father doesn't care about Nature."

Panorama: he had said the word in Greek. The closer he approached death, the more Greek he spoke, until the last few days before he slipped into a coma, his few words were those he had learned in the stark land where he had been born into the Greek race.

He was in his eighties on the fishing trip. I thought: standing on that plateau of many colors was he able at last, without worries, without responsibilities, to be free to respond with bliss to Nature.

Before I left, a priest or nun often came in to give them communion wafers. My father, who had carried on horrendous arguments with my mother because he would not kiss an archbishop's hand, now kissed the hand of a lowly priest or nun, whoever brought the wafer. He told Father George Politis, a youngish immigrant lay priest from the Island of Lefkas opposite the Grivas domain of Peratia, that he attended chapel on the second floor whenever he could and took communion. Father George told him he could attend chapel but should not take communion because the old trouble between Catholics and Orthodox had not been settled. "There's one Jesus Christ," my father said to me, "and I'll take communion whenever the nuns and priest bring it."

I remembered when he asked me to what church his grandson George Theodore's wife Sabrina belonged. "The Gregorian Armenian church. It was once Greek Orthodox, but broke away. It believes Jesus has one nature, divine, and the All–Holy is not the mother of God."

"Well, I don't believe She is either."

"If you're Orthodox, you have to believe it."

"Aaaa, I don't believe that."

Often my mother would break her silence and interrupt conversations. "Does Nick Zeese still live?"

"No. He died twenty years ago."

"He didn't believe in anything Greek," she said. "He never went to church."

"Yes," I said, "a few years before he died, he started coming to church."

"He came to church," my father said acidly, "like a certain villager. Whenever he was heard praying in church, people said, 'Whose sheep have been stolen?'"

"Does his wife still live?"

"No." I had heard of her death by chance. A woman who had lived in a Carbon County mining camp many years previously telephoned from Los Angeles to ask me for a copy of one of my publications. "It's too bad about Eileen Zeese," she said, and then I heard about her having been beaten to death. "She came down here after Nick died, wearing a new fur coat and lots of jewelry, and some man took up with her. Then he asked her for her money and she said she didn't have any. He didn't believe her and beat her up bad. They took her to the hospital and she died a few days later."

"That *kerata*," my father said about Nick Zeese. "When I was foreman of a railroad gang in Bozeman, Montana, the roadmaster asked me if I could spare one of the men to take over a gang on a short branch line of the Great Northern. Nick was with me, hiding to keep out of jail I guess, and I sent him. One day I had to go to the roadmaster's office. I walked in and there was Nick, his feet up on the desk, with a whiskey bottle between him and the roadmaster. The gang was off working by itself."

"Eight or ten miles out of Bozeman, Easter of 1911, I took thirty

311

Greeks from Pocatello to replace railroad ties. We bought two lambs for a dollar seventy-five cents each and barbecued them outside the railroad cars. We sang and ate. Chickens were fifteen cents each, roosters were free because they ate the grain chickens needed. We bought a calf one day from a farmer for four dollars and fifty cents. We had no way to kill it and shot it in the head with a rifle. We got on the handcar with it, but we were afraid a train would come and we wouldn't be able to jump and lift the car off the tracks in time because the calf was so heavy."

"I went into Oregon looking for some men for my Idaho railroad gang. In a Huntington saloon a cowboy walked in. People said he came in once a year. 'What are you playing?' he asked the dealer. The dealer said, 'Blackjack.' The cowboy asked what the limit was and the dealer said twenty dollars. The cowboy said, 'Make it higher.' The dealer asked permission from the saloon owner and they raised the limit to a hundred dollars. They played ten hands. If your points are below seventeen, you have to draw a card. On the tenth hand the cowboy said, 'I'm good for all.' The cowboy forced the dealer to draw and his hand added up to twenty-two points. The cowboy walked out with a thousand dollars."

For ten years I had been writing down my parents' recollections. I would sometimes think after a hiatus that they had nothing more to tell me, but memory is inexhaustible: "When I sent to Corfu to get money from my father to buy supplies and sell them to get enough money to come to America, my father didn't have any money. He sold his next year's wages at a discount to a moneylender to give me the money. Achh, my poor father."

My mother asked if Mrs. Dikaios, the College Grad, was still living. Yes, I told her. She was one of the few of my mother's old *parea,* her group, still alive, hardly ever leaving her house, arthritic herself and caring for her senile, invalid husband. I sometimes saw her at funerals wearing an out-of-date hat set with a touch of stylishness still on the side of her head.

"Does Efterpy Felis still live?"

Younger than my mother by twenty or more years, Mrs. Felis always searched me out at church functions to lament her life as a refugee after the Greek defeat in Asia Minor in 1922. Her grandmother had become separated from the family in the upheaval, and although they searched for years, they never found her. "My mother cried every day of her life."

"Does Mrs. Vassiliou still live?" my mother asked at times.

Mrs. Vassiliou, not of her *parea* but one of the women with whom she had exchanged ritual name day visits, was still alive. She had sold her little house in old Greek Town and moved to an apartment where everything was in spotless order for her death. It was rumored she had placed the three yards of burial cloth given her by her godfather at baptism in a plastic bag on top of a coffee table. No less could be expected of a woman who continued hanging up her wash while an earthquake was going on.

"Does Mrs. Souvall still live?"

"She died recently," I said without reminding my mother that I had brought her a packet of Mrs. Souvall's memorial wheat from her forty-day liturgy. I had emptied the small stapled, plastic packet of boiled wheat, almonds, parsley, and pomegranate seeds onto a paper plate for her. I handed her a spoon. "It's Mrs. Souvall's memorial wheat," I said. She burst into sobs. "No. No. I can't eat her kolivo. I can't!"

"It's our religion."

"No. I don't want her dead!"

Almost everyone they had eaten bread and salt with was dead. Louis and Nick Zeese; dead at forty-eight, my father's grocery store partner; Stylian Staes, the Greek vice-consul, interpreter, newspaper reporter, sometime Greek school teacher; Jim Galanis of the Golden Rule Store; my godfather; Theda Bara and her priggish husband; priests, chanters, labor agents, newspaper editors, and reporters.

The sheep people were all dead—the Diamantis, Pappases, Jouflases, Mahlerases, and Koulourises; Sam Sampinos; John Papoulas and his sheepherder, the "Crier," who had looked like movie versions of British colonels serving in India. After World War Two John Papoulas had taken a number of his big-headed, white-faced Rambouillets to his ancestral village Mavrolithari—Black Rock—

My scrapbook used for collecting material about my parents.

My cousin Ioanna Giovas's family history.

A page of my father's handwritten autobiography.

A page from one of my journals.

to help replenish the flocks devastated by the German invasion and the civil war that followed.

Two of the Pappas sisters visited their parents' village in the middle 1970s and saw again their mother's brother. He had worked as a sheepherder fourteen years in Colorado to gather enough dowry money to enable one daughter to marry a doctor, the other, a furniture manufacturer. On Good Friday, just before evening liturgy, Mary and her uncle walked to the outskirts of the village. They came upon grazing sheep which scattered in all directions at their approach. "We frightened your sheep," Mary said to the lolling shepherd.

"Eh, our sheep have been that way ever since the ewes took one look at those big-mugged rams the rich Greek–American brought here after the war."

Mary's uncle admonished the shepherd for not going to Great Friday services. He shrugged, "Is it my fault He gets Himself hanged every year?"

I brought one of the last of my father's *patriotes* with his wife to visit my parents. Gus Heleos was eighty-eight years of age. An old time Mormon had told me while I was gathering material on a coal strike: "I remember Gus Heleos when he worked in the Hiawatha mine. He batched it with some other Greeks but took care of his own food to save money. He wanted to open his own business. He ate the same thing every night, pork and beans. He marked the can in half with a pencil and ate that half cold with a hunk of bread and no matter how hungry he was, he never ate a bean more. He left it for the next night's supper."

Gus Heleos talked fast and excitedly to my father about their first years in the coal fields, about good men they remembered fondly, a vendetta, labor agents, recalcitrant priests. "Remember, George, when I was president of the church, when the priest got mixed up with the Greek school teacher and we closed the church because we were fighting the Cretans who took his side. I asked you to give me some money for the church expenses and you gave me three hundred fifty dollars and said, 'Don't give a penny of it to the priest'? And the Cretans were ready to kill you and we had to watch out for you?"

I took Mrs. Heleos into my mother's room where we talked about life in the mining towns. I asked if her family were really Austrians or Yugoslavs, called Austrians because they had been under Austro-Hungarian rule. To that moment my mother had gazed at us through sedated eyes. Suddenly she squirmed, arranged and rearranged the covering over her knees, clasped her hands, and said in Greek, "You shouldn't be talking like that."

I shook my head at her, but an old anger rose. Throughout my childhood, adult years, and now on the threshold of my own old age, I had seen her trying to control an agitation, squirming when people were present, and I did not know what I had said or done. At times I could trace her anxious misery to some foolish old-country idea of propriety, some genteel absurdity, an outright misinterpretation that she had gleaned from random phrases. Still she did not trust me to have the sense to be "proper."

She had gone through life in an invisible shell that had kept her as she had been since a child. Her ideas, old-country culture, her personality had not been touched by the passing years, change of country, the evolution of girl-woman-wife-mother-grandmother-great-grandmother.

In her extreme old age, senile, she retained an exasperating way of walking. I would take her by the arm to go from my father's room to her own because she had, as usual, forgotten her walker. She would walk slowly, independently, a little apart from me. She had always walked this way, to her own rhythm, straight ahead, alone, as if I were not there, never letting me lead her where we were going. Alone, as if she had never had anyone to go along with her, had always to depend on herself. She would look right and left, trying to decide where she should go, as if I were not there to help her in her old age.

The day after the visit my father told me about Gus Heleos's father coming from Greece to see his son. "By the time the old man came, Gus and his wife had ten children. [They eventually had thirteen.] The old man kept after Gus to return with him to Greece. Gus said, 'I've got ten children. How can I leave them?' The old man said, 'Aaa, they're not Greeks. Their mother's not Greek.' Gus humored him. It was hunting season and the old man said he'd like to do some shooting. Gus took him out into the sagebrush, set up camp. The old man picked up the rifle and said, 'You're coming back with me or I'll kill you!' Gus looked at those crazy eyes and said, 'Maybe you're right. When we get back to town, I'll see about our tickets.'

"When they got back to Price, Gus drove to the sheriff's office, pretending it was the ticket agency. In English he told the sheriff the story and asked him to keep his father locked up until he could make arrangements to send him back to Greece. Three days later the sheriff put the old man on the D&RGW and Gus never heard from him again."

Almost six years have gone by. We've come to know the office workers, kitchen help, patients, nurses, and aides, many of them young, obese women with pretty faces. Several nuns have left because of illness. Aides are constantly replaced. Patients who shuffled slowly up and down the halls for exercise, soon are seen less often, then not at all, and then die unobtrusively, the only clue to death their furniture in the hall while a full-scale cleaning goes on inside the rooms. The next day a new old-person sits in the freshly cleaned room with a familiar armchair, a desk, or a dresser brought along, but never the familiar bed. Only hospital beds that can be cranked up, oxygen tanks attached, are allowed.

The new old-person may sit and stare, shuffle down the hall, complain to maintenance men and nurses' aides about the rooms, the food, lights above the door that have not been answered. Mostly they sit, and those who can remember think about the past. A woman in a wheelchair, her crippled, useless hands on her lap, muses on the grandchildren she seldom sees: "They rush in for a minute on Easter, Christmas, once in a while on Mother's Day. They were my whole life."

A man pushes his wheelchair by the heels of his shoes, saying, "They can't wait for me to die, especially the son-in-law. Lazy, lightweight brain, thinks he's something special, expecting everything handed to him."

An old couple walk with identical, small jerky steps past my parents' doors. "It's not only our kids," the woman says, "it's everybody's. Our house was their house, but their house was not our house."

A thin alcoholic sits near the entrance of the nursing home all day, smoking one cigarette after another. We exchange pleasantries. "I was not a good father," he said once.

A woman screams incessantly. She thinks a black man is in her room. "Why does that child scream?" my mother asks. "I must help it." The woman who shares the screaming woman's room was once lovely, a friend tells me. She is tied up, "restrained" the polite word, because she constantly takes her clothes off. Another woman pleads in Dutch, but no one knows what she is saying. Down the hall an Italian man, not so old as the other patients, stands at his door and watches every nun, nurse, visitor suspiciously. He swears obscenely at the nurses and aides. His smiling wife, swaying stiffly, clutching her cane, a victim of muscular dystrophy, tells me, "My son is back again. Now there's so much washing to do. It takes me twenty minutes to go down the stairs to the basement with my basket and a lot longer to come up."

Middle-aged children come and go, bringing paper sacks of laundered clothing.

"I come in the morning so I can get it over with."

"I can't stand to see all these old people. How can you come so often?"

"I've got my daughter and her children to think of and yet I'm expected to come here regularly."

A woman with the remnants of her mother's life in a bag—her room is being cleaned thoroughly—tells me goodbye. "I know it's hard but you sisters will be glad you did so much."

My father relates a sardonic anecdote about the poverty of Greece. He is no longer afraid of dying. He prays for it, tries to will it. He does not listen to the tape recorder, wants only to hear the news read to him, is consumed with stopping his pain. My mother comes out of her sedated immobility to ask me what food I have prepared for dinner. "Stop at a grocery store. Buy some chops, braise them on both sides. Make a lettuce salad. Add feta and olives and your dinner will be ready in no time."

Our conversations begin, continue, and end with: "Now where

319

do your children live? Then they don't live in the same place? How many children do they have? Now where do they live? They don't live in the same place? How many children do they have? Now where do they. . . ." She stares at a photograph on the wall. "Is that Sophie, my Sophoula?" But she often plays simple card games with Jo and Demetra.

Often we return her belongings to the dresser and closet. She gathers them together periodically to return to her house. "It's the full moon," Sister Columba keeps saying. The full moon comes more often lately. If my mother is especially intransigent, slender, hazel-eyed Sister Columba calls me. She calls often. "Helen [she pronounces my name *Haylen*}, I gave your father a percadan just now and he'll be sleeping through lunchtime. When you come down, bring something nourishing, homemade soup or something." "Haylen, when you come down, bring a can of Drano. Your parents' bathroom sink is clogged up. I can take care of it much more quickly myself than waiting for Housekeeping to get around to it."

"How can she know when my father is worse?" I ask Sister Columba when I find my mother is looking at the door frantically, clasping and unclasping her skeletal, trembling hands.

"They just know."

"He can't last much longer," Sister Columba said as she left for a retreat and study at Gonzaga University. She has had a heart attack and will no longer be allowed to do active nursing. My father's pain became unbearable. "I think his appendix is ready to burst," the doctor says. The appendix is removed and is normal; the surgeon finds a gangrenous gallbladder on the verge of breaking open. Surely he will die. How can a man nearly ninety-seven last, we ask each other. He survives the horrible pain, the pounding on his back to clear his lungs and prevent pneumonia, the assault of laboratory and x-ray technicians on his body. He returns to Saint Joseph's, ten days later he hemorrhages, is taken to the hospital, given massive blood, is back again in the nursing home. "He's amazing," the surgeon says, but we sisters wish he had died. His hearing is almost gone; we read the newspaper loudly, repeat when we sense he has not heard. Without sight, without hearing, he will be completely isolated.

The week he lay dying, his fingers swelled. "You must remove his wedding band," the nurse told me. I hesitated: I was infringing on a private world. "We have to take your ring off. It's too tight." In the heavy drowse straddling the boundary over which death lay, he stirred and said clearly, harshly, "No!"

My mother most often forgot that he had died. When she remembered, her grieving was fresh, as if my father's death had just occurred. "I dreamed last night that I was in a big hall filled with people. Your father was there. He was the boss. I kept looking for him and looking for him, but I never found him."

I think as I drive home how quickly immigrant life vanished, Greek Towns long since gone, the young matriarchs and patriarchs sick to death or dead already, Greek schools and church affairs a vestige of former days, name day visiting diminished, icons and vigil lights seldom seen in houses, proverbs hardly ever heard. I think of them, my parents, in the early mornings when the grieving call of the mourning dove beyond the hollow comes with the fresh scent of water and greenness. I think of them at night when in the blackness a diesel whistle sounds across the Salt Lake Valley, its blare mitigated by distance. It is not the haunting call of the old steam engines, but it is better than nothing.

Notes

CHAPTER 1

4 "WHO NEVER ATE WARM BREAD": G. Athanas, *Traghoudia ton Vounon* ["Songs of the Mountains"] (Athens, 1953), p. 11.

CHAPTER 2

35 BECAUSE THE ORTHODOX CHURCH: The First Ecumenical Council of the church met in Nicae in 325 and decreed that Easter would be celebrated the Sunday following the first full moon after the vernal equinox and after Jewish Passover. The calculations were based on the Julian Calendar. A difference of thirteen days exists between the date of the vernal equinox then and at the present time. Western Christian churches adjusted the date of the vernal equinox by adopting the Gregorian Calendar. Some Orthodox churches, including the Greek Orthodox of North and South America, use the Gregorian Calendar for all immovable feast days, such as Christmas, Epiphany, and the Annunciation. (From the *Orthodox Observer*, 23 April 1986.)

CHAPTER 3

44 THE MEMBERS WENT ON STRIKE: See the author's, "Unionism, Communism, and the Great Depression: The Carbon County Strike of 1933," *Utah Historical Quarterly* 41 (1973): 254–300.

CHAPTER 4

54 "WINTER WAS A HORROR": Soteriou M. Kotsopoulou, *Nafpaktia: Apo Gheografikis, Istorikis, k.l.p, Apopsios* ["Nafpaktia: Of the Geographical, Historical, and Other Aspects"] (Athens, 1924), p. 127.

CHAPTER 5

57 "THE ABSOLUTE RULER OF AKARNANIA": X. G. Mavromatis, biographical essay of the Grivas clan in *Great Greek Encyclopedia of Pyrsos*, vol. 2, pp. 732–34. A biography of Theodore Grivas is: D. G. Kambouroglous, ed., *Theodhoros Grivas* (Athens, 1896).

57 "RESIGNED COMPLETELY . . . DIED IN MASSALIA": *Great Greek Encyclopedia*, 2:733.

64 THE ICON HAD BEEN THROWN: Kotsopoulou, *Nafpaktia*, pp. 103-6.

CHAPTER 6

74 OTHER SONGS FOLLOWED: This family story is recounted in Dimitri Fotiadhi, *Karaïskakis*, 3d ed. (Athens, 1959), pp. 378-81.

76 "WHAT HAVE I DONE TO YOU, MY GOD": For *mirologhia* see Margaret Alexiou, *The Ritual Lament in Greek Tradition* (London: Cambridge University Press, 1974). Numerous *mirologhia* are found in the publications of the Academy of Athens: Georghios K. Spyridakis and Spyros D. Peristeris, *Ellinika Dhimotika Traghoudhia* ["Greek Demotic Songs"], vol. C (1968), pp. 349-76; in Ghiannis Efthovoulos, *Krytika Mirologhia* [Cretan *Mirologhia*] (Athens, 1976); Athanasios H. Giakas, *Ipirotika Dhimotika Traghoudhia* ["Demotic Songs of Epirus"]1000-1958 (Athens, n.d.), pp. 529-55; and N. C. Politis, *Ekloghai apo ta Traghoudhia tou Ellinikou Laou* ["Selections from the Songs of the Greek People"] (Athens, 1985). The southern tip of Greece, the Mani, is noted for ritual keenings for the dead. See Patrick Leigh Fermor, *Mani: Travels in the Southern Peloponnese* (New York, 1958), chap. 5. Greek immigrants brought these laments to America. See Helen Z. Papanikolas, "Wrestling with Death: Greek Immigrant Funeral Customs in Utah," *Utah Historical Quarterly* 52 (1984): 29-49.

CHAPTER 7

83 YORYIS DID NOT KNOW THEN: *General Makrighiannis's Apominomonevmata* ["The Memoirs of Makrighiannis"], introduction by Spiros I. Asdrahas (Athens, n.d.), p. 61.

83 WITH TIME THEY BECAME TRADITIONAL ENEMIES: Biographical essay of the Grivas clan, *Great Greek Encyclopedia*, 2:732.

CHAPTER 8

85 EVEN IN OLD AGE: For *sawm* ("fasting") and Ramadan see Caesar E. Farah, *Islam: Beliefs and Observances* (Woodbury, N.Y., 1970), pp. 143-45.

91 OUTSIDE, THE TWIGS AND CHARCOAL: A classic work on the Sarakatsani is J. K. Campbell, *Honour, Family, and Patronage: A Study of Institutions and Moral Values in a Greek Mountain Community* (London: Oxford University Press, 1964).

CHAPTER 9

100 "I'M GOING TO KLEPA. . .AND OPEN MY OWN SHOP": For the Kravara and its secret language see Patrick Leigh Fermor, *Roumeli: Travels in Northern Greece* (New York, 1966), pp. 187-95.

103 TO SURVIVE HE PLAYED BOTH SIDES: Nikos Kazantzakis, *Report to Greco*, trans. P.A. Bien (New York, 1965), p. 141.

112 "AS LONG AS GRIVAS IS ALIVE": *Greek Demotic Songs (Selections)* (Athens: Academy of Athens, 1968), vol. A, p. 256, author's translation from the Greek.

112 "CRY, COUNTRY AND VILLAGES": Ibid., p. 257.

113 THE HILARIOUS LAUGHTER OF THE VILLAGERS: Wedding activities and songs for the province of Nafpaktias in which the village of Klepa is found are in Dimitris Douzos, *Laografika Nafpaktias* ["Folklore of Nafpaktias"] (Athens, 1961), pp. 85-91. Wedding songs with musical scores are found in Spyridhakis and Peristeris, *Greek Demotic Songs*, pp. 283-308.

CHAPTER 10

126 SHE CLOSED THE BOOK, HER HEART BEATING LOUDLY: Charos, the Charon of ancient Greek folklore who ferried the dead across the river Styx to the underworld, is Death himself in contemporary life. John Cuthbert Lawson, *Modern Greek Folklore and Ancient Greek Religion: A Study in Survivals* (London, 1892), pp. 98-117.

CHAPTER 12

145 THEY WERE FINALLY GOING TO AMERICA: For an account of immigrant life in industrial labor, see the author's, "Greek Workers in the Intermountain West: The Early Twentieth Century," *Byzantine and Modern Greek Studies* 5 (1979): 187-215; L.J. Cononelos, "Greek Immigrant Laborers in the Intermountain West: 1900–1920" (Master's thesis, University of Utah, 1978).

152 WELL-DRESSED LABOR AGENTS, CARDPLAYERS: A discussion of "flesh merchants" is found in Theodore Saloutos, *The Greeks in the United States* (Cambridge, Mass: Harvard University Press, 1964), pp. 48-56.

152 ON THE FOURTH DAY THEIR PAY CAME: Leonidas Skliris is discussed in the author's "Life and Labor among the Immigrants in Bingham Canyon," *Utah Historical Quarterly* 33 (Fall 1965): 294-303, and in "Greek Workers in the Intermountain West," 192-95, 204-7.

154 SHE WAS A MIDWIFE AND HAD USED FOLK CURES: For this midwife see the author's "Magerou, the Greek Midwife," *Utah Historical Quarterly* 38 (Winter 1970): 50-60.

157 RESPECTABLE CITIZENS COULD ENTER THE STOCKADE: John S. McCormick, "Red Lights in Zion: Salt Lake City's Stockade, 1908-11," *Utah Historical Quarterly* 50 (Spring 1982): 168-81.

CHAPTER 13

161 ON THE RAILROAD COACH TO NORTH PLATTE: A journal in the Greek Language kept by H. K. Kambouris for the years 1912–18 in the Ethnic Archives, Marriott Library, University of Utah, gives a vivid account of immigrant laborers on railroad gangs.

164 REMEMBERING HIS FATHER STANDING ON THE WHARF: A ledger kept by an *erminéas*, an uncle of the author's cousins, Thalia and Katherine Papachristos, in their possession, gives a record of his purchases and loans to railroad gang workers during 1911-14.

165 IN THE RAMPAGE THAT FOLLOWED, GREEK TOWN WAS SET AFIRE: J. G. Bitzes, "The Anti–Greek Riot of 1909—South Omaha," *Nebraska History* 51 (1970): 199-224; Thomas Burgess, *Greeks in America* (Boston, 1913), pp. 165-67; Theodore Saloutos, *The Greeks in the United States* (Cambridge, Mass.: Harvard University Press, 1964), pp. 66-69.

165 "THEY WERE AFRAID WE WERE GOING TO USE THEIR WOMEN": Another version gave the men twenty-four hours to leave: Saloutos, *Greeks in the United States*, p. 62.

CHAPTER 16

196–97 THE JOURNALIST BURST OUT, "AMERIKI SWALLOWS THEM!": The journalist's book was published in 1916. Maria S. Economidhou, *E Ellines tis Amerikis opous tous edha* ("The Greeks in America as I Saw Them") (New York, 1916).

CHAPTER 17

213 "AAA," NIKOS SCOFFED, "SKLIRIS IS IN BIG TROUBLE": This strike is described in the author's "Life and Labor Among the Immigrants of Bingham Canyon," pp. 289-315.

CHAPTER 18

225 A GREEK LABOR AGENT ARRIVED FROM PUEBLO: Zeese Papanikolas, *Buried Unsung: Louis Tikas and the Ludlow Massacre* (Salt Lake City: University of Utah Press, 1982).

CHAPTER 20

251 THE STRIKERS COOKED SPAGHETTI IN COFFEE CANS: Allan Kent Powell, *"The Next Time We Strike": Labor in Utah's Coal Fields 1900-1933.* (Logan: Utah State University Press), chaps. 3,4.

254 ACCOMPANIED BY VIOLIN AND LAUTO, KYRIA SOPHIA SANG: Economidhou, *The Greeks in America as I Saw Them*, pp. 62-63.

CHAPTER 21

264 BRAWLS ERUPTED ON THE BOARDWALK: For details see the author's "The Greeks of Carbon County," *Utah Historical Quarterly* 22 (April 1954): 150-53; for the Greek response to the war see the author's *Toil and Rage in a New Land: The Greek Immigrants in Utah*, 2d ed. rev. (Salt Lake City: Utah State Historical Society, 1974), reprinted from *Utah Historical Quarterly* 38 (Spring 1970): 153-56.

267 THE CROWD, MUTTERING, SLOWLY FANNED OUT: Papanikolas, *The Greeks of Carbon County*, pp. 153-54.

CHAPTER 22

271 YORYIS BID TO PROVIDE THE LABOR ON A WATER LINE: The successful bid made headlines in the *Helper Times*, 1 August 1919.

278 THEY LEFT THE OFFICE AND CALLED A STRIKE: Papanikolas, *Toil and Rage*, pp. 166-75.

CHAPTER 23

283 WHEN THE ROOM DARKENED: Several events in this chapter are discussed in Helen Zeese Papanikolas, "Greek Folklore of Carbon County," in *Lore of Faith and Folly*, ed. Thomas E. Cheney (Salt Lake City: University of Utah Press, 1971).

286 THE REMNANTS RUSHED INTO THE SEA: Marjorie Housepian, *The Smyrna Affair* (New York, 1966).

288 "THE CASTLE GATE NUMBER TWO HAS EXPLODED": Papanikolas, *Toil and Rage*, pp. 175-79; Powell, *"The Next Time We Strike,"* pp. 141-51.

292 ON MAIN STREET PEOPLE CLUSTERED, TALKING ABOUT IT: Larry R. Gerlach, *Blazing Crosses in Zion: the Ku Klux Klan in Utah* (Logan: Utah State University Press, 1982).

CPSIA information can be obtained
at www.ICGtesting.com
Printed in the USA
LVOW13s2339260318
571194LV00022B/331/P